HOLLYWOOD THEORY, NON-HOLLYWOOD PRACTICE

For my father,
in loving memory
of my mother,
and for Colin

Hollywood Theory, Non-Hollywood Practice

Cinema Soundtracks in the 1980s and 1990s

ANNETTE DAVISON
University of Leeds, UK

ASHGATE

Published by
Ashgate Publishing Limited
Gower House
Croft Road
Aldershot
Hants GU11 3HR
England

Ashgate Publishing Company
Suite 420
101 Cherry Street
Burlington
VT 05401-4405
USA

Ashgate website: http://www.ashgate.com

British Library Cataloguing in Publication Data
Davison, Annette
  Hollywood theory, non-Hollywood practice : cinema
  soundtracks in the 1980s and 1990s. – (Ashgate popular and
  folk music series)
  1. Motion picture music – History and criticism
  I. Title
  781.5'42

Library of Congress Cataloging-in-Publication Data
Davison, Annette, 1971–
    Hollywood theory, non-Hollywood practice : cinema soundtracks in the 1980s and 1990s
    / Annette Davison.
        p. cm. – (Ashgate popular and folk music series)
    Includes bibliographical references (p.).
    ISBN 0-7546-0582-5 (alk. paper)
        1. Motion picture music – Analysis, appreciation. 2. Motion picture music – History and
  criticism. I. Title. II. Series.

  ML2075.D39 2003
  781.5'42 – dc21

2003041873

ISBN 0 7546 0582 5

Typeset by Express Typesetters Ltd, Farnham
Printed and bound in Great Britain by MPG Books Ltd, Bodmin

Contents

List of illustrations

List of music examples

General Editor's preface

The upheaval that occurred in musicology during the last two decades of the twentieth century has created a new urgency for the study of popular music alongside the development of new critical and theoretical models. A relativistic outlook has replaced the universal perspective of modernism (the international ambitions of the 12-note style); the grand narrative of the evolution and dissolution of tonality has been challenged, and emphasis has shifted to cultural context, reception and subject position. Together, these have conspired to eat away at the status of canonical composers and categories of high and low in music. A need has arisen, also, to recognize and address the emergence of crossovers, mixed and new genres, to engage in debates concerning the vexed problem of what constitutes authenticity in music and to offer a critique of musical practice as the product of free, individual expression.

Popular musicology is now a vital and exciting area of scholarship, and the Ashgate Popular and Folk Music Series aims to present the best research in the field. Authors will be concerned with locating musical practices, values and meanings in cultural context, and may draw upon methodologies and theories developed in cultural studies, semiotics, poststructuralism, psychology and sociology. The series will focus on popular musics of the twentieth and twenty-first centuries. It is designed to embrace the world's popular musics from Acid Jazz to Zydeco, whether high tech or low tech, commercial or non-commercial, contemporary or traditional.

Professor Derek B. Scott
Chair of Music
University of Salford

Acknowledgements

The material in this book grew out of a concern that relatively little seemed to have been written about the film scores and soundtracks of films produced outside of Hollywood, particularly in terms of contemporary cinema. The project took several years to come to fruition, throughout which working with Eric Clarke and Erica Sheen proved to be an enormously valuable experience. I have learnt a great deal from them both and continue to do so.

Rachel Cowgill, John Croft, Kate Daubney, Nikki Dibben, Stephanie Pitts and Luke Windsor all encouraged the development of this work and helpfully commented on drafts at various stages of the project, for which I am also very grateful. Discussions about film music with Peter Franklin, Robynn Stilwell and David Cooper have always proved stimulating and have undoubtedly contributed to my exploration of some of the ideas to be found in the book. Jim Buhler provided useful comments on an earlier draft of the Godard chapter and Mark Butler was helpful in his editorial comments on an article which grew out of an earlier draft of the Jarman chapter. The case studies have all been presented as individual papers at conferences and research seminars at the Universities of Royal Holloway, Oxford, Keele, Sheffield, Leeds, Southampton, and Surrey, The Royal College of Music, London, and the University of the Applied Arts, Vienna. I would like to thank all those who shared with me their comments and ideas about these papers. Students and staff of the Departments of English and Music at the University of Sheffield, of Media and Cultural Studies at University College Warrington, and of the School of Music at the University of Leeds have all played a role in pushing forward my thinking about the issues discussed in this book, for which I am also grateful. Randy Thom and Simon Fisher Turner both kindly discussed their soundtrack work with me, and James MacKay was also extremely helpful in sharing material about the production of *The Garden* and in assisting me in the procurement of still images from this film. I would also like to thank Derek Scott (series editor), Rachel Lynch and other members of the editorial team at Ashgate Publishing for their continuing support when things kept going wrong.

Many other friends and colleagues offered encouragement during the development of this work and I am indebted to them for that support. In particular, I would like to thank Cindy Weber and Jayne Rodgers: great intellectual discussants, cinema-partners, friends and sources of fun.

I was fortunate in receiving British Academy funding for some of this research in the form of a PhD studentship, and would like to thank the Arts and Humanities

Research Board for their assistance with the cost of final research trips, stills and copyright permissions, which took the form of a small grant in the performing arts (B/SG/AN9026/APN14086).

I also thank the following for permission to reprint material that first appeared elsewhere:

Indiana Theory Review who published an earlier version of some of the material in Chapter 5 (on Derek Jarman's *The Garden*) as 'Playing in *The Garden*: sound, performance and images of persecution', Vol. 19 (Spring 1998), 35–54; Continuum Books who published a shorter version of some of the ideas discussed in Chapter 6 (on Wim Wenders's *Wings of Desire*) as 'Music to Desire By: Crossing the Berlin Wall with Wim Wenders' in J. Scanlon and A. Waste (eds), (2001), *Crossing Boundaries: Thinking Through Literature*, Sheffield: Sheffield Academic Press, pp. 161–8.

I have made every effort to trace the original copyright holders of material printed in this book to obtain their permission to do so. Any omissions brought to the attention of the publishers will be remedied in future editions.

Introduction

In a recent newspaper article, Scott Hughes pointed out that between 1986 and 1996 soundtrack album sales in the USA quadrupled (2000, p. 8). In the UK, 'two film themes – Bryan Adams's "Everything I Do (I Do It For You)" from *Robin Hood: Prince of Thieves* [1991], and Wet Wet Wet's "Love Is All Around" (*Four Weddings and a Funeral* [1994]) – became the longest-running singles chart number ones ever' (ibid.). Hughes states that along with the use of stars, today's Hollywood films are launched by expensive soundtracks which are focused more on record sales and brand strengthening than 'complementing a director's vision' (ibid.). Such statistics show how popular film soundtracks are, whether they feature pop songs, orchestral scoring or a mixture of both.[1] By the end of the 1970s, John Williams's score for *Star Wars* (1977) had sold over 4 million units, and had become the highest-selling non-pop album up to that point (Burlingame 2000, p. 17). Sales of James Horner's orchestral score to *Titanic* (1998), currently the highest-selling orchestral score soundtrack album of all time, have now reached over 11 million units (Hughes 2000, p. 9).

Academic research into film music – film musicology – has also been dramatically on the rise since the 1980s. One area of this research that has been particularly popular is that of the 'classical Hollywood score', which is considered to be the dominant scoring practice of Hollywood films made between the mid-1930s and the early 1950s. In *Settling the Score* Kathryn Kalinak defines classical scoring as an 'institutional practice for the regulation of nondiegetic music in film', where nondiegetic music is heard only by a film's audience since the characters presented on screen cannot hear it: it exists outside of, or beyond, the fictional world of the film, the diegesis (1992, p. xiv).[2] As is discussed below, there has been a resurgence of classical scoring practices in Hollywood's 'event' movies, the 'blockbusters', since the mid-1970s.

This study also takes classical Hollywood scoring as its starting point, but is primarily concerned with practices of film soundtrack composition for films made after 1980, outside of, and in relation to Hollywood, characterized here as 'Non-Hollywood'. In the second part of this book, a range of aesthetic, economic, and production practices are identified and analysed in case studies of soundtracks to particular Non-Hollywood films of the 1980s and early 1990s. Each of these soundtracks demonstrates an interesting – and often critical – relationship to classical Hollywood scores and soundtracks. Part of my argument here is that these soundtracks-as-critique may be read in relation to the re-emergence of classical scoring in the mid-to-late 1970s in the

Hollywood blockbusters which gradually became more visible and ubiquitous.[3]

Many consider the re-emergence of scoring techniques and orchestral forces associated with classical Hollywood to have started with John Williams's scores for a cycle of disaster movies in the early 1970s – *The Poseidon Adventure* (1972), *The Towering Inferno* (1974), *Earthquake* (1974) – closely followed by Williams's score for Steven Spielberg's *Jaws* (1975), and later those for George Lucas's initial *Star Wars* trilogy (1977; 1980; 1983), Spielberg's *Close Encounters of the Third Kind* (1977), *ET: The Extra-Terrestrial* (1982) and the Spielberg–Lucas devised *Indiana Jones* trilogy (1981; 1984; 1989).[4] These action-adventure films owe much to the serials and B-movies of the classical Hollywood era, though the films' promotion and publicity campaigns signalled a new era in the marketing and distribution of Hollywood cinema, as exemplified by advertisements for films on broadcast television and saturation booking in movie theatres across the US.[5] This was also the era of the VCR (video cassette recorder) and the rise of cable and satellite television channels, all of which offered further opportunities for the distribution of films. Did the presentation of these blockbuster films on smaller screens via a proliferation of distribution channels demand a 'larger' (that is, full orchestral) sound? What other reasons might the studios have had to decide to use classical scoring rather than the increasingly popular and generally more lucrative compilation scores which were often made up entirely of pop tracks, as with *The Graduate* (1967), *Easy Rider* (1969), *Mean Streets* (1973) and *American Graffiti* (1973)?

First it is important to explain what I mean by the term 'classical scoring', or 'classical Hollywood scoring'. These terms do not simply imply the use of the symphonic forces associated with music from the Classical period of European art music history (*c.* 1750–1820), or even those commonly associated with 'classical music' per se. As will be explored in more detail in the chapters which follow, the notion of classical scoring under discussion here is associated with what various film theorists and historians – such as Bordwell, Staiger and Thompson (1985) – have termed 'classical Hollywood cinema'. Drawing on theoretical conceptions of classical Hollywood filmmaking, a number of film musicologists – including Gorbman (1987), Kalinak (1992) and Flinn (1992) – have described the classical Hollywood film score as defined by a set of structural conventions originally institutionalized as a set of filmmaking practices in the 1930s and 1940s. These practices were united in the aim of heightening the fictive reality of a film's narrative. The mixing and audiovisual editing of classical film scores and soundtracks were also organized around these same conventions. These include privileging dialogue (as primary carrier of narrative information), the synchronization of music and action (though not *too* closely), the use of music as continuity and to 'control narrative connotation' (Kalinak 1992, p. xv). As will be discussed in Chapter 1, however, classical cinema is more than just a historical moment or set of conventions: it is 'a nexus of style, ideology, technology, and economics which coalesced during a particular time and particular place' (ibid., p. xiv).

There are a number of reasons why classical scoring might have been considered appropriate to the blockbuster movies which became gradually more prominent in the schedules from the mid-1970s. First, the narrative format of the blockbuster is often organized around that of the serial: a format associated with the B-movie adventure films popular in the 1930s and 1940s. For a number of critics, these films signalled a return to precise and efficient storytelling, to a narrative tautness more akin to classical Hollywood cinema than to the less teleological, more experimental Hollywood films which immediately preceded them in the late 1960s and early 1970s; films directed by Robert Altman, Dennis Hopper and Arthur Penn, for example, and influenced by both European art cinema and classical Hollywood. The return to classical scoring can thus be interpreted as operating in tandem with the films' references to the narrative techniques of classical Hollywood. As a result of adhering to classical conventions, this kind of scoring works hard to encourage the audience to surrender to the film and fully engage with the emotional worlds and action depicted on screen. On another level, it may operate as a nostalgic wink or nod to films from this earlier (studio) era to an audience familiar with them as a result of their exhibition on television and video.[6]

Second, and relatedly, it has been argued that the blockbuster's referencing of the serials and B-movies of the studio era brought with it a return to the conservative values proposed by the narratives of the earlier films, with their tendency towards encouraging white, Western-centric subject positions through bourgeois, heterosexual male heroes. Indeed, a number of studies interpret the return to conservatism as a direct reflection of US politics of the late 1970s into the 1980s: the rise of Reaganism (Ryan and Kellner 1988; Kolker 1988). The resurgence of the male action presence in films of this period has also been read as a reaction to burgeoning feminism (Tasker 1993). More importantly for *this* study, Anahid Kassabian (2001) has suggested that orchestral classical scoring also functions as an allusion to, or even a regeneration of, such values.

Third, the return to large orchestral forces might be seen to signal the return of high production values to the Hollywood soundtrack, following the shift to smaller jazz, rock, and pop combos through the 1960s which was often the combined result of financial constraints and hopes of profitable soundtrack albums. In this view the orchestra is interpreted as a demonstration of wealth, of opulence. As a cinematic practice this can be traced back to the use of large orchestras to accompany silent films and the rest of the programme in the urban picture palaces during the second and third decades of the twentieth century. The use of orchestral forces continued into the synchronized sound era, eventually with the music recorded (and thus fixed) on to the film strip itself.[7] Although the Big Five studios were forced to sell off their theatres in the early 1950s as a result of anti-trust proceedings first brought against them in 1938 – divorcement[8] –

large-scale orchestral forces continued to be used in high production value Hollywood films, such as biblical epics and glossy musical productions. In more general terms, music as a signifier of high production values may be considered to have a much longer history, connected to the patronage of composers and musicians by aristocrats of the European courts which dates back at least as far as the Renaissance.[9] Today the high production value of a soundtrack is most frequently demonstrated through the use of state-of-the-art technology; a strategy which can itself be traced back to the coming of sound, through to the development of stereo magnetic sound in the 1950s, to the upgrading of theatres to Dolby (optical) stereo in the late 1970s and to the more recent developments in digital sound.[10]

Fourth, the early 1970s saw the first major re-releases – and, in many cases, primary releases – on record of classical scores from the studio era by Max Steiner, Erich Wolfgang Korngold and other major studio film composers. What was to become a burgeoning revival of interest in classical scoring in the 1970s record market began with RCA's recording and release of an album of Korngold's film music entitled *The Sea Hawk* in late 1972 on its classical label, Red Seal (Burlingame 2000). This record became the fifth biggest selling classical album of 1973 and a series of 'Classic Film Scores' were commissioned by the label over the next six years as a result (pp. 14–15). Only one 'current' composer was featured in the series: John Williams, who was represented by re-recordings of extracts of his scores for *Close Encounters of the Third Kind* and *Star Wars*. A number of other labels also began to produce records of classical film scores during the 1970s.[11] It is possible that some of these records found their way into the collections of the young film-school-trained directors who were fast moving into mainstream Hollywood at this time. According to Burlingame, George Lucas made a 'temp track' for *Star Wars*; that is, a track, usually of recorded music, created to accompany a film through editing and early screenings and to stand in for the yet-to-be-composed score. This temporary music track included 'selections from Holst, Dvořák, Walton, [Miklós] Rózsa, and more, [and] convinced Williams that [Lucas's] film about events "a long time ago in a galaxy far, far away," demanded a score firmly rooted in the nineteenth-century romantic tradition' (Burlingame 2000, p. 17).[12] In reviews of the film, the stylistic references at the root of Williams's score were recognized and discussed by critics, though not always favourably. Following the success of the compilation score of contemporary art music which Stanley Kubrick had chosen over his commissioned score by Alex North for *2001: A Space Odyssey* (1968), it seems that some critics had expected a more 'futuristic' sound for the similarly space-set *Star Wars* (despite the film's classical style and the conventionality of Lucas's story).[13]

Although each of these factors probably played a role in the resurgence of classical scoring, the notion that the blockbusters of the mid-1970s signalled a return to the narrative tautness of classical Hollywood films of the studio era has been most often discussed (see Chapter 2). Indeed, in *The Classical Hollywood Cinema: Film Style and Mode of Production to 1960*, David Bordwell, Janet Staiger and Kristin Thompson argue that the classical style of filmmaking – of which classical scoring is considered to be a part – persists, to a certain degree at least, despite changes to the industrial organization of Hollywood since divorcement. On the other hand, some theorists propose that these transformations have resulted in the replacement of classicism by something different, such as the 'post-classical' or 'neo-classical', often linked to notions of a 'New Hollywood'.

In the 50 years since divorcement various 'New' Hollywoods have been determined. This is because conceptions of transformation during this period differ greatly contingent on whether issues of economics, aesthetics, technology, industry and institution, or audience (or a combination of these) are being addressed (M. Smith 1998; Krämer 2000; Tasker 1996). Thus, while some critics, theorists and historians emphasize continuity between contemporary and classical Hollywood practices and structures (in one or more of the spheres listed above), others argue that the differences outweigh the similarities. Whether Hollywood's blockbusters and/or its industrial organization are best described as 'classical' or 'post-classical', as they did in the studio era, the Hollywood majors maintain an oligopolistic stranglehold on market share globally. Today, however, the studios exist as part of giant communications conglomerates rather than the isolated but vertically integrated – production, distribution, exhibition – company structures of the classical era.

Investigating the relationship between 'Old' (classical) and various 'New' Hollywoods also involves consideration of the relationship between Hollywood and European cinema. A good deal has been written about various nation-state and other cinemas in relation to Hollywood (though less has been said about the relationship between New Hollywood and European cinema).[14] The dialogue between Hollywood and European cinema has been on-going for over a century. It has included the exchange of personnel, the exchange and interrelation of film form and content in terms of style, genre, narrative, and so on, and also trade discussions concerning the economic and cultural implications of America's domination of the European market. However, as Geoffrey Nowell-Smith points out, this conversation has often been marked by rhetoric: economic rhetoric from the US side, championing the free market and consumer choice; culturalist rhetoric from the European, which focuses on cultural and national identities and views Hollywood cinema as an hegemonic invader (1998, p. 2). In reality, this relationship is more complex, not least due to the ambiguous position cinema itself occupies in relation to modernity (Nowell-Smith 1998, p. 2; Morrison 1998, pp. 1–21; Branston 2000; Hansen 2000). Cinema's industrial production practices, its reliance on modern developments in technology and the position of cinema as a major form of mass communication make it a clear exemplar of social modernity. Definitions of cultural modernism which locate the modern in relation to the negation or disruption of the classical (allied to notions of stability and continuity), however, most often constitute 'alternative' (often including European) cinemas as modernist, and Hollywood as 'classical'.[15]

More recently there has been a shift towards highlighting the problems involved in conceiving of particular cinemas solely in relation to 'hegemonic' Hollywood.[16] Indeed, the debate about the various forms of interrelation between cinemas has begun to move toward a more inclusive approach to the full range of world cinemas. Hollywood does *not* always function as the dominant ideology against which these cinemas have developed. In all cases, however, very little attention has as yet been paid to such relations in terms of film soundtracks, particularly in terms of more recent cinema.[17] Thus, while acknowledging the problems of conceiving of cinemas and their soundtracks primarily in relation to Hollywood and understanding classical Hollywood scoring practice as a form of dominant ideology, this book is based on the idea that engaging with institutional issues in relation to film soundtracks and scores can prove fruitful. For the purposes of this study I argue that since the mid-1970s the model of the classical Hollywood score *has* functioned as a form of dominant ideology in relation to which alternative scoring and soundtrack practices may assert themselves.

An understanding of classical Hollywood scoring and soundtrack practice is important for a number of different reasons. First, and most obviously, it adds to our grasp and analysis of classical Hollywood cinema in general. Studies such as those by Gorbman (1987), Kalinak (1992) and Flinn (1992) demonstrate the usefulness of this approach. Second, in terms of the apparent resurgence of this scoring practice in the mid-to-late 1970s as part of the development of a successful formula for blockbuster movies, an understanding of classical Hollywood scoring assists consideration of the relationship between 'Old' Hollywood cinema and 'New' Hollywood. Third, by operating as a signifier of classical, and thus – by extension – also New Hollywood cinema, the return of classical Hollywood scoring offers filmmakers a further means by which they may demonstrate their relationship to Hollywood cinema through the production of scores and soundtracks which either critique or echo this practice. The first three chapters of the book take up each of these issues in turn. In Chapter 1, a number of key theoretical approaches to classical Hollywood scoring are explored in the context of some of the major film-theoretical accounts of classical Hollywood cinema. In Chapter 2, the apparent return of classical scoring in the mid-1970s is placed in the context of approaches to the relationship between 'Old' and 'New' Hollywood, classical and 'post-classical' cinema. Chapter 3 traces a history of some key theoretical approaches to alternative scoring and soundtrack practice. The film-theoretical work presented in these opening chapters is inevitably dealt with only summarily, but the intention is that such reviews will offer the reader less familiar with this literature a grounding which may enrich the discussions of theoretical approaches to classical, post-classical and alternative scoring practices which follow.

Drawing on this theoretical work, the case studies discussed in the second half of the book present a variety of approaches to scoring and soundtrack creation which, I argue, may be considered productively in terms of their relationship to classical scoring and soundtrack practice. As mentioned above, all of these films were produced during the 1980s and early 1990s; the period in which New Hollywood consolidated its control over both the European market and, through a series of mergers and acquisitions, the (previously independent, or semi-independent) American art film market. Three of them are clearly non-Hollywood films, that is, films made outside Hollywood: Jean Luc Godard's *Prénom: Carmen/First-name: Carmen* (1983), Derek Jarman's *The Garden* (1990) and Wim Wenders's *Der Himmel über Berlin/Wings of Desire* (1987). The fourth film, David Lynch's *Wild at Heart* (1990), is an example of the approach of New Hollywood to the co-financing and distribution of films which might otherwise have been lower-budget independent art films.

In the soundtracks to each of these films a different relationship to classical scoring and soundtrack practice is uncovered. The music to *Prénom: Carmen* offers a deconstruction of the relationship of sound and image proposed by the classical Hollywood film. Here, the presence of a diegetic string quartet produces both diegetic and nondiegetic music cues. Many of these cues can be considered to adhere to classical scoring practices, though in many cases they exaggerate these practices to the extreme and in doing so reveal their artifice. Relatedly, the soundtrack to *The Garden* exposes the risk of uncoupling the apparent unity of the sound and image track as expressed in classical soundtrack practice. Through the use of out-of-sync singing and of transformed 'real world' sounds and wholly acousmatic electroacoustic music and sound (that is, the presentation of music and sound with no visible sources depicted on-screen), this film explores the possibility that a film's soundtrack may be liberated from slavery to the image track.

By contrast to *Prénom: Carmen* and *The Garden*, *Wings of Desire* foregrounds a negotiation between classical and alternative scoring and soundtrack practices. This occurs through the film's presentation of two ontologically distinct realms – the mortal and the angelic – with the mortal representative of classical soundtrack practices and the angelic, alternative scoring and soundtrack practices. The mortal realm is associated with pop tracks which are played back or performed diegetically, with the valorization of sight over sound (ocularcentrism) and the use of colour – as opposed to black and white – film stock. The omnipresent angels are associated with Jürgen Knieper's nondiegetic score, the valorization of sound over sight exemplified by the angels' ability to hear the thoughts of the mortals unseen, and black and white film stock. Furthermore, it is possible to read the film's mortal realm as representative of Hollywood cinema, and the angelic, European cinema; in this way, the film's narrative depicts the relationship between these cinemas allegorically. Rather than privileging one realm over the other – and thus also, one form of scoring and soundtrack practice – the film presents the possibility of negotiation or compromise between them. In *Wild at Heart* the relationship between these scoring and soundtrack practices is fully integrated. Through collaborative production practice Lynch produces a score and soundtrack that present the utopian potential which was theoretically possible during the all-under-one-roof period of studio production, though rarely achieved. Sounds and dialogue are used in musical ways. Segues between different musical cues demonstrate a level of attention to detail which far surpasses the norm. Further, on a number of occasions the character of Sailor (played by Nicholas Cage) 'takes charge' of the soundtrack, and in this way functions as a stand-in for Lynch as soundtrack innovator.

Each of these analyses is an attempt to develop a synthesis of film studies and musicology. One intention of this book is to assist those who may be unfamiliar with the literature of film studies or film music studies to gain at least a basic understanding of some of the key theoretical issues and debates. The case studies are not intended to offer detailed insights into every musical cue of the scores to these films, however. Instead, they are organized to provide evidence to support the thesis of the book: that is, that it is not only productive to consider institutional issues in respect of Hollywood cinema, but also in terms of alternatives to this cinema(s), in particular, in relation to scoring practices. Thus, the interpretations of these scores and soundtracks offered in the case study chapters have been developed through the analysis of their relationship with, or opposition to, classical scoring and soundtrack practices. In providing evidence for these interpretations other material has inevitably been excluded from these analyses.

It is also important to highlight what I do *not* set out to achieve in this book. For example, I do not develop Grand Theory, but I draw on a range of theoretical frameworks in order to present an argument about film scores and soundtracks. Neither do I attempt to offer an overview of world cinema soundtracks or, indeed, world cinema theory, though some of the issues discussed here are certainly relevant to the analysis of other cinemas' soundtracks. This book is not, unfortunately, a sociological study of film soundtracks; such studies are desperately needed. Similarly, it is not primarily psychological or psychoanalytic in its approach either. Rather, in arguing for the usefulness of considering institutional issues in relation to cinema soundtracks, this book offers a tentative beginning: we are as yet a long way from connecting all of the elements which, when taken together, will offer a more complete picture of film soundtracks from within a variety of world cinema institutions at a global level to the more local considerations of the roles that film soundtracks play in people's lives, outside of the cinema. My hope is not that I have presented *the* answer to a particular question, but that this study will stimulate debate about the aesthetics and interpretation of film scores and soundtracks in general.

I use the term 'score' (and 'scoring') to refer to the solely musical element of a film soundtrack. Traditional conceptions of the term tend to focus on original instrumental music written for specific films at the expense of non-original material, such as pre-existent songs. Here I include *all* musical material used in the film under the heading of 'score'. By contrast, discussion of a film 'soundtrack' may include consideration of the other sonic elements of a film: dialogue and sound effects.

Where I was not able to locate a copy of the original score material to these films, the analyses are based on my own aural skills (and failings!). I am grateful to certain individuals for checking these transcriptions and analytical sketches, but all errors are my own.

Notes

1. Sales of soundtrack albums which predominantly feature pop songs tend to outsell orchestral score soundtracks. In the Top Ten list of 'America's biggest selling soundtracks of all time' featured in Hughes's article (source: Recording Industry Association of America), only one, *Titanic*, is an orchestral score and this album also features the film's theme song 'My Heart Will Go On' sung by Celine Dion (Hughes 2000, p. 9).
2. Nondiegetic music is thus opposed to diegetic music, which the film's characters can – in theory – hear. See Gorbman 1980 and 1987, pp. 11–30, for a discussion of this terminology.
3. Thomas Schatz (1993) traces the roots of the blockbuster back to big-budget, high production value, studio-financed independent productions of the 1950s and earlier.
4. *Star Wars* (Lucas, 1977), *The Empire Strikes Back* (Kershner, 1980), *The Return of the Jedi* (Marquand, 1983); *Raiders of the Lost Ark* (Spielberg, 1981), *Indiana Jones and the Temple of Doom* (Spielberg, 1984), *Indiana Jones and the Last Crusade* (Spielberg, 1989).
5. Relatedly, Peter Krämer (1998) suggests that many such films might be better classed as family films, due to Hollywood's attempt to reach a wider demographic and thus maximize profit potential.
6. See Carroll (1982). Also, Jeff Smith discusses Carroll's ideas concerning the use of 'allusion to film history as an expressive device' and argues that these ideas are helpful in explaining the function of pop music in films (1998, p. 167).
7. See Crafton (1999) for a detailed discussion of the formats tried and tested before sound-on-film was accepted as the norm.
8. For a useful summary of the impact of divorcement on the Hollywood industry, see Maltby 1995, pp. 71–3.
9. See, for example, Fenlon 1989.
10. It should be noted, however, that most such technologies were not developed (nor adopted) in a straightforwardly teleological manner. Rather, it is only in retrospect that attempts have been made to see such developments in evolutionary terms. See Armes 1988; Belton 1985b, 1992a and 1992b.
11. These labels included Angel, Seraphim, MGM Records, Warner Bros., Deutsche Gramaphonn, London, Polydor, Unicorn, London Phase 4, Citadel Records, Chalfont. Elmer Bernstein's mail order series 'Elmer Bernstein Film Music Collection' was also influential during the 1970s.
12. Kalinak states that Lucas 'had originally wanted to use classical music as accompaniment for the first *Star Wars* film, but Williams convinced him to try

original music' (1992, p. 198).

13. Kalinak 1992, pp. 198–9. Kalinak cites Greg Oatis writing for *Cinemafantastique*: 'One would think that faced with the limitless possibilities of space and the multiplicity of life forms Williams would explode with ideas. But in composing the sound to go with the future, Williams doesn't look to any of the "avant-garde" composers like Varese and Cage ... Instead Williams looks to the major-key flourishes of Wagner ... and Tchaikovsky ... and the swashbuckling *Captain Blood* and *Adventures of Robin Hood* soundtracks of Erich Wolfgang Korngold' (p. 184).

14. For recent approaches to the European–Hollywood cinema relationship see, for example, Nowell-Smith and Ricci 1998; Petrie 1992; Ellwood and Kroes 1994; Morrison 1998. Chapters 4 and 6 in this book include brief discussion of the relationship between French and German cinemas in relation to Hollywood.

15. Only a fraction of European cinema is actually 'modernist' in this manner, however, and as is discussed further in the chapters which follow, the notion of the 'classical' is also open to a range of interpretations.

16. See, for example, Shohat and Stam 1994; Stam 2000a, pp. 20–22; de Grazia 1998, p. 20.

17. There has been some discussion of the impact of the coming of sound on language and the development of different language versions of films, however. See, for example, Vincendeau 1999; Garncarz 1999; Claus and Jäckel 2000.

Chapter 1

Classical Hollywood cinema and scoring

Classical cinema and the realist aesthetic

Most critics agree that the term 'classical' was first used in relation to Hollywood cinema by French film critic and theorist André Bazin in lectures delivered in the 1950s. In part, this was a direct response to those French critics who were dismissive of the huge numbers of Hollywood films which flooded France in the years immediately following the Second World War. Bazin used the term 'classical' as a means of elevating Hollywood cinema's critical status. As he states in the essay 'The Evolution of the Language of Cinema':

> By 1938 or 1939 the talking film, particularly in France and in the United States, had reached a level of classical perfection as a result, on the one hand, of the maturing of different kinds of drama developed in part over the past ten years and in part inherited from the silent film, and, on the other, of the stabilization of technical progress. (Bazin 1967, p. 30.)

Here Bazin creates a notion of the classical informed by both the institutional and the aesthetic, and perhaps implicitly, their interdependence.[1] Eliding apparent stylistic differences between silent and sound films, he draws a distinction between directors who allow the 'plasticity' of the object(s) being photographed to shine through unproblematically – thus moving closer to depiction of the 'real', the teleological goal toward which Bazin believed cinema was headed – and those who are reliant on montage. In his view 'montage can be "invisible"' with scenes

> broken down ... to analyze an episode according to the material or dramatic logic of the scene. It is this logic which conceals the fact of the analysis, the mind of the spectator quite naturally accepting the viewpoints of the director which are justified by the geography of the action or the shifting emphasis of dramatic interest (1967, p. 24).

Here classical cinema is conceived as transparent in the seemingly direct presentation of the drama; a directness dependent upon spectators' attention being drawn away from the mechanisms of filmmaking, particularly editing. Bazin implies that the shift towards such 'invisible' forms of montage was inevitable and teleological.

According to Bazin, classical cinema reaches its zenith in 1939, shifting to, or incorporating, a more 'baroque' form of filmmaking in the 1940s due, at least in part, to the influence of thematic and stylistic developments within various national cinemas.[2] This transformation involves the incorporation of a range of devices in addition to the continuity system, including the development of the technique of 'depth of field' and its use by such US and French directors as Jean Renoir, Orson Welles and William Wyler. 'Depth of field' shots allow dramatic expression to unfold within a single camera set-up, and can thus function as a replacement for classical continuity editing techniques such as the shot/reverse-shot format so favoured during dialogue scenes, in which the spectating-subject is shown a view followed by the source of that view, or vice versa. Further, shots-in-depth inevitably involve montage in themselves, by making inter-relations and juxtapositions a part of the shot (1967, pp. 34–5). Indeed, by contrast with classical editing's 'insidiously substituted mental and abstract time', shots-in-depth enable 'real time' to be 'returned' to the objects depicted on screen (p. 39). Such techniques bring the cinema audience ever closer to the representation of the real, and involve a democratization of cinema for Bazin, making the spectator's experience more active, and enabling 'a sense of the ambiguity of reality' (p. 37).

For Bazin, the classical cinema is defined by a period of relative stability in institutional and aesthetic terms, during which large-scale technological developments such as synchronous sound and colour are also stabilized. It has the ability to please a 'worldwide public', and exhibits 'perfect balance' in matching its cinematography and editing to a film's subject matter.[3] Classical cinema is a staging post *en route* to the goal of the representation of the real; a representation surpassed with the development of techniques such as depth of field. Indeed, already implicit in Bazin's theorization is the notion that the depiction of the real presented by classical editing is in some sense surreptitious. As discussed below, this view was much developed by later *Cahier du cinéma* critics.

Classical cinema as ideological

> I love to go to the movies; the only thing that bothers me is the image on the screen.
>
> Theodor Adorno[4]

It was not long after the demonstrations and riots in France in May 1968 that *Cahier du cinéma* critics Jean-Luc Comolli and Jean Narboni ([1969] 1999) posited classical cinema's 'depiction of reality' to be ideological. In this manifesto-like Marxist editorial they argue that 'films ... are produced and distributed by the capitalist economic system and within the dominant ideology' (p. 753). While these critics concur with Bazin's suggestion that the essence of cinema is its reproduction of reality, they go on to argue that because the techniques and devices of filmmaking have been developed under dominant ideology, the 'reality' presented in films serves only to reproduce this ideology (p. 755).[5] Indeed, Comolli and Narboni state that it is virtually impossible for filmmakers to change the economic relations under which their films are produced and distributed (p. 754). Instead, they urge filmmakers to attempt to reveal the ideology inherent in classical cinema's 'so-called "depiction of reality"', so that it may become possible to 'be able to disrupt or possibly even sever the connection between the cinema and its ideological function' (p. 755). Comolli and Narboni categorize films according to their relationship with dominant ideology: from those which serve dominant ideology unproblematically, to those which are rendered subversive by their breaching of the conventions of 'realist' cinema by means of formal radicalism and oppositional content. A further category describes films that appear to conform to dominant ideology yet may be recuperated from it through the existence of internal tensions between film content and form, and the critic's ability to 'read against the grain'.[6]

Fellow *Cahiers* critic Jean-Louis Baudry initially also entertained the possibility of an oppositional cinema in which '[b]oth specular tranquility and the assurance of one's own identity collapse simultaneously with the revealing of the mechanism, that, is of the inscription of the film work [*sic*]'.[7] However, for Baudry, ideological intent at the level of the film text is preceded by that at the level of the mechanics of the cinematic apparatus, in particular, in terms of the camera and the projector:

> It is an apparatus destined to obtain a precise ideological effect, necessary to dominant ideology: creating a phantasmatization of the subject, it collaborates with a marked efficiency in the maintenance of idealism. ... The ideology of representation (as a principal axis orientating the notion of aesthetic 'creation') and specularization (which organises the *mise-en-scène* required to constitute the transcendental function) form a singularly coherent system in the cinema. Everything happens as if, the subject himself being unable – and for a reason – to account for his own situation, it was necessary to substitute secondary organs, grafted on to replace his own defective ones, instruments or ideological formations capable of filling his function as subject. In fact, this substitution is only possible on the condition that the instrumentation itself be hidden or repressed. ([1974–5] 1986, p. 295)

Baudry here argues that the act of looking is collapsed with that of cinematic representation. His work draws on a psychoanalytic framework: subjects comply with their suppression by dominant ideology because the cinematic experience is in some sense pleasurable.[8] This pleasure serves to mask the 'captivation' of the spectator by the image which results in a form of regressive dream state. Thus, the subject's identification with characters on screen is only *secondary* to identification with the cinematic apparatus – an identification unique to cinema, and one which places cinema alongside the other state apparatuses, such as schools and churches, which Louis Althusser defines as ideological.[9] However, locating ideological intent at the level of the apparatus, ultimately led Baudry to the view that resistance to dominant ideology is futile.[10] Not even alternative modes of representation can disrupt such powerful processes. Comolli also grew sceptical of the possibility of opposition and instead highlighted the collusion of the subject in its 'captivation'.[11]

In *The Imaginary Signifier* ([1975] 1982), Christian Metz combines, restates and redefines many of the points made earlier by *Cahiers* theorists.[12] In summary, he argues that, ideologically speaking, the classical Hollywood film encourages a particular screen–spectator relationship: the spectator – the 'I', or 'first person' of this spectator – is invited to identify with the space within the film's fiction which is occupied by the 'eye', or lens, of the camera. With the aid of Lacanian psychoanalysis Metz argues that the spectator's identification with a material representation of space (primary identification) is mapped on to a symbolic one (secondary identification): the spectator identifies this space as that held by various characters or positions of knowledge. This subsumption of the spectating-subject into the narrative – which basically describes what cinematic suture is – takes the form of various cinematic devices and their role in particular systems, perhaps best exemplified by the shot/reverse-shot operation (Heath 1977–78; Silverman 1983).

From the mid-1970s to the late 1980s, the framework offered by Metz's Marxist-psychoanalytic account of spectatorship became the dominant approach to Hollywood cinema in Anglo-American academic circles. However, increasingly this approach (and that of the earlier *Cahiers* critics) has come under attack.[13] Some critics have noted the ahistoricity of the approach, which once again reduces cinema to the realization of a teleological project à la Bazin. In doing so this approach constructs the viewing subject as 'abstract, essentialized and overly homogenous' (Jay 1994, p. 487). In focusing primarily on the cinematic apparatus and on film style the Marxist-psychoanalytic approach fails to take account of the person, the socialized individual watching the film. Particularly interesting to *this* study is the fact that this approach almost totally ignores any contribution made by a film's soundtrack, including music. This may be because the admission of sound or music into the model would allow the 'possibility of seeing tensions between aspects of the film experience that might work against ideological closure', which would, thus, undermine the argument presented (ibid.). Metz himself draws attention to the failure to consider sound on its own terms (rather than through visual-oriented language and theory) in his discussion of 'aural objects', under the heading 'Ideological Undermining of the Aural Dimension' ([1975] 1980, pp. 25–7).

'"To understand" a perceptual event is not to describe it exhaustively but to be able to classify and categorize it: to designate the object of which it is an example (Metz [1975] 1980, p. 27). By contrast to visual objects, sonic objects tend to be considered largely adjectival – attributes, characteristics – rather than nouns in themselves (p. 25). Sounds are considered as objects in terms of their sources rather than in their own right (p. 27). Off-screen sound is so-called when a sound's source is not visible onscreen (though the sound is heard). In fact, a sound is never 'off'; it is either audible or inaudible. Thus, 'the language used by technicians and studios, without realizing it, conceptualizes sound in a way that makes sense only for the image' (p. 29). This situation is partially due to the fact that the physical location of a sound's source is more 'vague and uncertain' than is the case with visual objects, with sound's relationship to space 'much less precise' (p. 30). But this doesn't wholly explain the confusion: the ideology behind it is due to the cultural 'conception of sound as an attribute' rather than an object in its own right (ibid.).

The conceptions of classical cinema advanced in *Cahiers* (and *Screen*) through the 1970s drew on Bazin's formulation of this cinema's transparency as a function of various stylistic devices, technological developments and the foregrounding of dramatic logic. These later critics interpreted this transparency as deeply ideological. Theorizations of classical cinema were focused primarily around the notion that the subject-position of the film spectator is constructed by the film text through its privileging of certain discourses over others – in the case of classical cinema, the transparency of the dominant discourse – but also in the way that the apparatus functions within these discourses (that is, the role of the camera in filming, and so on). Such approaches emphasized the identification and interpretation of aesthetic norms, and highlighted their function in the perpetuation of dominant ideology (bourgeois capitalism). The classical was assumed to be something relatively unchanging, though little or no empirical evidence was presented to support these accounts, in general. By contrast (and at least partially in response to this lack of data), in *The Classical Hollywood Cinema: Film Style and Mode of Production to 1960* (1985), David Bordwell, Janet Staiger and Kristin Thompson sought to produce a more empirically rigorous yet also systematic approach to classical Hollywood cinema. They describe theirs as 'an attempt to articulate a theoretical approach to film history' (p. xv).

Classical Hollywood cinema and historical poetics

> Before there are auteurs, there are constraints, before there are deviations, there are norms.
>
> David Bordwell, in Bordwell et al. 1985, p. 4

Bordwell, Staiger and Thompson's particular brand of historical poetics (also described as neo-formalism) is founded upon assumptions formed by cognitive psychology rather than psychoanalysis. Where Marxist-psychoanalytic theories emphasize the passivity of the viewing subject, fully constructed by the text and apparatus of classical Hollywood cinema, theorists such as Edward Branigan and Bordwell et al. suggest instead that '[c]lassical films call forth activities on the part of the spectator'.[14]

> Meir Sternberg characterizes following a tale as 'gap-filling', and just as we project motion on to a succession of frames, so we form hypotheses, make inferences, erect expectations, and draw conclusions about the film's characters and actions. ... [T]he spectator must co-operate in fulfilling the film's form. It is clear that the protocols which control this activity derive from the system of norms operating in the classical style. For example, an insistence on the primacy of narrative causality is a general feature of the classical system; the viewer translates this norm into a tacit strategy for spotting the work's unifying features, distinguishing significant information from 'noise,' sorting the film's stimuli into the most comprehensive pattern. (Bordwell et al. 1985, p. 8.)

Thus, rather than assuming that an audience's engagement with a film narrative is the result of appeals made to the unconscious, the proposition is that the classical systems of narrative causality, spatial and temporal representation encourage audiences to 'treat what they see *as if it were real*'.[15] Thus spectators are invited to bring their perceptions of the everyday world to bear on the world unfolding on screen, as Bazin too had suggested some years earlier. Bordwell et al. retain the notion of 'the classical' because 'the principles which Hollywood claims as its own rely on notions of decorum, proportion, formal harmony, respect for tradition, mimesis, self-effacing craftsmanship, and cool control of the perceiver's response – canons which critics in any medium usually call "classical"'(1985, pp. 3–4). The term serves as a shorthand to this cinema's 'aesthetic qualities ... and historical functions' (p. 4).

Bordwell et al. conceive of classical Hollywood cinema as a mode of film practice which persisted from 1917 to 1960 and comprised 'an integral system, including persons and groups but also rules, films, machinery, documents, institutions, work processes, and theoretical concepts' (1985, p. xiii). In particular they highlight that this period of Hollywood filmmaking is characterized by a stabilization of aesthetic norms and also the consolidation of the studio mode of production with its 'detailed division of labour, the continuity script, and a hierarchical managerial system' (p. 9); that is, procedures and practices which are organized around cost efficiency. For these authors the persistence of this industrialized mode of film production and the stability of aesthetic norms during this period were mutually reinforcing.

By contrast to the Marxist-psychoanalytic theorists of the 1970s, Bordwell, Staiger and Thompson in part base their findings on the analysis of a random sample of one hundred Hollywood films. They state that from around 1917, classical film style – as determined by aesthetic norms and economic imperatives – became the dominant mode. Although the specific devices of film style have changed over time (through technological development, for example), the more abstract systems governing the use of these devices (in particular, narrative causality, the representation of space, and time), and the interrelations between these systems endured. Of these, narrative causality (organized around human agency, particularly in terms of psychological motivation) is considered to be primary in classical cinema, with the systems of the representation of space and time subordinated to it. Thus the devices and conventions which depict space and time on-screen function to produce a verisimilitudinous and internally consistent representation of the fictional world in which the narrative takes place, but also work to efface their role and that of the cinematic apparatus, resulting in an apparently unmediated presentation of the narrative.[16] As Richard Maltby points out, '[f]rom this perspective, the typical Hollywood movie appears as a coherent, unified, story-telling whole' (1995, p. 333).

Bordwell et al. highlight the role that economic imperatives have played in technological change, demonstrating that moments of innovation can often be traced to 'a specific attempt to improve efficiency or differentiate the product' (1985, p. 367). However, they also argue that even the most dramatic technological developments did not challenge the classical style, but were instead quickly incorporated into it through its stable aesthetic norms. Pertinent here is the case of the shift to synchronized sound. Bordwell et al. verify their claims about the assimilation of new developments through highlighting that

> [t]hroughout the practices and discourses of the technical agencies from 1927 to 1932, one finds a highly coherent set of analogies between image and sound, between the visual and the auditory construction of narrative space and time. In these analogies, the recording of speech is modelled upon the way cinematography records visible material, and the treatment of music and sound effects is modelled upon the editing and laboratory work applied to the visual track. (1985, p. 301)

Their analysis of technical manuals and other documentation of the period demonstrates that, in aesthetic terms, throughout the 1930s sound recording was linked to cinematography by means of a biological analogy, with the camera and the microphone behaving as the eye and ear of an imaginary person watching and listening to the scene. Just as the cinematographer must 'work to create an impression of visual depth' so the sound recordist must work to create 'sound perspective'. 'Just as manipulation of focus and framing eliminates unwanted background detail, techniques for reducing ground noise create a "foreground" vocal space', in a similar manner to the way in which an imaginary person watching and listening to the scene would 'tune-in' to whichever sonic element they considered most important.[17] Further, just as characters in silent films were often highly mobile, so a means had to be found to enable these movements to be reflected in the recording of characters' voices in sound cinema. For example, norms had to be developed to define the relationship between the loudness of a recorded voice and the scale of a shot. Camera movement also created problems: if the camera and microphone were to generate the impression of a single coherent subject (the imaginary person mentioned above), a mobile microphone had to be developed. Early microphones were noisy when moved because they had their own amplifiers, so sound technicians had to use a number of fixed microphones and fade them up and down according to camera movement and action. By 1930, however, the first microphone boom had been developed. Dialogue gradually became the primary carrier of narrative action in the sound film. The technical innovations and developments in sound recording which followed were virtually all aimed at improving the ability of the equipment to capture better the subtleties of the human voice, and to inhibit the recording of unwanted background noise which could obscure the dialogue, such as that generated from the set and the cameras.

While acknowledging that the American film industry has undergone a number of changes since 1960 (such as saturation booking, recutting and redistributing a film, conglomerate ownership), Bordwell et al. argue that few such changes have affected the mode of production. Where these changes *have* affected production, many such modifications can be considered to be extensions of practices from the studio era, such as the continuation of the package-unit system, and similarities in the union contract agreements for recording musicians, although they are now freelance workers rather than studio employees (Bordwell et al. 1985, pp. 368–9). Indeed, the authors assert that 'the classical style remains the dominant model for feature filmmaking' (p. 370). Even though Bordwell et al. argue that more recent Hollywood cinema, or what they term 'New' Hollywood cinema (from *c*. 1970), has absorbed conventions of the art cinema, they state that it continues to wear its relationship to 'old Hollywood' on its sleeve (as do many of the European art films it draws on), with a conservative style and conformance to generic conventions (pp. 375, 377). Thus, '[i]n a sense, Bordwell's argument can be seen as the reiteration, within his own theoretical framework, of Bazin's famous remark concerning the "fertility" of the "classical art" of American cinema "when it comes into contact with new elements"' M. Smith 1998, p. 11).

This approach to classical Hollywood cinema has been highly influential though it has also received a certain amount of criticism. For Bill Nichols, the main problem is the idealization of the spectator: the failure to address viewing subjects as gendered and historically situated (1992, p. 75). This is a view echoed by Richard Maltby (1995), though primarily due to the fact that the emphasis on the centrality of coherent narrative delimits consideration of any of the other pleasures which movie-goers might attend to during their experience of a Hollywood film. A Hollywood movie's 'consumable identity' is such that it exploits a wide range of possible access routes in order to maximize profits, via its star performances or special effects, for example (Klinger 1989). Indeed, some argue that Hollywood cinema has always been too opportunistic to be defined by the high degree of standardization proposed by Bordwell et al. Furthermore, the assimilation of 'alien aesthetic norms into the dominant system' inevitably involves a 'necessary process of experimentation and accommodation' (Jenkins

1995, p. 114). In emphasizing the persistence and continuity of classical Hollywood filmmaking, however, Bordwell, Staiger and Thompson restrict discussion of these transitional moments.[18]

The Marxist-psychoanalytic and neo-formalist accounts share a number of features: both attempt to approach objectivity (one by revealing ideological positions, the other by using empirical evidence); both involve quasi-scientific theoretical bases (whether psychoanalytic, psychological or empirical).[19] Both also interpret classical Hollywood filmmaking as the embodiment of unity, coherence, and transparency, and the dominant form of filmmaking practice.[20] However, while the Marxist-psychoanalytic account makes no real attempt to consider the film soundtrack, for Bordwell et al. music provides the best example of the assimilation of sound to the aesthetic norms which define classical Hollywood cinema: classical Hollywood scoring.

Classical Hollywood scoring

By around 1910 it was usual practice for films to be exhibited with continuous musical accompaniment (Altman 1997; Marks 1997). While the audience of a silent film would very possibly hear a different accompaniment to the same film in a different cinema, or even from one screening to the next, in each case it would hear a continuous musical accompaniment which bore a loose relationship to the narrative action. At around the same time orchestral cue sheets – 'special scores' – were being prepared and distributed by the studios for their big features, signalling a first attempt by studios to take control of the music which accompanied the exhibition of their films (Marks 1997, p. 62). Throughout the silent era the choice of music and means of accompaniment had generally been decided by the theatre owners and their musicians (and before cinema became a fixed-site form of entertainment, by the showmen and women). With the coming of sound, studios became wholly responsible for the soundtracks to their films.[21] After an initial period of transition in which there was a good deal of experimentation (with a variety of coexistent practices), scoring-production practice necessarily became more uniform and led to a more standardized soundtrack than had ever previously existed.[22]

For maximum efficiency the studio sound and music departments were organized according to the same extreme specialization of labour as the rest of the production system. Indeed, the coming of sound standardized further the already industrialized mode of film production since more subdivisions of labour were required. These included dialogue coaches and directors, composers, arrangers, orchestrators, and a range of sound recording experts (Bordwell et al. 1985, p. 246). In the case of the music department, having 'spotted' the film (that is, having located the points at which music should be used), composers were frequently required to write only melodies and harmonies, which would then be realized by orchestrators. Copyists would write out the parts for performance, and salaried players performed them conducted by a musical director (who would sometimes also write the music for the credit sequences by cutting and pasting the film's big themes together).[23]

A number of the scoring functions which gradually became standardized after the coming of sound can be traced back to practices which developed during the silent era. These include: music's role as continuity device – that is, the use of music to cover over gaps and smooth over unevenness in a film's visuals (and possibly also to 'drown out' the sound of the projection equipment initially); the practice of 'sneaking in and out' – that is, of fading the amplitude of music up on entry and down on exit rather than drawing attention to the presence of music with abrupt starts and stops;[24] music as narrating device.

Bordwell et al. point to a range of possible predecessors of film music's narrating function. Background music was used intermittently in nineteenth-century melodrama, for example, to 'underscore dramatic points' (though it was used throughout spectacle plays and pantomimes; 1985, p. 33). Nineteenth-century composer Richard Wagner also used music continuously and narratively in his operas, following his conception of 'unending melody'. Again musical material was used to 'underscore dramatic points', but here music was on a more equal footing with the drama than was the case with melodrama, to the extent that it could be used to offer information to the audience which was not yet presented on stage, or which conflicted with what was presented on stage, in particular, through the use of leitmotifs. These are musical units which may be distinguished through either their melody, harmony, rhythm, or orchestration, and which become associated, by repetition, with a character, situation or idea. As a number of commentators have noted, discussion of Wagnerian theory and practice was featured prominently in articles and manuals concerned with the musical accompaniment of films during the silent and early sound periods.[25] Sections of the score which did not use leitmotivic organization 'functioned as a recitative to cue specific attitudes to the scene (e.g. comic music, suspense music)' (Bordwell et al. 1985, p. 34).

In their most complex incarnation – in Wagner's *Ring* cycle of four operas originally intended to be performed on consecutive evenings – these leitmotifs fulfilled a range of functions: assisting audience recognition (or memory) of particular characters, events or ideas across the operas by operating as musical signifiers generating connections through association; highlighting connections between such elements which may or may not be presented on stage, taking the form of characters' thoughts, for example; and generating coherence and unity across these lengthy works. For all of these reasons, leitmotivic organization proved to be a popular means by which film music operated in narrative terms in both the silent and the sound eras. However, while in Wagner's operas music could 'flaunt its omniscience by ironic or prophetic uses of motifs', Bordwell et al. state that in the classical film the narrating function of music is limited to character causality; it must be motivated by the story, not vice versa (p. 35). The score can, though, be considered to offer brief 'glimpses' of omniscience through the presentation of motifs during the opening credits sequence and through its occasional anticipation of developments in the storyline (p. 34). Indeed, the very existence of nondiegetic music indicates a certain self-consciousness in film scoring: this is music for the film's audience but is not accessible to the film's characters.

Making reference to Adorno and Brecht, Bordwell et al. connect the conventions of classical filmmaking and classical scoring still further by suggesting that the 'scale of the orchestral forces employed and the symphonic tradition itself create an impersonal wash of sound befitting the unspecific narrator of the classical film' (1985, p. 34). The moments at which the music *may* become more foregrounded are, as with classical camerawork, the points at which there is little dialogue with which to compete. By the mid-1930s, classical scoring was able to function similarly to classical camerawork in its ability to move seamlessly across different levels of narration: from semi-objective or 'unrestricted' positions in which music is used to assist in establishing the locale or period of the diegetic world, to more 'restricted' ones in which it is used to express characters' mental states, thoughts and desires: 'subjective musical point-of-view' (ibid.).

Although the practice of 'sneaking' in and out of the frame had been discussed by critics and in handbooks and manuals since the silent era, with the coming of sound attention became focused on the more general issue of 'unobtrusiveness'. In his handbook for composers and conductors of 1935, Leonid Sabaneev stated that film music must not draw attention to itself, but should retain its musicality in terms of form, which should 'in some way [be] subordinated to the rhythms of the screen, but not destroyed by them'.[26] Music must be true to its character: a symbolic language, extended and developed in time. It 'must not be asked to suffer dilution by the rhythms and occurrences of the picture' by being asked 'to follow events in detail' (1935, p. 22). The *close* synchronization of music to picture should thus be avoided, since it works against the true nature of music; it is 'anti-musical' (p. 22).

Sabaneev describes film music as the 'left hand' to the (right hand) melody presented on screen. With the exception of moments at which the left hand is *meant* to move into the foreground, in general it should not draw attention to itself, but should offer support to the right hand (the narrative). Indeed, as a 'romantic, irrational element' music is able to heighten the emotional effects of the images on screen (1935, p. 18). In order for the musical background to serve 'as a sort of psychological resonator of the screen, enhancing its effect and augmenting its emotional passages', music and picture must synchronize to the extent that their 'rhythms should coincide' (pp. 22, 23). As long as these rhythms work in harmony, attention will not be drawn to the music but 'the aesthetic effect of the stage action will be strengthened' (p. 23). This is a view shared by Gerald

Cockshott, writing in 1946: film music must function as an unobtrusive servant. It should 'discreetly [heighten] the spectator's emotional response', but not 'keep nudging him violently in the ribs' (1946, p. 6).

Most of these critics agreed that film music should avoid the imitation of natural sounds, which is better served by the then-possible synchronized sound effects, although Sabaneev suggests that musical imitation has its place when 'symbolism ... is required' (1935, p. 24). The usefulness of music as continuity – assisting smooth transitions between scenes and gap-filling between sections of dialogue – is considered important, as is the notion of a sonic hierarchy: film music must not compete with dialogue or sound effects, though it may be used to draw attention to particularly significant lines of dialogue. Both Sabaneev and Cockshott suggest that ideally music should be completely absent when dialogue is present, with music written *around* it. Sabaneev's position on this may well have been due to the technical limitations of sound recording, editing, mixing and playback apparatus in the early 1930s. A number of commentators writing during this period discuss the pragmatics of orchestrating music for the sound film in some detail in an attempt to assist composers avoid the detrimental impact of the microphone and post-production on the sound of the recorded music and its relationship with the other sonic elements. However, as Claudia Gorbman points out, the practice of fading music down during dialogue rather than leaving such sequences unscored had become the norm by the mid-1930s.[27] By contrast to Sabaneev, Cockshott suggests writing music *around* dialogue in an attempt to steer the industry away from the practice of fading music down at musically illogical points (1946, p. 2).

Certain classical scoring practices can therefore usefully be conceived of in terms of a continuation of practices developed during the silent era. However, the shift to synchronized sound and the rapidity of technological innovation during the early years of the sound film resulted in the transformation of a number of these practices, such as the shift from saturation scores to intermittent scoring. Further, in some senses the crystallization of the classical score into the format discussed here was highly dependent upon the technological development of, for example, post-synchronization, dubbing, and multi-track recording. Most commentators agree that by the mid-1930s – for good or bad – Hollywood scoring practice had settled into a fairly stable set of conventions. For Theodor Adorno and Hanns Eisler, writing in 1947, classical scoring conventions were certainly 'bad' in ideological terms.[28] It was Adorno and Eisler who first proposed the idea that classical Hollywood film scoring operated as a signifier of classical Hollywood cinema (albeit implicitly). In many ways their study presaged later film theory: they pre-empted Bazin's ideas about the transparency of classical cinema and Marxist-psychoanalytic approaches to transparency as ideological, for example. They also presaged the conception of cinema as institution and made connections between film style and mode of production. *Composing for the Films* has also influenced a good deal of film musicology. In the following section I summarize what I consider to be the most salient points of their critique of classical Hollywood scoring. Brief consideration is also given to the wider context of this critique, in particular in relation to Theodor Adorno and Max Horkheimer's *Dialectic of Enlightenment* ([1944] 1979).

Composing for the Films: **Adorno and Eisler's critique of classical Hollywood scoring**

In one sense *Composing for the Films* ([1947] 1994) functions as a critique of Hollywood as 'culture industry', in particular, in terms of the passive screen–spectator relationship that Adorno and Eisler believed it encouraged. This was a view of Hollywood that Adorno had developed in collaboration with Max Horkheimer and which had been published three years before the book he co-authored with Eisler, as *Dialectic of Enlightenment* ([1944] 1979). In *Composing for the Films* Adorno and Eisler suggested that Hollywood scoring conventions of the 1930s and 1940s played a vital role in setting up and maintaining this passive screen–spectator relationship. In doing so such conventions assisted the culture industry in its manipulation of the masses and also denied music its potential. Thus, in another sense the book functioned as an attempt to urge film composers to be true to the historical dialectic of musical material that Adorno had developed elsewhere in relation to autonomous music; music which has no other function than to stand for itself.[29] With this historical dialectic – a particular instantiation of a universal 'truth' which underpinned all of his philosophical arguments – he argued that what appears to be fixed by natural law is in fact only convention. This notion is underpinned by Adorno's refusal to grant either history or nature the status of ontological given. Rather, each is knowable only through its dialectical relationship with the other. In the case of musical material, following Schoenberg he stated that through composers' increasing technical control over – or rationalization of – the musical materials handed down to them from the previous generation, they are able to demonstrate the conventional nature of this material and so emancipate themselves from its demands by revealing that it is not 'natural law'.[30]

At times these agendas conflict with the declared premise of Eisler's original commission which, as Graham McCann explains in the introduction to the 1994 edition of *Composing for the Films*, was intended to be an investigation of 'the relationship between the movie, music, original sound and synthetic sound with a view to discovering new possibilities. The hypothesis was that radically new music could be much more constructive and effective in movies than the now clichéd traditional music' (p. xxxii). The main conflict in the book is to be found between the descriptive elements – which McCann argues express a predominantly Adornian critique of Hollywood – and the prescriptive elements – which he suggests sit more comfortably with Eisler's views (pp. xxviii–xxxiii).

This conflict can also be read as a reflection of Adorno and Eisler's radically different views on the role of music in direct political action and, indeed, on direct political action itself: unlike Eisler, Adorno did not believe that direct political action could bring about real change at this point in late capitalism. However, Adornian critique does not preclude the possibility that, at the very least, ideological machinations can be revealed as such (Paddison 1993, pp. 97–105).

It is necessary at this stage to give a brief summary of the view of Hollywood presented by Adorno and Horkheimer in the section of *Dialectic of Enlightenment* entitled 'The Culture Industry'. Here they argued that Hollywood cinema offered the culture industry – a centralized, all-controlling administration – the means to manipulate the 'masses'. The culture industry's dictum that 'the masses must get what they want' simply perpetuated the dominance of mechanized industrialization. Indeed, the culture industry was itself a creation of this same mechanized industrialization. However, Adorno and Horkheimer argued that its real agenda was to provide an illusory escape from the drudgery and alienation which constituted reality for these people. It enabled the masses to employ their leisure time in the pursuit of relaxation and entertainment in order to regain their strength to return to work the next day:

> Amusement under late capitalism is the prolongation of work. ... What happens at work, in the factory, or in the office can only be escaped from by approximation to it in one's leisure time. All amusement suffers from this incurable malady. Pleasure hardens into boredom because, if it is to remain pleasure, it must not demand any effort and therefore moves rigorously in the worn grooves of association. No independent thinking must be expected from the audience: the product prescribes every reaction. ... Even the set pattern itself still seems dangerous, offering some meaning – wretched as it might be – where only meaninglessness is acceptable. ([1944] 1979, p. 137)

Taste and receptivity were thus only apparent freedoms created by the culture industry in order to perpetuate the duping of the consumer by the (pseudo-)individualization of the object. Indeed, all products, or commodities, 'created' by the culture industry, including films, were heavily standardized, with each component interchangeable. It should be noted, however, that it was not the movie production process that Adorno considered to be standardized; writing later in 'The Culture Industry Reconsidered', he referred rather to 'the standardization of the thing itself – such as that of the Western, familiar to every movie-goer – and to the rationalisation of distribution techniques' (1991, p. 87).

In particular, Adorno and Horkheimer criticized the mode of reception they believed Hollywood cinema imposed upon its audience: passivity. They argued that this was due to the fact that it was becoming difficult to distinguish between the movies and real life; a situation brought about, at least in part, by the coming of sound.

> The sound film, far surpassing the theatre of illusion, leaves no room for

imagination or reflection on the part of the audience, who is unable to respond within the structure of the film, yet deviate from its precise detail without losing the thread of the story; hence the film forces its victims to equate it directly with reality. The stunting of the mass-media consumer's powers of imagination and spontaneity does not have to be traced back to any psychological mechanisms; he must ascribe the loss of these attributes to the objective nature of the products themselves, especially the most characteristic of them, the sound film. They are so designed that quickness, powers of observation, and experience are undeniably needed to apprehend them at all; yet sustained thought is out of the question if the spectator is not to miss the relentless rush of facts. Even though the effort required for his response is semi-automatic, no scope is left for the imagination. Those who are so absorbed by the world of the movie – by its images, gestures and words – that they are unable to supply what really makes it a world, do not have to dwell on particular parts of its mechanics during a screening. ([1944] 1979, pp. 126–7)

In this passage Adorno and Horkheimer hint at the ideological nature of the apparent transparency of a Hollywood film's diegetic world: its ability to draw the audience's attention away from the cinematic apparatus and, thus, away from the realization that the film is a product created for an audience. As mentioned above, it was not until the late 1960s and early 1970s that film theorists such as Jean-Louis Baudry (1974–75) began to consider such issues in detail, and most did so solely in terms of the visual apparatus. Indeed, it was not until the early 1980s that cinema's sonic apparatus – in terms of both production and representation – began to be investigated in this way (see Belton 1985a and Doane 1985, for example). Baudry et al. could not see any way out of the subject's unknowing 'captivation' by the ideology of the apparatus. However, in *Composing for the Films* Adorno and Eisler suggest (albeit implicitly) that film music has the potential to reveal this ideological machinery at work.

According to Adorno and Horkheimer, technological development, which had been engineered in the name of the liberation of the worker, now controlled both the working hours and the leisure time of the worker. Others, such as Walter Benjamin, saw the invasion of technology into the sphere of aesthetic production as harbouring the potential for a politically progressive mass art. For Adorno, however, film reproduced the structure of the commodity in the aesthetic realm. As Richard Allen points out:

The relationship between image and referent in the mechanically reproduced image mirrors the relationship established between use value and exchange value in the commodity. Just as use value appears to ensure that exchange value can function as an index of need, so the referent appears to anchor the image in reality. (1987, p. 236)

Thus, rather than seeing the principal exponents of the culture industry – radio and cinema – as leading to Benjamin's collective self-emancipation, Adorno and Horkheimer saw them leading to collective narcotization, and to the perpetuation of the masses' domination at the hands of the late capitalist regime. In *Composing for the Films*, Adorno and Eisler argued that Hollywood uses the particular nature of music and the auditory senses to assist in this narcotization. They were critical of the conventions by which music was composed and placed into the classical Hollywood film. They believed that a serious discrepancy had developed between what they saw as pseudo-traditional conventions and the technological foundations of the motion picture.

In their critique of the scoring conventions which they saw as symptomatic of classical Hollywood, Adorno and Eisler identified many of the same conventions discussed above. The first of these was the leitmotif which, as in Wagnerian music drama, was used as a structuring principle. However, whereas the grandiose scale of the latter meant that these easily recognizable musical units provided the audience of these operas with much-needed signposts through the work, Adorno and Eisler argued that the leitmotif was largely redundant in Hollywood cinema. By contrast to Wagner's operas, Hollywood films were relatively short and tended towards representation of the real.

Adorno and Eisler next turned their attention to the symmetrical melodies frequently used in classical scoring, which were supported by conventional harmonies so that their continuation could be easily predicted by a film's audience, and had their origins in nineteenth-century Romanticism. They argued that such symmetry was unsuited to the 'prosaic irregularity and asymmetry' of movies' visual action and, furthermore, that it conflicted with film music's utilitarian nature ([1947] 1994, p. 8). In order to work with the image, melody must be freed from its tonal and symmetrical fetters. Thus they argue in opposition to the view put forward by a number of the commentators discussed above, who argued that film music must adhere to musical form.

The next convention listed is particularly important for Adorno and Eisler: unobtrusiveness. While they concurred that moments exist in movies in which dialogue must be heard, and under which complex musical development would be disturbing, they argued that to ask for music but stipulate that it must not draw attention to itself is to consider only one possible solution, and one to which 'banal' music is the only answer (p. 10). Adorno and Eisler suggested that non-musical sound would better fit the realist goal instead.

They also argued that the musical illustration of visual action was used too much: given the hyper-explicit visuals of cinema, musical illustration offered only redundancy. The use of music to assist in the characterization of location or era was also criticized. In particular they disagreed with the use of musical arrangements which were intended to typify the music of the period being depicted, arguing that such writing conflicted with the modern technology involved in filmmaking. A number of other conventions were also mentioned in passing, including the use of music to create atmosphere or mood, to express the conflicts of individual characters, or to persuade the spectator to identify with the hero. They concluded their overview with a brief discussion of cliché which, they suggested, had claimed all of the aforementioned conventions. Many individual musical effects have been so overused that all they serve to demonstrate is the tiredness of their expression.[31] Clearly, Adorno's notion of the historical dialectic of musical material is central to these criticisms, as it is to the notion of convention itself.

In *Composing for the Films* Adorno and Eisler create a model of Hollywood in order to critique it, to demonstrate the extent to which rationalization has taken over society, and in which the spectator's (passive) relationship to a film is wholly constructed (and contained) by the film. In particular, they criticize such films for wasting music's potential, for making its contribution redundant by limiting it to assisting further with the film's construction of the subject. However, as I discuss below, music's character made it particularly appropriate to perform this task, for it did so while appearing to deny any part in such a calculated agenda.

Adorno and Eisler were particularly critical of what they saw as the culture industry's manipulation of the specific nature of the auditory sense, and its divergence from the optical. While the eye perceives the world as made up of distinct, separate objects, in general the ear is incapable of such clear-cut differentiation. Where the 'swift, actively selective eye' can see clearly the commodified character of the late capitalist world (in that it distinguishes easily between separate objects), the more passive (always open) ear has simply not adapted to rationalization and industrialization as well as the eye (p. 20). Instead, 'ordinary listening' appears to have a stronger relation to 'pre-individualistic collectivities' than optical perception (ibid.). In order to demonstrate their point further, Adorno and Eisler quote J. W. Goethe on the 'cultural anthropology' of the Enlightenment age:

> 'According to my father everyone should learn to draw. ... He also more seriously urged me to practice drawing rather than music, which, on the other hand, he recommended to my sister, even keeping her at the piano for a good part of the day, in addition to her regular lessons.' (*Dichtung und Wahrheit*, Part I, Book IV.) The boy, visualised by the father as a representative of progress and enlightenment, is supposed to train his eye, while the girl, who represents historically outmoded domesticity and has no real share in public life and economic production, is confined to music, as was generally the case with young upper-class women in the nineteenth century, quite apart from the role of music throughout oriental society. ([1947] 1994, pp. 20–21)

While auditory perception 'preserves comparably more traits of the long by-gone, pre-individualistic collectivities than optical perception' (p. 21), this does not mean that it offers a utopian escape from the administered and alienating world of late capitalism. Instead, the 'amorphous nature [of collectivity] leads itself to deliberate misuse for ideological purposes' (ibid.). Autonomous music is also related to this collectivity, partly due to its nonconceptual nature – '[it] is in a certain sense pre-capitalistic, direct' (p. 22) – but has a dual nature. Following Max Weber, Adorno and Eisler argued that in some respects, music is 'rationalised, extensively technified, and just as modern as it is archaic' (p. 21). Part of music's job is to attempt to 'circumvent [the] taboo' of lazy and passive auditory perception: Adorno and Eisler contrast the 'indolent and dull' ear of the layman to that of the musical expert – an ear of 'concentration, effort, and serious work' (p. 23). However, as a result of its dual nature, music is also the auditory form most open to manipulative effects: it is '*par excellence* the medium in which irrationality can be practised rationally' (p. 22). While it appears to be a medium of direct self-expression, it is actually a mediated discourse underpinned by rationalization, which can be 'managed': '[s]uch a rationally planned irrationality is the very essence of the amusement industry in all its branches. Music perfectly fits this pattern' (p. 23).

This management of music by the culture industry was used to perpetuate further the circularity of its control: keeping the spectator-auditor coming back for more of the same. It is due to this notion of music as potentially, yet surreptitiously, manipulable and manipulating that Adorno and Eisler were so damning of the 'false' conventions and 'tired' clichés of the Hollywood score. By feeding off what essentially amounts to a Romantic view of music – a view of music as unmediated and, thus, *unmanipulated* – the culture industry is able to manage music's rationalization for its own ends, to propagate its own ideology. However, as mentioned above, inherent in Adorno and Eisler's critique is the possibility that music *could* be used in such a way that it would reveal what they saw as the culture industry's controlling, 'management' of Hollywood cinema. Their study berates classical scoring conventions for failing to employ music in relation to this redemptive potential. I return to this issue in Chapter 3, where I consider some of the prescriptions Adorno and Eisler suggested in *Composing for the Films* as alternative scoring practices. In the next section I turn to more recent theories of classical Hollywood scoring.

Classical Hollywood scoring: recent film musicology

In Claudia Gorbman's 1987 account, *Unheard Melodies: narrative film music*, the notion that classical scoring practices are based on the same principles as classical filmmaking is made explicit.[32] Indeed, she states that classical scoring practices cannot be considered separately from classical cinema, which in turn involves a consideration of cinema as an institution and of the texts it produces. Gorbman draws upon the work of Bazin and French Marxist-psychoanalytic accounts, identifying the classical age of cinema as the late 1930s into the 1940s in France and the USA. She defines cinema as 'a conjuncture of several economies, a narrative discourse determined by the organization of labour and money in the cinema industry, by/in ideology, and by the mechanisms of pleasure operating on subjects in this culture' (1987, p. 70). The theoretical model of the classical film is precisely that, however: a theoretical model. No actual film exists which is fully determined by this model. Thus, rather than defining classical cinema as a rigid set of rules, Gorbman presents it as a set of conventions which, when followed, produce a text which is recognizable as a classical film. Such conventions cover duration, plot development, elements of the *mise-en-scène*, editing, sound recording and mixing. Gorbman's account adds scoring practices to this list.

Gorbman follows psycho-structuralist Christian Metz in suggesting that cinema constructs its spectator ideologically, along with his or her desires to know. This is achieved predominantly through classical editing strategies, which attempt to mask the traces of filmic discourse and the role of the cinematic apparatus in narration: the aesthetic of transparency. Through collating evidence from manuals and articles on sound recording and mixing, aesthetic and practical writing on music composition for cinema, as well as analysing a number of the finished texts – movies – Gorbman demonstrates that the principles of music composition for classical films are subject to similar, if not exactly the same ideological premises.

These principles are usefully grouped under seven headings which here, too, combine to produce a pool of conventions rather than a set of obligatory rules: invisibility; inaudibility ('unobtrusiveness' in Adorno and Eisler's terms); signifier of emotion; narrative cueing; continuity; unity; and the possible violation of any of the previous principles in the service of the others. Operating together, these principles promote the spectator's absorption in the narrative and divert attention away from the cinematic apparatus and the mode of production. Invisibility and inaudibility are directly concerned with concealing the presence of nondiegetic music: music created by an extradiegetic persona.[33] Just as the camera must be hidden from view in order to conceal the film's nature as 'product', so too must the sound recording equipment. As was first stated by the theorists and critics writing during the classical period mentioned above, nondiegetic music must not draw attention to its presence but must 'creep' or 'sneak' in under dialogue or sound effects, or arrive with a scene change. It must be appropriate to the scene, subordinate to dialogue, and its form must be dependent on the demands of narrative action so as not to draw attention to itself as music to-be-listened-to.

As signifier of emotion and provider of narrative cues, classical scoring aids the spectator's subsumption into the narrative, once again diverting attention away from the film as technologically created product, albeit indirectly by redirecting attention towards the diegetic world of the film. In particular, certain kinds of musical language have become associated with emotional cues which Gorbman categorizes as the representation of the irrational, of Woman, and of the epic. In the latter case, music assists in '[elevating] the individuality of the represented characters to universal significance'.[34] Scoring which functions in this way is more likely to be heard than other nondiegetic music. It 'invites the spectator to contemplate; it is helping to *make a spectacle* of the images it accompanies' (1987, p. 68; original emphasis); thus, the musical representation of the 'epic' frequently occurs at moments in which the narrative is temporarily halted. The aim of such cues is less to 'bond' spectators to the film's characters and their feelings than with their fellow spectators in the auditorium (ibid.).

Classical scoring can also '[refer] the spectator to demarcations and levels of the narration' (p. 82). These levels range from elements which might be considered external to the diegetic world, such as opening and closing credits music, through to quasi-objective diegetic levels of narration, in which music assists in the denotation of the time and place in which the action takes place, the mood and illustration of the action itself, and to forms of subjective narration in which music assists with the signification of a character's thoughts, feelings and desires.[35] Thus, classical scoring may involve the expression of concepts or ideas, but can also be used to mimic, or make explicit, physical actions depicted on screen ('mickey-mousing') or draw attention to 'sudden dramatic tension' via a 'stinger' (an accented chord synchronized to a specific moment on screen). A spectator's understanding of extra-musical meaning is dependent upon their recognition of 'cultural musical codes' in which particular musical ideas have become associated with particular meanings through convention. Many such conventions are the result of connections formed between music and text and/or drama in song, opera or programme music written across centuries of Western music. Lexicons of mood music compiled during the silent era to assist with the generation of cue sheets – for example, Becce (1919) or Rapee ([1924] 1970) – highlight the degree to which such meaning was codified. These musical ideas accrue further meanings through their placement within the film as a result of their association with the image and/or the narrative: 'cinematic musical codes'.[36] The striven-for transparency of classical cinema requires that meanings are overdetermined. Music offers a further means of underlining and supporting meanings which may also be signified by other filmic components.

Music also works with classical techniques of editing to produce continuity, providing a sonic bridge across cuts (whether these are discontinuities of a spatial, temporal or geographical kind). Similarly, classical film music assists in creating formal and narrative unity in an otherwise discontinuous medium, most often through the 'repetition, interaction and variation of musical themes' (Gorbman 1987, p. 91). Gorbman provides a brief analysis of musical themes and their development in *Mildred Pierce* (Curtiz, 1945) in order to demonstrate their role in generating unity across the film and assisting in narrative cueing through musical conventions. With the final principle she adds a degree of flexibility: music cues may transgress any of the previous principles as long as this transgression operates at the service of the other principles. For example, 'in its illustrative function (IV), music which mickey-mouses the action often becomes noticeable, violating the principle of inaudibility (II)' (ibid.). Indeed, if music and action are too closely synchronized 'we would be ... made conscious of a perversely manipulative narrator' (p. 16).

Gorbman characterizes the medium of the classical Hollywood score during the studio era as that of the symphony orchestra, with nineteenth-century Romantic music its idiom. This has provided the mainstay of narrative film music because 'its purpose is quick and efficient signification to a mass audience' (p. 4). While Gorbman accepts that deviations from this musical language, such as jazz and electronic music, did occur (more often in the 1950s and 1960s), so convinced is she of the communicability of this musical language to this audience that she suggests that 'the reading position of spectators in the thirties and forties was so thoroughly defined by the classical norm that the rare music composed with subversive intentions was most probably perceived as conforming, by and large, to the established canon' (p. 86). However, with the exception of the views of critics and those in the industry at the time, the relative lack of published research on the reception of film music as part of the cinematic experience in any era, means that there is, as yet, little hope of supporting such a view with evidence.

In *Settling the Score: Music and the Classical Hollywood Film* (1992), Kathryn Kalinak presents a view of classical Hollywood scoring which is much in accordance with Gorbman's. She too sees it as defined by a set of structural conventions that were originally institutionalized as a set of practices in the 1930s and 1940s united in the aim of heightening the fictive reality of a film's narrative. Kalinak's view differs from Gorbman's in at least two respects, however. First, Kalinak makes a distinction 'between implicit and explicit content as a determinant on the composer' (1992, pp. 220–21, n.17), where Gorbman makes no distinction as to whether the meaning generated by the music is related to action made visible on screen or something less tangible and implicit, such as an emotion or mood. Second, Kalinak places more emphasis on the 'classical score's symphonic medium and romantic idiom as determining characteristics' (p. 221). Where Gorbman argues that the late Romantic idiom was the norm for classical Hollywood scoring because it offered a stable and well understood signifying system, Kalinak suggests that there are a number of additional reasons why this particular idiom was favoured during the studio era.[37]

First, Kalinak points to the background of the composers who worked in Hollywood in the period during which the conventions were stabilized (the early-to-mid 1930s) and argues that they were predominantly European émigrés 'who brought with them a musical predilection for the nineteenth century' (p. 100).[38] However, the impact of their classical training before emigrating should perhaps not be overestimated: a number of these composers, such as Max Steiner, had been writing 'light' music rather than serious art music before moving to Hollywood (in Europe and on Broadway, for example). In general, light music is based on a more conservative aesthetic than art music.[39]

Second, Kalinak points to producers' conservative tastes and lack of musical acumen. Following the development of synchronized sound, power and control over a score generally belonged to the studio rather than to the composer and/or director. Part of the reason for this was that during the studio era the majority of individual agents (composers and directors, for example) were contractually bound to the studios rather than to particular projects. Just as the coming of sound allowed studios to take full control of their film soundtracks (and take it away from the exhibitors, the cinema managers), so they also usurped power from their employees. Kalinak sees the predominance of the Romantic idiom as further evidence of the control that the studio wielded over its products: studio executives had very conservative tastes, and favoured the melodies and harmonic familiarity of the late Romantic style to that of Stravinsky or the Second Viennese School, for example. Kalinak presents documentary evidence to support this view.[40]

Third, Kalinak suggests that there may be ontological reasons why Romantic music was the predominant idiom of the classical Hollywood film score:

> Film is a discontinuous medium, made up of a veritable kaleidoscope of shots from different angles, distances, and focal depths, and of varying duration. Romanticism, on the other hand, depends upon the subordination of all elements in the musical texture to melody, giving the auditors a clear point of focus in the dense sound. (1992, p. 101)

Thus the focus on melody in Romantic music offered a clear sense of (diversionary) continuity to the film spectator.

Fourth, following Caryl Flinn (1992), Kalinak suggests that the classical Hollywood composers' turn to the Romantic idiom during the studio era may have been a consolatory move: an appeal to the Romantic aesthetic and its association with notions of creative genius and the direct, unmediated power of music to help them cope with the suppression of their artistic sensibilities as part of the heavily industrialized machinery of studio film production. Kalinak sees classical Hollywood score-production practice as defined by the same efficient assembly line mode of production that was a 'determining characteristic of the studio model' with its highly specialized division of labour. Scores were usually composed post-production, and were expected to be finished in four to six weeks (sometimes in a much shorter period of time).[41]

Kalinak's study includes an analysis of Erich Wolfgang Korngold's music for the Errol Flynn swashbuckler, *Captain Blood* (Curtiz, 1935) which is seen as exemplary of the classical Hollywood film score (1992, pp. 79–110). Analyses of four further Hollywood film scores follow. Max Steiner's score for John Ford's *The Informer* (1935) and John Williams's score for George Lucas's *Star Wars* (1977) are discussed explicitly as expressions of the classical Hollywood score (or, in the latter case, a contemporary version of it). The other two scores analysed – Bernard Herrmann's music for Orson Welles's *The Magnificent Ambersons* (1942), which RKO re-edited and partially rescored after Wells had completed it, and David Raksin's score for Otto Preminger's *Laura* (1944) – are considered exemplary in demonstrating the flexibility of classical scoring practices as they developed over time, with both the idiom and medium of the classical Hollywood score undergoing a certain amount of transformation. For Kalinak, however, the 'most consistent and distinctive feature of the classical score' remained constant: 'a structural foundation which bound music and image in service to the narrative' (p. 159).

In *Strains of Utopia: Gender, Nostalgia, and Hollywood Film Music* (1992), Caryl Flinn argues that there were economic, critical, and ideological reasons for the dominance of classical Hollywood scoring during the studio era. In particular, Flinn is concerned with the extent to which the Romantic aesthetic's construction of music as utopian pervaded both institutional practice and critical discourse surrounding it at the time. The Romantic aesthetic originally developed in reaction to advancing industrialization, and signified the triumph of human subjectivity over machinery. It was founded on an 'exalted notion of consciousness of a very singular, individual subject' in combination with a vast universality: the notion of composer as genius, for example (1992, p. 25). The Romantic aesthetic perceived the artist in opposition to society, and great art as always necessarily out-of-step with its immediate context. Music was considered the most Romantic of the arts due to its more abstract, non-representational nature (by comparison with literature and figurative painting, for example), and was thus seen to be connected with other-worldly qualities.[42]

Flinn suggests that Romantic ideology informed the choice of musical style used during the studio era as an antidote to the highly industrial nature of score production: in this way scores would bear the mark of human subjectivity. To a certain extent this ideology was proposed by the composers themselves, but it was also upheld by the studios because it helped to divert attention away from the industrialized nature of their products. As far back as the silent era studios had realized the economic advantage of having new music composed to accompany films, as it was generally cheaper than having to obtain licences for pre-composed music. The copyright control of commissioned film music belonged to the studios and, as mentioned above, Flinn suggests that this too may explain why Hollywood film composers turned, in vain, to the Romantic aesthetic for consolation, given the fact that they had little or no control over their scores. However, film composers' Romantic ideas about authorship resulted in the worsening of their working situation. By disputing that they were employees, and claiming instead to be 'independent contractors', composers lost their rights to rudimentary privileges of employment such as a basic wage and regular breaks.

Flinn demonstrates how influential Wagner's operas and his theoretical principle of the *Gesamtkunstwerk* were to classical cinema's investment in unity (where *Gesamtkunstwerk* may be translated as the 'total work of art', in which the whole adds up to more than the sum of all the parts, that is, the music, the text, the dramatic action, the lighting, and so on). Yet Flinn argues that a good deal of criticism and theoretical work written during the studio era and concerned with classical Hollywood cinema constructed an appearance of unity at the expense of music, in that it didn't allow film music to generate its own meaning: film music must always be subservient to the narrative. The apparent role of music is further compromised by the suggestion that its position in the production schedule – that is, *post*-production – makes it auxiliary to meaning production. Flinn finds such a 'passive', 'inactive' model of the film score difficult to believe given the character of the scores themselves.[43] She cites several composers who discuss the techniques of thematic organization and orchestration they use to avoid clashing with dialogue. Such techniques suggest that a more *contrapuntal* (as opposed to parallel) relationship exists between film music and the other elements of the classical film's complex. Indeed, several composers state that they consider their most successful scores to be those which are 'integrated' most wholly with the film. Thus, Flinn argues that the practice of classical Hollywood scoring exceeds the dominant view that the soundtrack must parallel the image and/or the narrative.[44]

Flinn's position is underpinned by a notion of utopia which is rooted in socio-historical reality, in which subjects' utopian thoughts at a particular point in history reveal what they consider to be deficient or lacking in society at that given time. Thus she suggests that classical Hollywood's turn to the Romantic aesthetic and its subsequent alignment of film music with utopia reveals Hollywood's own belief that the film text of the period was in some sense lacking, that is, in need of completion by music. Furthermore, Flinn proposes that Hollywood attempted to conceal this deficiency of the film text by displacing it on to the film's music, that is, by considering the score's signifying differently – non-representationally – to be evidence of its own incompleteness. In hiding the problems of the film text, music also proved potentially threatening to the appearance of the film complex's unity in that it could reveal that it comprised a soundtrack *plus* an image track: that is, is materially heterogeneous. Flinn believes that this is why such a passive, inactive notion of classical scoring emerged (as limited to paralleling the narrative, and so on). In reality, classical scoring contributes in more constructively integrated ways than simple repetition of the narrative or the image. Further, the alignment of music – as non-representational sign – with an impossible, idealized utopia also meant that it was placed outside of discourse, and could (conveniently) never be adequately spoken of by language. According to Flinn, in making film music its scapegoat, Hollywood was able to conceal the fact that it considered its film texts (and its cinematic apparatus and the viewing-listening situation) to be deficient.

Film musicologists James Buhler and David Neumeyer (1994) also consider the ideological underpinning of film theory's tendency to limit its conception of classical scoring: that the music must parallel, and be subservient to the narrative. In agreement with Flinn, Buhler and Neumeyer argue that film theory of the classical era constructed music in such a way that it was considered to be ontologically different in order to avoid comparison with a film's representational signifiers. However, while Flinn proposes that 'music' was constructed in this way so that it could deflect attention away from deficiencies in the film text, following recent film theoretical considerations of the nondiegetic *voice*, Buhler and Neumeyer argue that this limiting account of nondiegetic scoring is due to the more specific threat of its authority over the other narrative elements. The nondiegetic voice (or voice-over) is considered authoritative because it has the power of narration: it 'creates the diegetic world in its recounting' (1994, p. 379). Thus, because nondiegetic music is generated in the same realm, it must also be capable of this power. Furthermore,

[following] the tradition of 19th century opera, film invests music with moral force, however, music also possesses the potential to disrupt the moral authority not only of the nondiegetic voice, but of the central narrative itself. Worse yet – at least to anyone concerned about preserving the concept of singular, transcendent truths – music might indicate the presence of an alternative moral vision, a presence that would cast doubt on the moral authority that narrative claims. Hence classical film theory has strictly enforced an epistemological difference between nondiegetic voice and nondiegetic music, one that renders music's narrating voice mute, or at least unintelligible. As Gorbman notes, the voice-over 'is perceived as a narrative intrusion,' an intrusion of a narrating voice, while nondiegetic music is not. (ibid.)

Thus, the presence of nondiegetic music brings with it the threat of another transcendental truth in the implication that the narrative may not necessarily be 'the whole story'. Classical film theory stills nondiegetic music's threat by proposing that it is *not* a threat: music must parallel the image, be synchronized to it, because it signifies differently. However, as Gorbman also suggests, Buhler and Neumeyer add that synchronizing image and music too closely can produce an uncanny effect, due to the fact that the music appears to create the image: 'music seems to narrate' (1994, p. 379). In doing so, 'music transgresses (and imperils) the usual epistemological order that places image above music' (ibid.). Nonetheless, Buhler and Neumeyer state that on the whole synchronization *weakens* music's claim to 'discursive authority', since the more that film music is truly synchronized with the image, the more discontinuous and fragmentary it is likely to become.

Buhler and Neumeyer also suggest a similarity between the (apparently threatening) position of nondiegetic music and that of the female voice in cinema as theorized by Kaja Silverman in *The Acoustic Mirror* (1988). Just as classical film theory confines classical scoring to the synchronization of the image, or narrative, so classical cinema confines woman's voice to her body: while a handful of embodied female voice-over narrators exist in classical cinema (such as Lisa in Max Ophuls's *Letter from an Unknown Woman* (1948)), *dis*embodied female voice-overs are rare. Silverman argues that this confinement strips woman of her discursive authority when considered in comparison with the authority that the disembodied voice-over enjoys. For Buhler and Neumeyer:

Just as the illusion of unity between voice and body is consistently upheld in the

> female characters so as not to disrupt the discursive authority of the male subject, so too music that mimics the image allows music to be integrated into the filmic world without challenging the discursive or narrative authority of the image. (1994, pp. 379–80)

Thus, classical Hollywood scoring 'effaces itself in order not to unsettle the epistemological order that film theory has constructed on the basis of the moral authority of a unified, consistent point of view' (1994, p. 381). This view is thus congruent with Martin Jay's critique of the Marxist-psychoanalytic approach to classical cinema discussed earlier in this chapter and which draws on the work of Peter Wollen. Wollen and Jay draw attention to the lack of discussion concerning sound or music in this model, and suggest that to do so would have meant admitting the possibility of unravelling the ideological closure the model otherwise proposes.

So, while Gorbman and Kalinak provide relatively value-free discussions of classical scoring practice and some of the discourses surrounding it, Flinn, Buhler and Neumeyer are more concerned with the ideological implications of such discourses and propose that classical scoring is more transgressive than theoretical discourse suggests. Buhler and Neumeyer also highlight the role that modernist musicology has played in constructing film music as regressive and anachronistic through its predilection for the late Romantic style.[45] They argue that this style predominates 'less for the characteristic sounds than for its flexibility. The late Romantic style flows easily between motivic and tonal modes of organization and can readily absorb such features as touches of local colour, quotations from existing music, and imitations of earlier styles' (p. 383). Indeed, Buhler and Neumeyer suggest that consideration should be given instead to the *variety* of writing encompassed in the typical classical Hollywood score.[46]

Flinn suggests that film composers were, in general, happy to play along with a somewhat constricted notion of what classical scoring *could* or *should* do in a classical film because, with this construction of music as a non-representational, other-worldly discourse which speaks of 'something better' they could associate themselves with the Romantic aesthetic's notion of creative genius. In doing so, film composters were able to deny the industrial reality of their working situation: that they were part of the industrialized studio system, churning out scores at an exceptionally fast rate. Kalinak, for one, suggests that, in this respect, little has changed for many Hollywood composers in terms of their relationship to the industrial machinery of big-budget feature film production (1992, pp. 190–91). Although composers now work freelance (they are no longer salaried staff members of the studios), scoring for television functions for many as a training ground and fulfils one of the roles of the old studio music department. But have classical scores themselves changed? Kalinak's analysis of Williams's score for *The Empire Strikes Back* (1980) suggests that the answer may be: not much. By contrast, the industry itself has been subject to some major structural transformations. In the next chapter, the impact of these changes and others on the aesthetic of Hollywood cinema are considered in relation to the score and soundtrack.

Notes

1. Bazin's conception of the classical as at least partially due to a particular institutional framework is even more explicit in 'On the *politique des auteurs*' ([1957] 1985). In this essay, Bazin praises classical Hollywood cinema above all others, for what he considers 'most admirable' in it, 'i.e. not only the talent of this or that filmmaker, but *the genius of the system*, the richness of its ever-vigorous tradition, and its fertility when it comes into contact with new elements' (p. 258, my emphasis).
2. Krämer suggests that perhaps this periodization might be considered the first appearance of a notion of the 'post-classical' (2000, p. 64).
3. Bazin 1967, p. 29. Bazin finds in such films 'all the characteristics of the ripeness of a classical art', which is defined by 'its perfect balance, its ideal form of expression, and reciprocally one admires them for dramatic and moral themes to which the cinema, while it may not have created them, has given a grandeur, an artistic effectiveness, that they would not have otherwise have had' (ibid.).
4. Attributed to Theodor Adorno; cited in Hansen 1981, p. 194.
5. Thus the Bazinian notion the 'camera as an impartial instrument' is critiqued (Comolli and Narboni [1969]1999, p. 755).
6. See, for example, 'A collective text by the Editors: [John Ford's] *Young Mr Lincoln*', *Cahiers du Cinéma*, no. 223 (August 1970), translated in *Screen*, 13, Autumn 1972, pp. 5–44.
7. Baudry [1974–5] 1986: p. 296. The article was first published in *Cinéthique*, Nos. 7–8 (1970); reprinted in translation in *Film Quarterly*, 28 (2), Winter 1974–75, 39–47, and later in Rosen 1986. Page numbers given here relate to Rosen 1986.
8. Susan Hayward (2000) has produced a useful definition of the term 'subject' as used by structuralist and post-structuralist theorists. Used by structuralists (such as Baudry), the term was

    > based primarily in Marxian-Althusserian thinking which perceived the subject as a construct of material structures. Thus we are the subjects of such structures as language, cultural codes and conventions, institutions – what Althusser called Ideological State Apparatuses (ISAs). We are, he argued, interpellated as subjects ... by ISAs such as the church, education, police, family and the media. ... Film, as a pre-existing structure, is like all other ISAs in its ideological functioning, and as such interpellates the spectator, thereby constituting her or him as a subject. Post-structuralists (Michel Foucault, Jacques Derrida, Jean-François Lyotard) argued against this totalizing theory and proposed a different vision of the subject as simultaneously constituted and constituting – as both effect and agent of the text (pp. 375–6).

    With reference to the structuralist/post-structuralist debate Hayward highlights that

    > the spectating subject is, in a sense, a divided subject (dialectically positioned as constituted or constituting) in relation to the filmic text. Because film projects before us ideal images in the form of stars and a seamless reality that disguises its illusory unity ..., film functions metonymically for this imagined unity of the ego-ideal and as such allows us to identify with that ego-ideal. But film also does something else. It projects our desires onto the screen, it functions as a release for our repressed unconscious state and our fantasies. ...

> So film is, simultaneously, the place where the spectator can find imaginary unity *and* the site where the unspoken can be spoken – that is, a 'safe' place from which to observe our lack of unity (p. 377).

9. Althusser 1971; see, in particular, 'Ideology and Ideological State Apparatuses (Notes towards an investigation)'. It should be noted that this group of French film theorists, including Baudry, considered the 'state' in the more general terms of dominant ideology. See Jay 1994, p. 476.

10. Baudry ([1976] 1986), "The Apparatus: Metapsychological Approaches to the Impression of Reality in the Cinema'. This article was first published in *Communications*, no. 23, 1975; reprinted in translation (by Jean Andrews and Bertrand Augst) in *Camera Obscura*, no. 1, Fall 1976, 104–28, and later in Rosen 1986.

11. For example, in 'Machines of the Visible', Comolli stated that the spectator may not be entirely passive, but his/her work 'is not only a work of decipherment, reading, elaboration of signs. It is first of all and just as much, if not more, to play the game … it is to maintain … the mechanism of disavowal at its highest level of intensity' (Comolli cited in Jay 1994, p. 477).

12. In particular, Metz reintroduced the concept of voyeurism to film theory (this time, however, it was based on Jacques Lacan's notion of the scopic drive), and also the Freudian notions of disavowal and fetishism.

13. Both Jay 1994, pp. 486–90, and Maltby 1995, pp. 434–47, provide useful summaries of the various critiques.

14. Bordwell et al. 1985, p. 7; see also Branigan 1992. However, as discussed above, a number of Marxist-psychoanalytic studies highlight the importance of the collusion of the subject in undertaking the role allotted to them by the cinematic text and apparatus.

15. Maltby 1995, p. 333; emphasis original. However, as Bordwell et al. state, their study is limited to questions of form and style and to an exploration of the relationship of these to the mode of production: it does not extend to the consideration of ideological issues concerning the institution of Hollywood cinema.

16. For example, the 'invisibility' of editing is a result of its being successfully motivated by the narrative.

17. Bordwell et al. 1985, p. 301. The wording of an early advertisement for Vitaphone Talking Pictures demonstrates this in its emphasis on the 'life-like' and 'real' quality of its sound:

> Audiences are saying it, everywhere: At last '*pictures* that *talk* like *living people!*' *Vitaphone* Talking Pictures are electrifying audiences the country over! For *Vitaphone* brings to you the greatest of the world's great entertainers … Screen stars! Stage stars! Opera stars! Famous orchestras! Master musicians! *Vitaphone* recreates them ALL before your eyes. You see and hear them act, talk, sing and play – like human beings in the flesh! Do not confuse *Vitaphone* with mere 'sound effects'. *Vitaphone* is the ONE proved successful talking picture – exclusive product of Warner Bros. Remember this – if it's not Warner Bros. *Vitaphone*, it's NOT the real, life-like talking picture. *Vitaphone* climaxes all previous entertainment achievements. See and hear this marvel of the age – *Vitaphone*. (Reproduced in Maltby 1995, p. 161)

18. See also M. Smith 1998. It should also be noted that the historical poetics of Bordwell et al.'s account *could* be used to focus upon 'the periods of transition and experimentation before the system stabilizes around new elements', as Henry Jenkins points out (1995, p. 114). For some critics, the emphasis on narrative coherence above all else has had a detrimental effect on Bordwell et al.'s

consideration of possible disruptive functions *within* Hollywood cinema, rather than just in terms of other cinemas, for example in terms of the roles played by popular stage melodrama and consumer culture in the history of Hollywood cinema (Altman 1992; Kaplan 2000). According to Kaplan, it was not until feminist film criticism began to approach women's melodramas that 'the rigid totalizing tendencies in both conceptions of classical cinema' were challenged, in particular through the need to allow for multiple forms of identification (p. 55). Of course, Laura Mulvey's now infamous essay 'Visual Pleasure and Narrative Cinema' ([1975] 1986) drew attention to the male-centredness of the ideology-based approach to classical cinema (and the oppression of woman at hands of apparent 'realism').

19. See, for example, Altman 1992; Kaplan 2000.

20. However, it should be noted that, although both approaches are concerned with classical Hollywood cinema, each has a different object: the Marxist-psychoanalytic account is primarily concerned with the revelation of cinema's ideological imperatives; the neo-formalist account focuses on producing an historical poetics of this cinema – a poetics which assumes an active spectator constantly working to decode the film's narrative meaning.

21. It should be noted that music had already established a place for itself within the production system during the silent era. Producers recognized that it was cheaper to commission original music for their films than to license material now under copyright to the growing number of publishing houses. Thus, they began to hire composers and also to develop their own publishing houses. This music was for the cue sheets and scores then being generated by the studios. See Flinn 1992, p. 15.

22. See Kalinak 1992, pp. 66–8. For more on the scores produced during this period of experimentation, see chapters 6 and 7 of Gorbman's *Unheard Melodies* (1987): these offer analyses of two very interesting transitional – and indeed sonically experimental – films: Jean Vigo's *Zéro de conduite* (1933) with music by Maurice Jaubert, and René Clair's *Sous les toits de Paris* (1930) with music by Armand Bernard.

23. High profile composers were able to choose their orchestrators and many, such as Max Steiner and Erich Wolfgang Korngold, developed long-standing relationships with particular orchestrators, such as Hugo Friedhofer, who were often composers in their own right. As Kalinak notes, Friedhofer orchestrated 17 of Korngold's 18 original film scores (1992, p. 74). For a brief discussion of Steiner's collaboration with Hugo Friedhofer, see Daubney 2000, pp. 13–16, and Duchen 1997, pp. 164–5.

24. Sinn 1911, p. 27; Sabaneev 1935, pp. 20-21, 29; both are cited in Bordwell et al. 1985, p. 418, nn. 31, 32. On the use of these practices in the synchronized sound era see Sabaneev 1935, pp. 19–20, 41.

25. For example, Sinn (1911, p. 76) quotes a silent film pianist as follows: 'I attach a certain theme to each person in the picture and work them out, in whatever form the occasion may call for, not forgetting to use popular strains if necessary' (cited in Bordwell et al. 1985, p. 33). Marks (1997, p. 103) cites Joseph Carl Breil writing in 1916 of his 1912 score for Sarah Bernhardt's *Queen Elizabeth*: 'Here was a real drama played by the greatest of artists. I realized at once that trivial music would not do, and set to work to write a score that would portray human emotions from a truly dignified point of view. With the limited means of a small orchestra put at my disposal then, I set to work and wrote a dramatic score built very much upon the motif lines set down by Richard Wagner.' Breil is perhaps most famous as the compiler and composer of a score to D.W. Griffith's *The Birth of a Nation* (1915). See Marks 1997, pp. 109–66 and Flinn 1992, pp. 14–17.

26. Sabaneev 1935, p. 21. Sabaneev offers some practical guidance for composers to assist them in producing what he calls 'elastic or extensile music' (p. 43) – music which can be stretched or shrunk to fit the narrative without compromising musical

form. Suggestions include adding pauses, writing shorter musical phrases, making use of sequences and progressions (pp. 43–5).

27. Around this time an 'up-and-downer' machine was devised, which automatically lowered the music signal when dialogue was detected. See W. A. Mueller, 'A Device for Automatically Controlling Balance Between Recorded Sounds', *Journal of the Society of Motion Picture Engineers*, 25(1), July 1935, pp. 79-86; cited in Gorbman 1987, p. 171, n. 11.

28. As Philip Rosen states, 'External evidence regarding authorship [of *Composing for the Films*] is murky' (1980, p. 157). The book originally appeared in English in 1947 under the sole authorship of Eisler. Claudia Gorbman (1991) attributes authorship of the book to Eisler following the appearance of an earlier draft of the manuscript from 1944 in Eisler's writings. In his preface to the 1969 German edition of the book, however, Adorno suggested that he had written at least nine-tenths of it. Miriam Hansen (1981) asserts that stylistic analysis of Adorno's edition of the German text substantiates his claim; in his study of Eisler, Albrecht Betz (1982) attributes co-authorship of the book to Adorno for the same reason. For the purposes of this study I have credited Adorno and Eisler with co-authorship of the text, both for the reasons suggested by Hansen and also because of the connections between parts of the text and Adorno and Horkheimer's *Dialectic of Enlightenment* ([1944] 1979) which are explored in more detail below.

29. Adorno [1949] 1973.

30. See Schoenberg [1911] 1978 and 1975, pp. 216–17.

31. Further, 'Only because definite musical configurations become patterns that are resorted to over and over again can these configurations be automatically associated with certain expressive value and in the end seem to be "expressive" in themselves' ([1947] 1994, p. 35). Such clichés are thus fixed wholly by convention according to Adorno and Eisler.

32. It should be noted that consideration of classical scoring practices is not the primary focus of *Unheard Melodies*; here I am concerned particularly with chapter 4, 'Classical Hollywood Practice: The Model of Max Steiner', pp. 70–98.

33. I use the term 'extradiegetic' rather than 'nondiegetic' to refer to people, such as a score's composer.

34. Gorbman 1987, p. 81. The 'orchestral grandeur of the theme in *Star Wars* that plays as spaceships speed through the galaxy' is cited as an example here (p. 68).

35. In terms of film music which, it is implied, has a subjective origin, Gorbman follows Gérard Genette: she prefers the term 'meta-diegetic' to describe 'narration by a secondary narrator' (ibid., p. 22).

36. Following Kalinak and Chion, Simon Frith highlights the 'wonderful' circularity of this situation: 'scorers bring sounds *to* films, for their everyday semantic connotations, from their roots in Western art music and musicology; listeners take musical meanings *from* films, from the cinemas in which we've learned what emotions and cultures and stories sound like' (1998, p. 122).

37. A further difference between the views of Gorbman and Kalinak can be found in their positions on psychoanalytic approaches, with Kalinak only tentatively accepting the validity of such approaches by comparison with Gorbman: 'Such new terrain ... is not yet fully explored, and the application of psychoanalysis raises many questions that have yet to be answered' (Kalinak 1992, p. 38).

38. Gorbman also sees this as a possible reason for the dominance of this idiom (1987, p. 171, n. 15).

39. I am grateful to Kate Daubney for bringing this issue to my attention. See, for example, the discussion of Max Steiner's musical background in Daubney 2000, pp. 1–11. Jeff Smith (1998), and James Buhler and David Neumeyer (1994) express

similar views.

40. Such evidence takes the form of sketches, autograph scores, departmental memos and other production records, alongside oral histories and interviews. Kalinak also discusses the role that the studio music departments and their key personnel played in mediating between composers and studio executives (1992, pp. 75–6).

41. Kalinak 1992, p. 72. The pressure on film composers to work extremely quickly, often for very concentrated periods of time, is made clear in this quote from studio composer Max Steiner:

> The prospective film composer should be in good physical condition, as we musicians are always the last people to get the picture and almost constantly have to work under terrific pressure. Many times I have to work two days and two nights in succession without an hour's sleep. The reason for this is that pictures are sold in advance and if thru [*sic*] any fault of the studio, delays occur, such as changes in the script, illness of the players, and numerable unforeseen 'accidents,' the picture still has to be completed and ready to start on its engagement on the day scheduled, so the only thing to do in this case is to work day and night to get it out. I wrote and recorded 'We Are Not Alone,' which has a continuous score of one hour and ten minutes, in six days. During these six days, I slept eighteen hours at most. This is a terrific strain on the eyes and heart, so I would not advise anyone who is not in good physical condition to undertake this vocation, especially as this pressure occurs almost constantly. (Cited in Daubney 2000, pp. 9–10.)

42. See, for example, the work of Arthur Schopenhauer (1788–1860) – one of the most Romantic of philosophers – on music (Schopenhauer 1966).

43. Unfortunately Flinn does not really provide concrete evidence from particular films to support her argument here, though she does offer analyses of the role of music in two films – Edgar G. Ulmer's *Detour* (1945) and George Stevens's *Penny Serenade* (1941). It should, however, be pointed out that Flinn's project was not intended to be a 'strictly' musicological one: 'I leave it for persons with more rigorous musical training than I have to perform close formal analyses of individual film scores. My chief interests lie instead in highlighting the ways in which music has operated in the critical discourse surrounding Hollywood film – and not just in the films "themselves"' (1992, p. 12).

44. Gorbman too draws attention to the fact that 'most film scholars [limit the music narrative relationship] to the concepts of *parallelism* and *counterpoint*' (1987, p. 15; emphasis original). It would be hard *not* to see this as a demonstration of the influence of the position proposed by Eisenstein, Pudovkin and Alexandrov in their 1928 manifesto, 'A Statement on Sound Film,' in which sound is split into categories according to whether it parallels, or is in counterpoint with, the image. This issue is discussed in more detail in Chapter 3. By contrast, Gorbman suggests that the notion of *mutual implication* better expresses the reality of the relationship between music and the narrative, in which music can have an altering effect upon an image, which may then call for a reassessment of the image as a result.

45. From the modernist perspective, film music's stylistic promiscuity (although often constrained within the boundaries of the late Romantic style) demonstrates a 'lack of firm artistic resolve', which is further compounded by Hollywood's connection with commerce (Buhler and Neumeyer 1994, pp. 384–5).

46. For example, Franz Waxman's score to James Whale's *The Bride of Frankenstein* (1935) encompasses Wagnerian leitmotifs, early Schoenbergian expressionism, Strauss's post-Romantic music and pastiche eighteenth-century dance music (ibid., p. 384).

Chapter 2

New Hollywood cinema and ('post-'?)classical scoring

In the first section of this chapter I introduce some of the key theoretical approaches to 'New Hollywood' or 'post-classical' cinema, which a number of theorists and historians argue emerged in the mid-1970s. In particular, I am concerned with the relationship between this cinema(s) and classical Hollywood cinema. In the second part of the chapter I review theoretical approaches to the apparent return of classical scoring in these films, particularly in terms of the relationship between these more recent scores and those of the studio era. While some focus on the similarities between these practices, others emphasize difference and suggest that such practices exemplify the existence of 'post-classical' scoring, rather than a return to classical scoring of the studio era.

Classical Hollywood and the post-classical and/or New Hollywood(s)

Recently a number of theorists have produced surveys of the various notions of 'post-classical' or 'New' Hollywood cinema(s) (for example, Krämer 2000; Tasker 1996; M. Smith 1998; Maltby 1998). These surveys demonstrate not only that various theorists, critics and historians define these terms differently, but that the urge to identify such shifts in film style and in the economic and institutional organization of the film industry dates back to the 1950s, if not earlier. As Peter Krämer (2000, p. 74) points out, developments in film history and theory in the 1970s–1980s elided many of these earlier views of transition through their expansion of the notion of classical Hollywood filmmaking: extending the period covered by classical Hollywood (the 1930s–1940s) to a much longer one (1910s–1960s). For a number of critics, apparently 'novel' (and thus, defining) elements of New Hollywood cinema are evolutionary with, or intensifications of, aspects of classical Hollywood cinema (Tasker 1996, p. 214). Thus, identifying *the*, or *a* moment at which New Hollywood begins and classical Hollywood ends is wholly dependent upon the criteria against which these transformations are being judged. For example, a history of Hollywood based on a history of narrative form would be very different to one constructed in relation to the history of economic relations in the film industry (Maltby 1998).

Most critics agree, however, that the single most important factor that began the shift from classical to New Hollywood was the break-up of the studio system as a result of the US Supreme Court ruling in 1948 which found the studios guilty of adopting anti-trust practices. In being forced to sell off its theatre chains and put an end to distribution practices such as 'block-' and 'blind booking' the majors lost their previously guaranteed exhibition market.[1] A number of other (often related) determinants have been highlighted as contributory to subsequent transformations of Hollywood cinema. These include: the suburbanization of America with the concomitant replacement of cinema by television as the focus of habitual viewing, and the need for cinema to redefine itself as a result; the rise of independent modes of production; the shift from a notion of the cinema audience as undifferentiated to a fragmentary one, and the role that the demise of the Production Code and the development of a ratings system played in this; the development of alternative modes of storytelling in Hollywood cinema in response to influences from television, avant-garde and European art cinemas; the large-scale mergers and acquisitions of film production companies by transnational corporations which began in the mid-1960s and which led to the horizontal integration of the entertainment industry and the drive toward 'synergy' (that is, the mutually beneficial cross-promotion of products across different media).

Although debates about the periodization of New Hollywood continue, Yvonne Tasker believes that film studies is now moving towards a consensus view which defines the era as beginning around 1975 with *Jaws*. Rather than seeing changes in film *style* from this era as the sole defining factor of New Hollywood, she suggests that it is perhaps better to read such shifts 'in terms of a postmodern multi-media world which undermines the very notion of "film as a distinct medium"' (1996, p. 226).[2] This view – similar to accounts proposed by Schatz (1993), Wyatt (1994), Monaco (1979), Maltby (1998), and others – foregrounds the adaptability and the commercial aesthetic of Hollywood cinema, in particular since the 1950s. It focuses primarily on the rise of the blockbuster in relation to changes within the industrial organization of the entertainment industry and, in turn, the impact of these developments on aesthetic decisions. A brief history of these transformations follows.

During the studio era, the period in which the so-called Big Five film studios – Warner Bros., Loew's-MGM, Paramount, Fox and Radio-Keith-Orpheum (RKO) – were vertically integrated (that is, had holdings in production, distribution and exhibition), exhibition was by far the most profitable element of the system. In order to stay profitable the industry attempted to develop filmgoing into a habit for consumers; it produced a large number of movies with relatively low budgets, in order to provide a continuous 'stream of "new-and-different" products' as quickly and efficiently as possible (Gomery 1986, p. 15). Productions were graded as 'prestige', A- or B-pictures, with B-pictures produced in the highest volume with the lowest budgets, and prestige pictures made in the smallest numbers with the highest budgets. During the 1950s the cinema as site of regularized viewing was usurped by television. This was also partially due to migration from the cities (where the majority of first-run cinemas were located) to the newly built suburbs in the immediate post-war era into what Schatz calls the 'family/housing/baby boom' (1993, p. 9). Overseas rentals of American films were also not as high as they could have been, due to the post-war quota systems enforced by a number of European nation-states, and restrictions on taking profits out of these countries. This led to a rise in co-production deals overseas, 'runaway' productions (films with the majority of production located outside the USA) and in the import of films.

The decline in audience figures through the 1950s and 1960s did not affect the studios as much as it affected exhibitors; the studios had already begun to use television as an alternative exhibition site.[3] However, Hollywood also recognized the need to differentiate its cinematic product from that which it produced for television. Thus, the studios began to focus on developing their programme of blockbuster, or 'prestige' pictures; they produced fewer films for increasingly large budgets (which were often spent on top stars and costly state-of-the-art technology), with the financial risk of this strategy off-set by regular sales to television (Maltby 1998, p. 31). Following divorcement in the late 1940s, the studios began to function less as production houses than as leasers of production facilities, financiers and distributors of independently 'packaged' productions. However, it should be pointed out that even during the studio era a number of 'prestige' pictures had been produced in this way, that is, as 'major independent' package productions: *Gone With the Wind* (1939), for example, and David O. Selznick's *Duel in the Sun* (1946). Thomas Schatz argues that such films should be read as 'prototype New Hollywood blockbuster[s]': each was a '"pre-sold" spectacle (based on a popular historical novel) with top stars, an excessive budget, a sprawling story, and state-of-the-art production values' (1993, p. 11). *Duel in the Sun* was also significant as a forerunner of New Hollywood in its distribution and exhibition strategy (discussed in more detail below); it opened nationwide following poorly received sneak previews (ibid.).

During the 1950s and into the 1960s the financial success of these prestige pictures continued, but as budgets rose, so the financial risks also grew. The studios began to diversify their interests in order both to off-set these risks and to respond to the changing market-place with the postwar 'boom in entertainment and leisure activities', population growth, and the fragmentation of a single audience.[4] While various new cinematic consumer groups emerged – the youth market, the cine-literate audience, for example – the blockbuster continued to dominate the box-office. However, the enormous successes of *The Sound of Music* and *Dr Zhivago* in 1965 were followed by a series of costly flops which almost bankrupted several of the studios.

This period of overproduction led the majors into a state of financial crisis and a sequence of mergers and acquisitions.[5] Television again played an important role in the rescue of Hollywood cinema: networks placed feature films at the heart of their programming, which led to a rise in value of the majors' film libraries (Maltby 1998, p. 31). Douglas Gomery argues that the innovative business practices of Lew Wasserman, president of talent agency MCA (Music Corporation of America), were also influential. Wasserman developed the practice of packaging and selling talent to studios and networks in such a way that tax costs were avoided, and percentage profits for his clients were secured. He bought up Paramount's film library and, in 1962, acquired Universal Studios.[6] Through the 1960s and 1970s MCA/Universal produced television shows and feature films, and also pioneered the made-for-television movie which led to Universal becoming the 'largest supplier of network broadcast television programming' (Gomery 1998, p. 48). In order to increase the profits of the company's feature filmmaking, with the release of *Jaws* in 1975 Wasserman combined 'mass-saturated advertising on prime-time television with simultaneous bookings in new shopping mall cineplexes across the United States' (p. 51). Although *Jaws* was not the first film to be marketed and distributed in this way, it was the first so promoted to achieve such a degree of success.

With the rise of pay- and cable-TV and home video in the late 1970s into the 1980s, Warner's Steven J. Ross played an important role in maximising the potential that Wasserman developed. Ross 'took Hollywood to a new era of vertically integrated conglomerate power that led to more economic might and profits than had ever been realized' (Gomery 1998, p. 51). This new format of vertically integrated conglomeration enables a company's productions (and/or production rights) to be sold to other companies within the conglomeration for distribution and exhibition at a low cost.[7] This approach thus not only yields higher profits but also enables each company to take advantage of the added value of cross-promotional tied-in products: synergy.[8] Relevant ancillary markets include the sale or rental of software (such as prints, videos, DVDs of the film; the film's soundtrack; spin-off computer games; television shows) through various channels of distribution (such as cable and satellite TV companies, video/DVD sale and rental companies, record companies, shops), and through merchandizing (a *Jurassic Park* poster, lunchbox or dinosaur toy, for example[9]). As a number of critics have highlighted, ancillary markets for blockbusters are frequently more profitable than film exhibition.[10] As a result, the sale of product to ancillary markets now has an impact on the character of the product during development. This is most noticeable in three areas: the computer game (and its relationship with the first-person chase/race/find sequence), TV/video as distribution channel (which has affected widescreen compositional practices; Neale 1998) and the soundtrack, which often includes at least some popular music (of whatever genre).[11]

To return briefly to the late 1960s and early 1970s. The financial instability of Hollywood during this period was matched in the instability in Hollywood's modes of representation. Indeed, it is considered by many to have been a period of 'relative experimentation' in Hollywood history, resulting in films such as *Bonnie and Clyde* (1967), *2001: A Space Odyssey* (1968), *Easy Rider* (1969),

McCabe and Mrs Miller (1971). The replacement of the Production Code by a ratings system in 1968 had had a clear impact on such films through their testing of new boundaries in relation to admissible film themes and the depiction of sex and violence. Many of them assimilated aspects of European art filmmaking, particularly in terms of non-linear, non-teleological plots focused around counter-culture anti-heroes (Elsaesser; 1975, Kolker 1988). Murray Smith (1998) detects a dialectical tension between these films and the cycle of disaster movies from the same period which – by contrast – were often organized around a return to narrative tautness. However, this tension is further complicated by the referential, yet ambivalent, relationship between European art films of the late 1950s and 1960s and the genre conventions of the B-movies and *films noirs* of the studio era.

Thomas Schatz interprets the relative experimentation of the late 1960s and early 1970s not as a break with classical modes of filmmaking but as a phase in the restabilization of the Hollywood industry achieved in full in the mid-1970s with the success of blockbuster movies as 'hyperbolic simulations of Hollywood B-movies' (Hoberman 1991, p. 284). Similarly, Richard Maltby interprets the studio experiments of the early 1970s as attempts to target the younger demographic attending the new cinemas located in suburban shopping malls. Box-office success continued through the 1970s: indeed, in 1974 it '[surpassed] Hollywood's postwar box-office peak' (1998, p. 16). The cycle of disaster films which followed the success of *Airport* (1970) were seen as key here: *The Poseidon Adventure* (1972), *Earthquake* (1974), and *The Towering Inferno* (1974), each of which was scored by John Williams (*Airport* was scored by Alfred Newman).[12] However, the film that really secured Williams's future was *Jaws* (1975).

As already mentioned, *Jaws* is seen by some to signal the end of Hollywood's downturn and marks the beginning of a new period in Hollywood history. There was a good plot which was packaged effectively as a film, but at least part of its success was due to the successful combination and consolidation of a number of different business practices. The film was pre-sold with Peter Benchley's novel (with film rights secured before the book's publication). The film deal was packaged by MCA/Universal, with Steven Spielberg as its young director. Unusually for a blockbuster, on account of its subject matter *Jaws* was released during the summer (thus signalling a dramatic shift in subsequent release strategies) and was booked into a large number – 464 – of screens simultaneously nationwide (that is, used saturation booking). A huge amount of money was spent on promotion in the days immediately prior to the film's release, in the form of television and radio advertising (which featured Williams's atmospheric yet succinct 'Jaws theme') and sensationalist artwork on the posters (a lone swimmer unaware of a disproportionately huge shark beneath, with mouth open and teeth bared). This kind of 'front-loading' of exhibition and promotion across a range of media has since become the norm with summer blockbusters; it both builds anticipation of the film as 'event' and lessens the impact of poor reviews.

Stylistically, too, *Jaws* has been seen by some to signify a shift, or turning point, in film history. As with many of the blockbusters which followed it, the film draws on a range of genres, thus addressing as wide a cross-section of the population as possible (Schatz 1993; Tasker 1996). It also functions particularly efficiently as a 'chase' film, but with an affective component which encourages the audience to submit to the film and experience it as an 'emotional roller coaster' which, through this emotional engagement, implies a return to classical cinema (Schatz 1993, p. 18). The chase element has also been incorporated into a high proportion of blockbusters since, not least due to the benefits of pre-selling computer game spin-offs. The narrative is fast-paced and taut by comparison with some of the more experimental fare produced by Hollywood in the early 1970s, though some argue that with post-*Jaws* blockbusters, narrative tends to be plot- rather than character-driven. This suggests a distinction between these more recent films and classical Hollywood cinema as defined by Bordwell, Staiger and Thompson (1985), for example.[13] Yet Murray Smith points out that 'narrative has certainly not disappeared under a cloud of special effects. In action films, the plot advances *through* spectacle; the spectacular elements are, generally speaking, as "narrativized" as are the less ostentatious spaces of other genres' (1998, p. 13). For some, however, the distinction is that in New Hollywood cinema, the narrativization of these elements is driven purely by the hope of high-yield returns from ancillary markets. Writing of high-concept movies in particular, Richard Maltby states:

> Designed to accommodate multiple acts of consumption across different formats, high concept has little commercial investment in narrative except as a vehicle for the movie's other pleasures, and equally little commitment to a classical hierarchicization of a narrative system over those of space and time. Tie-in products – novelizations, soundtrack albums, TV spin-offs – have no obligation to preserve the narrative line of the 'original' against the obvious economic benefits of multiplication, which maintains the product range in the marketplace and encourages repeat viewings. (1998, p. 39)

Although the aesthetics of Hollywood cinema may have changed (particularly in terms of blockbusters), and despite the shift from the vertically integrated industry of the studio era, to the vertically *and* horizontally integrated and 'tightly diversified'[14] entertainment conglomerates of the 1980s, the majors have continued their stranglehold on the film industry, particularly in terms of finance and distribution. Recent acquisitions have signalled the majors' return to exhibition too. Indeed, the majors' domination of the market would appear to be *more* consolidated – and more globalized – than ever before (M. Smith 1998, p. 9).

Although Hollywood blockbusters dominate American (and other) cinema(s),

Thomas Schatz points out that blockbusters also advance the production of other types of films and modes of filmmaking practice (1993, p. 34). In order to ensure that the industry can function in a state of relative stability, New Hollywood delivers three different classes of films (and note here the similarity to the three classes of films offered by classical Hollywood): first, the blockbuster with franchise potential and lots of commercial opportunities to exploit; then the A class star vehicle with sleeper potential (that is, to become a hit slowly and without recourse to blockbuster-sized promotion budgets); and third, the low-budget 'indie' (or 'semi-indie') feature going for a niche audience and occasionally gaining cult status.[15] Relatedly, rather than seeing the majors' on-going control of the market as constraining independent film production, Murray Smith argues that this environment has led to the development of a symbiotic business relationship between independent and New Hollywood cinema: 'industrial dualism'. Here, 'independent production companies act at once as "shock absorbers" and research arms ("pilot fish") for the majors, "by attracting risk capital and creative talent which the majors can then exploit through their control of distribution"' (1998, p. 9).[16] There is a good deal of evidence to support this view in the majors' gradual takeover of the art film market into the 1990s (Balio, 1998b).

In summary then, in the majority of the accounts discussed above, New Hollywood cinema is more commercially driven than its counterpart from the classical era, particularly in terms of its ancillary markets. This is at least partially the result of transformations which have taken place in the industrial structure of the studios: from being vertically integrated during the classical era, to being vertically and horizontally integrated, with the majors now a part of tightly diversified entertainment conglomerates. These changes are also reflected in the aesthetics of New Hollywood cinema to a certain extent, though in some respects this cinema also signals a return to the values of classical filmmaking. In the following section I consider the apparent return of classical scoring in New Hollywood cinema in relation to this context.

Post-classical scoring: the return of classical scoring?

In *Settling the Score* (1992), Kathryn Kalinak argues that while classical scoring has changed over time it remains a stable set of practices which continue to exert a strong influence over more recent scores. Although the pop score represented a 'serious challenge to the classical score' with its 'insistence on the integrity and marketability of the nondiegetic song' actively opposing a number of the conventions of the classical model, alongside the jazz, synth and theme scores which also initially appeared to challenge classical scoring and present radical alternatives to it, they gradually began to conform to the structural conventions of the classical model.[17] With Williams's scores for a series of disaster movies in the early 1970s, *Jaws* in 1975, and particularly *Star Wars* (1977), however, the structural conventions of classical scoring were emphatically reunited with the idiom and the medium of the classical Hollywood scores produced during the 1930s and 1940s. Kalinak produces an analysis of some of the leitmotifs and musical functions of Williams's score for *The Empire Strikes Back* (1980) as evidence (1992, pp. 190–202).

As Kalinak points out with regard to John Williams, and as a number of other composers working in Hollywood today have themselves stated in interview, the structure of their work remains remarkably similar to that of the composers employed by the studio system in the 1930s–1940s, although contemporary composers now work freelance.[18] Indeed, Kalinak implies that Williams's score for *The Empire Strikes Back* was produced by the same assembly-line mode of production that was a 'determining characteristic of the studio model' (p. 72). Even today the composer is still most often first involved in film score production at the post-production stage. Film composers often work to a four- to six-week production schedule, sometimes less (particularly if theirs is the second score, commissioned after a film's first score has been thrown out). Many of them work with orchestrators, and sometimes also computer and synthesizer programmers. These composers often have little or no contact or discussion with those producing sound for the film and, in the main, producers continue to have the last word on musical decisions.[19]

Anahid Kassabian agrees with Kalinak that the mid-to-late 1970s saw a resurgence of classical Hollywood scoring. However, rather than being concerned with defining current instantiations of this scoring practice, in *Hearing Film: Tracking Identifications in Contemporary Hollywood Film Music* (2001), Kassabian focuses on the ideological positioning it encourages. She is concerned with the potential range of meaning production and identificatory possibilities offered to perceivers through the use of different musical styles and idioms in contemporary scoring practice.[20] In particular, Kassabian makes a distinction between scoring practices which produce a narrowing track of identificatory possibilities and those which open them up to include a wider range of possibilities. As with classical filmmaking of the studio era, Kassabian argues, the narratives, editing and camera techniques of recent 'hyperclassical' Hollywood films such as *Star Wars* work to limit the range of subject-positions perceivers are 'invited' to occupy; these subject-positions are usually those associated with the films' white, Western, bourgeois, male protagonists. Similarly, Kassabian argues that the late Romantic symphonic classical scoring which is frequently used to score these films also works to construct a 'privileged subject position' and attempts to lure, or assimilate, the perceiver into occupying that position (2001, pp. 114, 89).

Kassabian supports her argument with the results of a large-scale listening experiment conducted by Philip Tagg and Bob Clarida.[21] Subjects were asked to respond to ten instrumental film and television themes (previously unknown to them) by writing down what they imagined or thought of when they heard the themes. Although the responses were fairly varied when considered individually, when they were grouped together they 'read like descriptions of the series or films to which the theme belonged, particularly in regard to genre and style'.[22] The agreement of specific meanings in the subjects' responses suggests that there is a high degree of correspondence between the intentions of the composers writing the themes, and in their reception by the subjects, that is, in the encoding and decoding of these meanings: communication. The consistency with which the musical meanings of these themes are encoded and decoded is determined by the composers' and subjects' 'competence' with this musical language, where competence is here defined as a 'culturally acquired skill possessed to varying degrees in varying genres by all hearing people in a given culture' (p. 20). Kassabian proposes that a high proportion of Westerners are competent in their understanding of classical film scoring due, in part, to its reliance on 'late-Romantic (especially German) art music practices' (p. 24). Competence in decoding these meanings can also be developed through watching films.[23]

By contrast to these hyperclassical films, Kassabian states that since the mid-1980s many films with female protagonists have replaced classical Hollywood scoring with pop scoring.[24] Though there are clearly financial reasons why pop soundtracks may have become more popular, she argues that this does not explain the 'particularly widespread use of compiled [pop] scores in films with "updated" female characters' (2001, p. 105). According to Kassabian, contemporary films which challenge the more conservative views of gender, sexuality and race represented in the classical Hollywood films of the studio era, for example, effectively *need* to use alternative scoring practices to late Romantic classical scoring since 'the possibilities for female characters in classical Hollywood scoring are severely limited ... a fallen woman or a virtuous wife' (p. 70). Popular music, by contrast, allows a more 'diffuse' (and thus more appropriate) range of identifications than those encouraged by classical scoring practices in the Romantic idiom which are more 'heavy handed' in enforcing particular meanings and guiding perceivers into a narrow range of possible subject-positions (pp. 84–5). Popular music 'proliferates [identificatory] possibilities by opening perception onto perceivers' own (socially conditioned) histories' (p. 113). Kassabian labels the processes of identification facilitated by popular music '*affiliating* identifications'. These are contrasted with the '*assimilating* identifications' produced by late Romantic classical scoring which 'track perceivers toward a rigid, tightly controlled position that tends to line up comfortably with aspects of dominant ideologies' (p. 141).

While pop songs can be used in conformity with the structural conventions of classical Hollywood scoring, the use of pop has the potential to offer the perceiver a qualitatively different experience of musical meaning and a wider range of identificatory possibilities than classical scoring practices according to Kassabian.[25] This is not to say that late Romantic classical scoring is necessarily monolithic in the meanings it creates, however, for '[n]o film can force a perceiver to engage in a particular way. Even the most rigidly assimilating of film scores cannot guarantee the cooperation of perceiving subjects. ... But such resistances should not be taken to mean that any identification is plausible in any film' (p. 138). Although classical scoring could theoretically be used to privilege a wide variety of subject-positions, alternative readings are more difficult to sustain. Kassabian offers brief analyses of three films to support this view: Spielberg's *Indiana Jones and the Temple of Doom* (1984), McTiernan's *The Hunt for Red October* (1990) and Donner's *Lethal Weapon 2* (1989). However, as Robynn Stilwell points out in her analysis of Michael Kamen's score to McTiernan's *Die Hard* (1988), while the dominant narrative of the film points to a conservative Reaganite product (superficially at least), the score (working with certain camera flourishes and the acting of Alan Rickman/Hans) encourages an alternative reading.

Kassabian suggests that there is a distinction between the way in which pop scoring and classical scoring function in relation to a film's perceivers: pop scoring has the potential to enable a variety of subject-positions, while classical scoring narrows perceivers' identificatory possibilities because it is based on competence with a familiar musical language. Yet to a certain extent the enabling of a variety of subject-positions by pop is also based on the perceiver's familiarity with musical languages. What interests me about Kassabian's view in relation to this study is the implication that Romantic symphonic scoring practices, expressed in whatever instrumental idiom, may operate as signifiers to a particular kind of classical Hollywood narrative in which a limited number of subject-positions are made available to perceivers, and which most often privilege white, Western-centric, middle-class male protagonists. Indeed, the resurgence, or revival, of classical Hollywood scoring techniques since *Star Wars* (1977) is synchronous with a move to a 'new conservative spirit in American culture' (Ryan and Kellner 1988, p. 11). Thus, Kassabian also suggests that a pop score may be considered a necessary, though perhaps not sufficient, signifier of narratives which challenge those of classical Hollywood cinema.

Following the 'explicit return to the style and sound of the classical film score in the wake of John Williams' music for George Lucas' *Star Wars* trilogy', K. J. Donnelly agrees with Kalinak (and, by extension, Kassabian) that there are substantial continuities between classical scoring and what he terms the post-classical scores of the 1980s and 1990s (1998, p. 143). Indeed, in 'The classical film score forever? *Batman* [1989], *Batman Returns* [1992] and post-classical film music' Donnelly argues that Danny Elfman's scores for these films manifest 'explicit allusions to particular stylistic aspects of studio era film music' (pp. 143–4). These include the use of a very large orchestra (up to 110 pieces) with a high proportion of the film scored by nondiegetic orchestral music, much of which is organized leitmotivically. However, Donnelly also states that there are important differences between classical and postclassical scoring practices due, at least in part, to changes in the economic and industrial organization of the Hollywood studios, which have occurred since the classical era (as discussed above). While Elfman's scores for these films certainly reference classical Hollywood scoring practice, Donnelly argues that they 'appear distorted by the music's distinctive character and its conspicuousness in the film'.[26] Rather than appearing 'unobtrusive', this music has the effect of being 'overblown and parodic', though this is to be expected given the 'generally hyperbolic and self-conscious character of the films themselves' (p. 150). The scores draw on the kind of musical clichés associated with the self-conscious humour of spoof films in which a spectator's conscious recognition of these codes is necessary to appreciate a musical joke (often at the expense of classical scoring conventions, as with Mel Brooks's *Blazing Saddles* (1974) for example). In this way, Elfman's scores for these films depart from classical scoring practice, since to remain unobtrusive film music should be appropriate to a film's narrative action and not draw attention to itself through the exaggeration of these scoring principles.

In the case of *Batman* the obtrusiveness of the film's music is due, at least partially, to the fact that the film yielded two soundtrack albums: one comprising Elfman's symphonic score for the film; the other, a collection of songs written for the film by the pop star Prince (now The Artist Formerly Known As Prince), many of which were featured diegetically *during* the film and which, in turn, also featured dialogue *from* the film.[27] The production of multiple soundtrack albums for films emphasizes the synergy at work between the horizontally integrated music and film industries – in this case, both owned by Warner Brothers – in the promotion of a single 'franchise' product or 'brand' – here, 'Batman'. As discussed above, these (tightly) diversified interests function to lessen the financial risks involved in big-budget film production through advancing the sales of a number of related products across a range of media via cross-promotional tie-ins. Ultimately, Donnelly argues that '[p]ost-classical cinema seems to display a proliferation of music that is unified at the point of the film as both text *and* as commodity' (p. 154; emphasis original). In the case of both *Batman* and *Batman Returns* this occurs as a result of raising the status of music in the films, through the exaggerated use of clichéd musical codes and, in the case of *Batman*, pop. Donnelly suggests that these divergences from the classical Hollywood score have been motivated by changes in 'industrial imperatives' and 'aesthetic concerns' and reflect the ownership of film production companies by huge global conglomerates which also have holdings in the music industry and thus promote synergetic cross-promotion.

The impact of the conglomeration and concentration of the media industry is evident in the highly orchestrated, multi-media promotional campaigns for blockbuster movies and the variety of tied-in products which operate as additional points-of-entry into the films. However, in some respects, the strategy of unifying a film's music 'as both text and commodity' is not particularly new: indeed, it can be traced back to the development of business enterprise between music publishers and exhibitors during the silent era.[28] The major film studios later got involved in the cross-promotional exploitation of film and music through setting up new, or buying out extant, music publishing houses in order to gain control of the licensing rights to back catalogues of music and song, and newly composed material. When sheet music sales began to decline and the popularity of records began to swell a number of the majors set up or acquired record labels. During this post-divorcement period, many of the studios were facing a financial squeeze. It was hoped that the marketing of film music would not only assist in the promotion of their films, but would offer an alternative revenue stream for relatively little extra outlay (since film music had to be composed, recorded and/or licences gained anyway). As Jeff Smith (1998) highlights, these economic imperatives began to have an impact on aesthetic decisions too.

From the 1960s particularly, composers were put under pressure to produce film music which was commercially viable in its own right, and which would advance sales of the film's soundtrack on record. This had clear effects on the historical development of the film score. For economic reasons there was a shift from scoring for orchestra to smaller, often jazz-influenced ensembles: smaller ensembles were cheaper; jazz-influenced idioms were popular at the time and likely to sell well. To enable the film to operate as promotion for the score, composers developed a range of aesthetic strategies by which music cues could be foregrounded.[29] A number of orchestral scores also sold well as soundtrack albums during this period, particularly those associated with successful big-budget pictures; the LP of Maurice Jarre's music to David Lean's *Dr Zhivago* (1965) spent over three years on the album chart, no doubt assisted by the numerous repetitions of 'Lara's theme' in the film.[30]

Nonetheless, whether or not the late Romantic orchestral scores featured in the films associated with New Hollywood are considered to be post-classical or to signal a return to classical Hollywood scoring, these theorists agree that the classical Hollywood score is referenced clearly in many of the highest grossing films of the period. As shown in the table below (Illustration 2.1), of the top ten highest grossing films of all time in the USA, all of which are post-*Jaws*, eight have primarily classical (or post-classical) orchestral scores.[31] The popularity of these scores is also demonstrated through sales of soundtrack albums.

Histories of the various forms of negotiation that have taken place between Hollywood and a number of other cinemas have been well-rehearsed elsewhere.[32] This study is focused on the impact of *New* Hollywood – with its concomitant resurgence of classical Hollywood scoring practices – upon a small selection of other cinemas in terms of their scoring and soundtrack strategies and practices. Through the analyses featured in later chapters attention is drawn to the ways in which these film scores and soundtracks have been produced in relation to, and often in opposition to, classical scoring practices. However, it is perhaps important first to highlight just how ubiquitous and dominant within the European film market New Hollywood has become. While Hollywood cinema has *always* been international in its scope, 'US film revenue from members of the European Community increased throughout the 1980s, to 90 per cent of cinema receipts there by 1990' (Miller 2000, pp. 152–3). Ginette Vincendeau sees this 'fiercer than ever competition from Hollywood' as the cause of the 'severe difficulties experienced by film industries throughout Europe. ... [It] has produced a sense of a beleaguered (perhaps even doomed) cinema' (2000, p. 63).

No.	Film	Box-office gross ($ millions)	Composer
1	*Titanic* (1997)	$601	James Horner (and theme song)
2	*Star Wars* (1977)	$461	John Williams
3	*E.T.* (1982)	$435	John Williams
4	*Star Wars: The Phantom Menace* (1999)	$431	John Williams
5	*Spider-Man* (2002)	$404	Danny Elfman
6	*Jurassic Park* (1993)	$357	John Williams
7	*Forrest Gump* (1994)	$330	Alan Silvestri (plus use of pre-existent pop songs)
8	*Harry Potter and the Sorcerer's Stone* (2001)	$318	John Williams
9	*Lord of the Rings: The Fellowship of the Ring* (2001)	$313	Howard Shore
10	*Lion King* (1994)	$313	Hans Zimmer (musical)

Source: http://movieweb.com/movie/alltime/html

Illustration 2.1   The top ten highest grossing films in the USA (November 2002)

One reason for the tremendous growth in the overseas market experienced by US cinema during the 1980s was the rebuilding and renovation of cinemas across a range of European countries; the majors played an important role in this. As Tino Balio points out, up until then Western Europe had only a third as many screens per capita as the USA, though it had roughly the same number of people (1998a, p. 60). Balio also highlights the importance of more effective promotional campaigns in this growth, and 'the emancipation of state-controlled broadcasting, [and] the spread of cable and satellite services' as contributory (p. 59). The freeing-up of commercial television in Europe and the developing satellite and cable markets offered Hollywood new distribution channels for both its products and the advertisement of its products to both mass and niche markets.

Europe's fears of its markets being overrun by cultural products from the USA were strongly expressed during the Uruguay round of negotiations between members of the General Agreement on Tariffs and Trade (GATT) which took place between 1986 and 1993 (Jarvie 1998; Jeancolas 1998; Mattelart 2000). Since the inception of the GATT the USA have consistently pressed for free trade to include films; in Article IV they agreed to exempt films from the Agreement during the very first rounds of talks in Geneva through accepting a simplification of the complicated screen quotas then in place across the overseas market to protect national cinemas. By recourse to paragraph 4 of Article III of the GATT, the USA argued that it was being subjected to discrimination, since this paragraph states that, effectively, 'imported good will be treated the same as domestic products' in the signatory countries (Jarvie 1998, p. 40). France, in particular, argued vehemently for the 'cultural exception' to remain part of the Agreement. If screen quotas were taken out of the Agreement, they stated, free trade with the USA (in terms of films and television programming) would not be reciprocated since, effectively, the American market is closed to France.[33] This view would seem to be supported by a comparison of import-export revenues between the USA and Europe which reveals the enormous disparity between them.[34] Film and television were eventually removed from the Uruguay round of the GATT talks.

Clearly the growing ubiquity of Hollywood cinema (and American television programming) during the 1980s and 1990s has been a sensitive issue across Europe. This period also saw the rise of the blockbuster, which in turn brought with it a return to classical scoring practices (as discussed above). Through analysing the scores and soundtracks from films produced in Europe and, in one case, on the margins of Hollywood during this period I suggest that the directors and composers of these films turned to the soundtrack (as well as to the organization of narrative, camerawork, and so on) as a possible means of critiquing, or resisting, classical Hollywood scoring and soundtrack practices. A history of theoretical approaches to alternative scoring and soundtrack practices follows in Chapter 3.

Notes

1. Though, as a result of the loss of its theatres, Hollywood was able to avoid the worst of the decline in audience figures through the 1950s and 1960s (Maltby 1998).
2. For Tasker, at least, a distinction is drawn between 'New Hollywood' and 'post-classicism', with the latter term used to refer to stylistic changes alone in post-1960 mainstream American cinema, and which can be defined in relation to Bordwell et al.'s account of the aesthetic norms of classical Hollywood cinema.
3. Michelle Hilmes; cited in Maltby 1998, p. 30, and Schatz 1993, p. 12. The curtailment of the distributors' practice of block-booking was also a factor in this. It

'undermined the economies of scale which sustained the distribution companies' financial dealings with small independent exhibitors whose audience were most vulnerable to the lures of television' (Maltby 1998, p. 30).

4. Schatz 1993, p. 13.

5. Maltby (1998) argues that this series of mergers and acquisitions began with Gulf and Western's acquisition of Paramount in 1965. Gomery (1998) traces it back to MCA's takeover of Universal in 1962.

6. Wasserman was then forced to sell off the talent agency component of MCA in order to avoid an anti-trust lawsuit, however.

7. Indeed, according to Herman and McChesney (1997, p. 54): 'Firms without cross-selling and cross-promotional potential are at a serious disadvantage in competing in the global marketplace.'

8. '[W]hile vertical integration describes the economic relationship between business sectors, "synergy" instead imagines a "creative" and horizontal relationship between practices and products, between hardware and software, between media, and between interpretations' (Maltby 1998, pp. 39–40).

9. Indeed, ancillary markets were a self-conscious plot element in *Jurassic Park* (1993), in which *Jurassic Park* merchandise is available in the (fictional) theme park's shop.

10. *Star Wars* (1977) was reputedly the first film to make more money from its ancillary markets than from the film's sales and rentals. As Richard Maltby points out: 'Ultra-high budgets, generated by spiralling star salaries and the costs of spectacular special effects, act as effective barriers to entry into the profits of synergy, securing the majors' control of the most profitable sectors. The existence of stable secondary markets has made the risk-taking involved acceptable, by providing a financial cushion for movies that fail at the theatrical box office. ... While in the late 1960s only one movie in ten made a profit, by 1985, the existence of secondary markets in cable television and video ensured that half the films with negative costs over $14 million went into profit' (1998, p. 37). See also Gomery (1998) and Schamus (1998).

11. Whereas *Star Wars* was the runaway hit of the late 1970s, Schatz draws particular attention to the importance of *Saturday Night Fever* for its 'erosion of various industry barriers and also the multimedia potential of movie hits' (1993, p. 22): it starred John Travolta, a familiar face from television; the Bee-Gees' soundtrack dominated the charts and initiated a new strategy in the cross-promotion of movie soundtracks, in which the music is used to pre-sell the film (see J. Smith 1998, pp. 197–8); and it assisted in the transformation of the 'golden age' Hollywood musical to 'music movie', a category which became increasingly popular through the 1980s with such hits as *Flashdance* (1983) and *Footloose* (1984).

12. A change in the mid-1970s to US tax laws which had previously benefited the investors of independently financed experimental films was probably also a determining factor in the shift towards more conservative cycles of films: series, reissues, and so on (Schatz 1993, pp. 20–21).

13. 'From *The Godfather* to *Jaws* to *Star Wars*, we see films that are increasingly plot-driven, increasingly visceral, kinetic, and fast-paced, increasingly reliant on special effects, increasingly 'fantastic' (and thus apolitical), and increasingly targeted at younger audiences' (Schatz 1993, p. 23). See also Maltby 1998.

14. Here Schatz makes a distinction between the *highly* diversified conglomerates of the late 1960s to early 1970s, with their holdings in variety of industries, and the *tightly* diversified conglomerates of the 1980s on, with their holdings focused in particular and related industries.

15. See also Wyatt 1998; Schamus 1998; and Balio 1998a. However, in 'The art film

market in the new Hollywood', Tino Balio questions how long the art film can continue as an 'alternative cinema' due to today's 'ruthless and competitive commercial environment' (1998b, p. 72). The result of this situation has been that the previously independent companies Miramax, New Line Cinema, and Samuel Goldwyn Co. have been subject to mergers and acquisitions and are now better described by the term 'major-independents', due to their being subsumed into global conglomerates.

16. Interestingly, this view has also been influential in studies of the popular music industry, an entertainment industry which has a similar history in terms of industrial organization. See Peterson and Berger [1975] 1990.

17. Kalinak 1992, pp. 186–7. Here Kalinak's argument echoes the view of Bordwell, Staiger and Thompson on Hollywood cinema's assimilation of the conventions of the art film into classical practice; see Bordwell et al. pp. 378–85, 'Alternative modes of film practice'.

18. By contrast, for K. J. Donnelly (1998), the fact that composers and orchestrators are no longer full-time employees of the studios has led to the much less standardized scoring in the 'post-classical' era (by comparison with that of the 1930s–1940s).

19. A number of composers have made this explicit: Rick Wentworth (oral presentation at 'Film Music Conference', University of Leeds, UK, 6 July 1998); Julian Nott (discussion panel, 'School of Sound', Institut français, London, UK, 16–19 April 1998) and Simon Fisher-Turner (oral presentation at 'School of Sound', Institut français, London, UK, 15-18 April 1999).

20. '*Perceivers* is the word I have chosen to designate the theoretical placeholder for audience members; it cannot be reduced to either textuality or an extratextual "real." While perceivers, as theoretical constructs, can never be the same as "real" audience members, they mark an important distinction from previous theoretical positions both because they are decidedly multiple and because they have ears' (Kassabian 2001, pp. 110–11).

21. The details of these experiments can be found in Tagg and Clarida (forthcoming). This research has been awaiting publication for some time.

22. Kassabian 2001, p. 19. In studying the responses of the subjects in the Tagg and Clarida experiment, Kassabian also discovered that 'while gendered identities and their articulations in culture may be quite complex, respondents in this study heard a very untroubled and traditional regime of gender' (p. 30). For example, subjects' imaginary female protagonists were associated with musical signifiers heard as 'rural', 'pastoral', the 'romantic' and the 'pre-industrial', while the male was associated with those thought to signify the 'urban' and 'industrial' (pp. 30–36).

23. Ibid., p. 24. See also Frith 1998, p. 122.

24. Kassabian acknowledges that this excludes a number of counterexamples from the sci-fi and action-adventure films which do use 'Romantic classical scores', however (2001 p. 177, n. 1).

25. Though this is also dependent upon the identificatory possibilities produced by the film's narrative, editing, and so on.

26. Donnelly 1998, p. 150. Indeed, Elfman himself has stated that when composing film music in a traditional style he tries to approach the scores of Korngold and Rózsa, though he adds that his music always 'goes through some funny circus mirrors in my head' and ends up being more 'twisted' (Elfman, cited in Donnelly, ibid.).

27. However, Prince's songs are generally sidelined in favour of Elfman's symphonic score which is 'constantly foregrounded in a non-classical fashion' (ibid., p. 146).

28. Both exhibitors and sheet music publishers gained financially from the cross-promotion of songs during film programmes in the form of 'song-slides' or 'musical

   illustration', with the sheet music of 'plugged' songs sold by exhibitors in their
   theatre foyers for a percentage commission. See J. Smith 1998, p. 28.

29. See chapters 4, 5 and 6 of Jeff Smith's study (1998) for a discussion of the variety of
    means used by Henry Mancini, John Barry and Ennio Morricone to foreground their
    music.

30. Burlingame 2000, p. 8. Jeff Smith points out that some historians have suggested that
    '*Zhivago*'s director, David Lean, went back after the score was finished and added
    more cues featuring 'Lara's Theme' to boost the score's profit potential' (1998, p.
    17).

31. This chart accessed at http://movieweb.com/movie/alltime/html on 24 November
    2002 (with which figures updated on 18 November, 2002) and relates to US box-
    office figures. The same chart is available from www.imdb.com, which also lists
    charts for top grossing films in non-US countries and worldwide. Although the
    positions of the films in these charts are slightly different, in the main the same films
    are featured. It should be noted, however, that the figures for these charts have not
    been adjusted to reflect inflation.

32. Nowell-Smith and Ricci 1998; Bordwell, Staiger et al. 1985, pp. 378-85; Morrison
    1998; Balio 1998a; Mattelart 2000; Miller 2000; Bordwell 1979 (on art cinema). For
    a discussion of how the US dominates trade in films, see Hoskins et al. 1997, ch. 4,
    esp. pp. 37–50.

33. As Jean-Pierre Jeancolas points out, in the ten years prior to the culmination of this
    round of talks 'French cinema ... lost 15% of its share of the market [in France],
    while the American cinema ... gained 20%' (1998, p. 57).

34. As Toby Miller points out: 'If we consolidate television, film, and video texts as at
    mid-1994, the American industry relied on exports for $8 billion of its annual
    revenue of $18 billion, with 55 per cent from Western Europe (*Daily Variety* 1994:
    16). Europe imported $3.7 billion in 1992, compared to $288 million in reciprocal
    sales; and the disparity is increasing. Overseas hard-top exhibition is now a more
    significant source of Hollywood's revenue than domestic receipts, as the new
    multiplexes have massively increased attendances throughout Europe over the 1990s
    (2000, p. 153).

Chapter 3

Alternatives to classical Hollywood scoring

In the previous two chapters I presented some key approaches to classical Hollywood scoring as it has been theorized since the coming of sound, and pointed to the apparent return of this scoring practice in New Hollywood cinema. I also highlighted that during the 1980s New Hollywood began to occupy an increasingly ubiquitous position in European film markets. The central argument of this book is that, by operating as a signifier of classical – and, indeed, New Hollywood cinema – the classical Hollywood score offered those making films outside and on the margins of Hollywood cinema in the 1980s and 1990s a further means by which they could differentiate their cinemas from Hollywood's, through the production of scores and soundtracks which critique or refer to this practice in particular ways.

The idea that alternatives to classical Hollywood scoring exist is not in itself new, although it has been relatively little discussed in theoretical terms.[1] In this chapter I introduce some of the most influential theoretical approaches to these alternative scoring practices: in particular, those of Eisenstein, and Adorno and Eisler. I begin, however, with Eisenstein, Pudovkin and Alexandrov's 'Statement [on Sound]' ([1928] 1985) which focused on the potential of film sound in general that had been enabled by synchronization. In this 'Statement' they proposed a 'contrapuntal' approach which would 'weaken' the dominant soundtrack practices of the 'international cinema'. As is discussed in more detail below, this terminology was later used by Eisenstein, and Adorno and Eisler to describe scoring practices opposed to those used in classical scoring, with counterpoint celebrated for its additive properties and parallelism viewed negatively as producing redundancy.

Eisenstein: counterpoint or unity?

With the coming of sound, a number of silent era theorists and filmmakers argued against what they saw as a threat to the dream-like, non-realistic qualities of silent cinema, in particular to the potentially regressive naturalism of synchronized, on-screen dialogue.[2] Many of the same writers celebrated the possibilities that *a*synchronous sound (as opposed to naturalistic dialogue) offered to the sound film, in the representation of subjective or emotional realities rather than naturalistic ones.[3] In their 'Statement [on Sound]' written in 1928, Sergei

Eisenstein, V. I. Pudovkin and G. V. Alexandrov also warned against the use of synchronous sound in a 'naturalistic' manner after the first 'novelty' period of its development. To continue to do so would lead to its 'automatic' use in '"highly cultured dramas" and other photographed performances of a theatrical sort' ([1928] 1985, p. 84). This was considered detrimental to cinema because the authors believed that cinema's specificity was built on montage: that is, the placing of individually neutral shots into a sequence from which meaning emerges. Adding synchronous (and naturalistic) sound to an individual shot 'increases the independence of [the shot's] meaning' and would thus work against the emergence of meaning through the *juxtaposition* of individual shots in montage (ibid.). Using sound *a*synchronously – in *counterpoint* to the image – on the other hand, would enable sound to *add* potential meanings through its juxtaposition with the visuals; sound could thereby operate as a further montage element. Ultimately Eisenstein et al. hoped that experimentation with synchronized sound in 'distinct nonsynchronization' with the visuals would lead to 'the creation of an orchestral counterpoint of visual and aural images' (ibid.).

Synchronized sound also offered a useful answer to problems caused by the use of inter-titles as a montage element[4] and 'explanatory pieces' such as close-ups, which could slow down the overall tempo of a sequence. As film narrative grew ever more complicated, the addition of another montage element offered a 'new means of enormous power to the expression and solution' of these problems (ibid.). Eisenstein et al. saw the 'contrapuntal' method as a means of weakening and perhaps even overthrowing 'international cinema'; that is, films made outside the Soviet Union (including, of course, Hollywood cinema). Rather, the mode of filmmaking these authors advocated apparently offered the potential for a truly international cinema, since '[s]uch a method of constructing the sound film will not confine it to a national market, as must happen with the photographing of plays'. Instead it 'will give a greater possibility than ever before for the circulation throughout the world of a filmically expressed idea' (p. 85). It is clear that Eisenstein et al. associated the specificity of theatre with language and speech, and the ontology of cinema with the image and non-verbal sound.

The view of filmmaking presented by these theorists, and by Eisenstein in particular, was organized around a notion of 'conflict'. It was based on bringing dialectical thought to bear on artistic creativity; mobilizing the theoretical work of Georg Hegel and Karl Marx in relation to the assemblage of films. Eisenstein saw the development of Soviet cinema to be based on a progression from the use of quite basic forms of montage through to montage forms which stimulated intellectual thought. It was his intention that a film's spectator should be actively involved in the production of a film's meaning. Through the juxtaposition of different montage elements or the interpolation of seemingly incongruous shots into the structure of a sequence, spectators would be led to question the role of such shots, and ultimately (when montage was used correctly) to recognize their social situation.[5]

In the section of *The Film Sense* titled 'The Synchronization of Senses', Eisenstein explained the difference between vertical and horizontal montage: a distinction made possible by synchronized sound (1942, pp. 69–109). Vertical montage is here defined by recourse to an analogy with a musical score for more than one instrument or voice, with each instrumental or vocal part represented on a different stave or line, and in which the diagrammatic character of the score makes explicit *which* instruments are playing and *what* they are playing at any given point in time. With audio-visual media another stave or line is needed in order to demonstrate what is happening in the image at the same moment. Similarly, horizontal montage is explained as the continuation and development of each individual line or stave through time. By combining both horizontal and vertical montage, Eisenstein aimed to create an organic whole, with sounds (and music) 'welded' or fused with the image through an '*inner synchronization*', a '"hidden" inner synchronization', a synchronization which must be '*dictated* solely by the demands of the expressive work in progress' through the common language of 'movement' (pp. 77–83; emphasis original). Making reference to further musical analogies – that is, the use of musical terms to explain non-musical events, relationships, procedures – Eisenstein suggested that such cross-media synchronization might take the form of rhythm (musical rhythm, rhythm of movement in and between pictoral shots) and melody (melody in music, play of light and colour in the image through time), for example.[6] However, this 'synchronization does not presume consonance': for, as long as a picture–sound relationship is '*compositionally controlled*' according to the particular theme or idea generating the sequence, such movements may either correspond or not-correspond (p. 85; emphasis original).

Part of the confusion engendered by Eisenstein's theory of audio–visual interaction is due to the fact that it includes the meaningful and productive use of both unity and disunity between cross-media elements, *provided* that in either case it is in service to the theme or idea underlying the sequence in question. Thus, a more general tendency can be located in Eisenstein's writings which is organized around unity, albeit a higher (or deeper) level of unity in which disunity may play a part; that is, where the same theme or idea may generate (and 'compositionally control') apparent surface-level disjunction across different media or individual montage elements. Although Eisenstein continually called for counterpoint between media, this was usually at the service of unity at a deeper level.[7]

Pudovkin expressed much the same view in his discussion of music as a sonic element of montage in 'Asynchronism as a Principle of Sound Film' ([1929] 1985). He stressed the difference between objective and subjective perception of the world and argued that asynchronous sound could assist in the depiction of this disjunction. To support this view he gives the example of a sequence from the second half of his film, *Deserter* (1933), in which an uprising builds, is quashed, and then finally builds again. Although '[t]he image's progress curves like a sick man's temperature chart: ... the music in direct contrast is firm and steady' (pp. 90–91). Rather than matching the progress of the sequence directly as an accompaniment and thus presenting 'only the superficial aspect of the scene', Pudovkin asked his composer, Shaporin, to create music which would represent the constant emotional theme of 'courage and the certainty of ultimate victory', which would 'develop in a gradual growth of power' (p. 90). He argues that, while the image depicts the events objectively, the music 'expresses the subjective appreciation of this objectivity. The sound reminds the audience that with every defeat the fighting spirit only receives new impetus to the struggle for final victory in the future' (p. 91). The music seemingly operates in counterpoint to the image, though in fact it works in the service of unity between image and sound at a deeper level.

The explicit use of music as a montage element was discussed in some detail by Eisenstein in the section of *The Film Sense* entitled 'Form and Content: Practice' (1942, pp. 157–216). Here he used a sequence from his film *Alexander Nevsky* (1938) – with music by Sergei Prokofiev – as a case study, and provided an analysis of the 'Attack of the Knights' which takes place just before the start of 'The Battle on the Ice'.[8] As with Eisenstein's earlier writing, musical analogies also featured prominently.

Eisenstein stated that music cannot 'mean' in any concrete way, though he argued that it could create meaning through structural means such as rhythm and movement. Upon hearing music, he suggested, we often visualize something in plastic terms (however vaguely or abstractly): in this way we may grasp the 'inner movement' of a segment of music. Such (musical) compositional lines can also assist filmmakers in deciding on the horizontal organization of visual shot materials – that is, through time. This occurred with the 'Battle on the Ice' sequence, which was cut to a pre-recorded track of Prokofiev's music (p. 174). Equally, however, visuals may be recorded and edited prior to the composition of the music, as was the case with the 'Attack of the Knights'. A match on 'inner movement' between audio and visual media is not enough on its own though. The 'inner movement' of the individual media must embody, in plastic terms, the expression of the theme too.[9]

Eisenstein's analysis of this attack sequence from *Nevsky* is an attempt to explain how it was bound together 'organically *through movement*' (1942, p. 174; emphasis original). Drawing on the classical painterly tradition, in which the eye of the viewer of a painting is directed to particular points on the canvas through graphic means, Eisenstein focused on the movement of the film spectator's eye gazing upon the series of shots which make up the sequence. In viewing each shot, and being directed to particular salient points in graphic terms (as organized in relation to the dramatic theme), a temporal element is added, generated by the spectator. This experience of horizontal movement through the shots of the sequence, and the spectator's experience of the temporality and rhythms of this movement, should be correlated with the music by the composer, or vice versa (pp. 172–4).

According to Eisenstein, shots from the *Nevsky* 'Attack of the Knights' sequence attained unity across the different media through a correlation of movements generated by a variety of means: graphically, for example, with the eye led from the front of the diegesis at the bottom left of the frame to the background at the top right of the frame; and temporally, through the play of light and gradations of tone colour.[10] A correlation exists between the music and the graphic and temporal elements of shot VIII in the cited sequence, for example: the quavers on the second, third and fourth crotchets of bar 13 which all recur at the same pitch assist the spectator in picking out a number of the spears (which disappear off towards the horizon at the top of the frame, as the line of soldiers tail off into the distance on the right of the frame) and are also matched temporally with glinting lights on the soldiers' helmets. Further, Eistenstein suggests that the spectator relates the chord of bar 13 (which occurs just after the transition from shot VII to VIII of the excerpt) to the warrior who looms at the foreground of the frame in close-up.

According to Eisenstein, general movements can also occur horizontally through a sequence (that is, not only through individual shots) – or indeed a general movement may be composed of the movements *between* individual shots. In the sequence under analysis Eisenstein argued that there was a general movement from left to right within the frame across this sequence of shots (in temporal terms, from the beginning to the end of the sequence). This is underpinned by the dramatic idea of the prince (shown on the left side of the frame with each recurrence) awaiting the enemy army and his desire to catch a glimpse of it (1942, p. 175). Thus Eisenstein argued that both music and image present the same underlying theme in this sequence, though in different ways. As Royal S. Brown points out, both composer and director have taken care to 'consistently avoid ... the kinds of direct interactions between music, action, and characters one finds in Hollywood' (1994, p. 138). In doing so *Alexander Nevsky* maintains, indeed promotes, a 'certain separation between the musical score and narrative' with neither privileged above the other (ibid.).[11]

As Nicholas Cook also points out in *Analysing Musical Multimedia* (1998), for all the valorization of counterpoint and the critique of parallelism Eisenstein's theory of audio–visual interaction as a possible means of alternative soundtrack practice to 'international' (or non-Soviet Union) cinema is built, at root, on a notion of unity. Adorno and Eisler critique this aspect of Eisenstein's approach too, as is discussed in more detail below. For Cook, however, both Eisenstein, and Adorno and Eisler 'end up going round in circles because they are trying to use a language predicated on similarity in order to articulate a principle predicated on difference' (1998, p. 65). Cook grounds this view of the Adorno and Eisler text, at least partially, on a critique of Eisler's music for Joris Ivens's film *Rain* (op. 70). (This was one of several scores Eisler composed as part of the Film Music Project funded by the Rockefeller Foundation to explore the use of new musical resources in film scoring during the period 1940–42; it is discussed at the end of

Composing for the Films ([1947] 1994), pp. xlix–l, 135–65.) Cook accuses Eisler of producing a score which focuses predominantly on the description of the image, and which thus contradicts the prescriptions proposed earlier in the book. Although Cook acknowledges that the book's joint authorship offers a possible explanation for such 'inconsistencies', ultimately he suggests that the problem is actually a 'conceptual' one, with the study's 'fundamental model for the relationship between different media ... [based on] identity' (1998, pp. 64–5). In each case, counterpoint either operates only at surface level and works to assist the expression of unity at a deeper level, or, if image and sound contradict one another, then in directly opposing unity, Cook argues that their relationship is also based upon unity. Although these authors assert difference, they cannot theorize it because they are constrained by the similarity-based terminology they use.

Adorno and Eisler: prescriptions for an alternative scoring practice

As was mentioned briefly in Chapter 1, part of Adorno and Eisler's problem with classical Hollywood scoring discussed in *Composing for the Films* ([1947] 1994) was the tendency to use regressive musical materials: music's potential was being 'dumbed down' in service to the image.[12] They argued that new musical idioms were more appropriate to film because they were more flexible and broke through the conventions of traditional musical styles, which were subordinated first to tonality, and only second to the dramatic task. Where a conventionalized musical idiom required extension – and thus 'superfluousness' – in order to establish its tonal centre, new musical materials were better suited to films' sequences of quick inter-cutting, for example, due to their brevity and lack of 'padding'.[13] The new musical resources did not require the same kinds of extension as tonal music: decoration and symmetry could be avoided. Brevity was also a function of the prevalence of discords in these materials, which, in turn, had led to the 'dissolution of tonality' (p. 41, n. 2). Adorno and Eisler suggested that because 'there is no room in [motion-picture music] for the formally satisfactory expansion of tonality', then it 'is driven to atonality' (ibid.). With free atonality and total serialism the teleology of tension and resolution associated with the establishment of, and return to, tonal centres does not apply: dissonant pitches no longer carry a sensuous 'pull' towards moments of resolution, because dissonance is the norm rather than the exception. Here '[s]ound is robbed of its static quality and made dynamic by the ever-present factor of the "unresolved"' (p. 41).

As a result of their brevity, the new musical resources were also capable of more concentrated expression. In classical scoring, with its use of traditional musical styles built upon the conventions of functional harmony, the representation of particular mood states or feelings 'preserves a certain restraint', whereas 'the new style tends to be unrestrained. Sorrow can turn into appalling despair, repose into glassy rigidity, fear into panic' (p. 40). Where the music of the Romantic period (and thus, classical scoring) could be used to *represent* emotions, the new musical resources had the potential to intensify this expressive embodiment and *express* fervent bursts of emotion. Indeed, as Adorno stated in his *Philosophy of Modern Music*: 'Music, compressed into a moment, is valid as an eruptive revelation of negative experience. It is closely related to actual suffering.'[14] Further, in contrast to the stylized and conventionalized qualities of traditional musical materials, the intense emotion of these concentrated musical units was also more fitting to the 'sensationalism' of the movies, Adorno and Eisler argued (pp. 35–6). Since traditional materials 'present themselves as something that has always been known, [they are] therefore ... deprived in advance of the power to express the unfamiliar and unexplored' (p. 37). Thus, modern musical materials are much better at expressing fear and horror than traditional musical idioms: 'The fear expressed in the dissonances of Schoenberg's most radical period far surpasses the measure of fear conceivable to the average middle-class individual; it is a historical fear, a sense of impending doom.'[15]

Adorno and Eisler argued that music should not confirm, or duplicate the screen action in a direct or immediate way, though music and picture must 'correspond', 'however indirectly or even antithetically' (p. 69). Nonetheless, they were critical of Eisenstein's apparent advocacy of levels of abstraction as offering a means of avoiding duplication between media. Eisenstein recounted the use of the 'Barcarolle' from Jacques Offenbach's *Tales of Hoffmann* in a film to depict a pair of lovers 'embracing against a background of Venetian scenery'. Eisenstein suggested that taking from these scenes

> only the *approaching and receding* movements of the water combined with the reflected *scampering and retreating play of light* over the surface of the canals, and you immediately remove yourself, by at least one degree, from the series of 'illustration' fragments, and you are closer to finding a response to the *sensed inner movement* of a barcarolle. (Eisenstein 1942, p. 161, cited in Adorno and Eisler [1947] 1994, p. 66.)

Here, Adorno and Eisler argued that Eisenstein merely 'transfers the principle [of identity] to a more abstract level, on which its crudeness and redundant character are less obvious' ([1947] 1994, p. 67). Similarly, they found Eisenstein's suggestions that the music–picture interrelation be organized around 'movement' (or 'rhythm' in Kurt London's view) to be too general. Such suggestions would more than likely result in 'an affinity of moods – in other words, something suspiciously trite that contradicts the very principle of adequacy to the motion picture in the name of which that "rhythm" or "higher movement" is invoked' (p. 69).

In agreement with Eisenstein, however, Adorno and Eisler considered montage to offer a potentially productive technique for combining music and image. It allowed the different media to maintain independence from one another, yet also to be considered in combination as a whole which would add up to more than the sum of its constituent elements. The relationship of music and image should not be organized around similarity, however, but instead by 'question and answer, affirmation and negation, appearance and essence', as '[t]his is dictated by the divergence of the media in question and the specific nature of each' (p. 70). Further,

> [t]he alienation of the media from each other reflects a society alienated from itself, men whose functions are severed from each other even within each individual, therefore, the aesthetic divergence of the media is potentially a legitimate means of expression, not merely a regrettable deficiency that has to be concealed as well as possible. (p. 74).

Indeed, Adorno and Eisler argued that the 'specific nature' of each media is so different that even when unified in terms of intended meaning they diverge.[16] Where the image is effectively static, music is all about motion. In fact, they argued, music is required to breathe life into the static, frozen images presented on screen: it should supply 'momentum, muscular energy, a sense of corporeity. Its aesthetic effect is that of a stimulus of motion, not a reduplication of motion. ... Thus, the relation between music and pictures is antithetic at the very moment when the deepest unity is achieved' (p. 78). Music should be used in such a way that it creates a productive antithetical relationship with the image: this would then dispel the myth that the media must be unified and would create a larger and more flexible pool of resources for the music–image relationship. Thus, Adorno and Eisler suggest that music should avoid standardized moments of entry and exit, and focus instead on interpolations which highlight the heterogeneity of music and image, such as halting the music abruptly rather than fading it down, or using it to 'outshout' the image presented on screen. Noise tracks may be used in place of music, or combined with music.[17] Traditional musical resources may also be used productively, but must be 'clarified and "alienated" in the light of advanced practice' (p. 34). Adorno and Eisler state explicitly that if such prescriptions were carried out the subject's actual situation (alienated from others, alienated from the products of its labour) could be revealed, which would thus undermine the ideological construction of the subject by the culture industry.[18]

Many of Adorno and Eisler's suggestions were targeted at pulling the spectator-auditor out of a direct, passive relationship with the cinematic action on screen which, they believed, constituted Hollywood cinema. Some of these prescriptions are based loosely on Berthold Brecht's idea of theatrical 'alienation' in which he argued that theatre and opera audiences should not be left to absorb passively what happens on stage and mistake it for real life: such forms of theatre drugged the audience into a state of identification with the play and thus seduced them into an acceptance of what was said. Instead, for Brecht, theatre should reveal the contradictions in society by dramatizing situations in such a way that they are made unfamiliar and, thus, less straightforwardly acceptable. Writers and directors were encouraged to separate the elements of the drama in such a way that they would not cohere into an integrated whole. Music, for example, should not be integrated so that it can induce empathy and identification with characters. Rather, it should be separated into musical interludes which interrupt the action and encourage the audience to contemplate the bigger picture. Indeed, though the topical songs and production numbers found in musical comedies were musically limited, the interruptions they created offered good aesthetic models of montage in practice, since their presence served to express the illusory character of the fictive reality portrayed, creating obstacles to 'aesthetic empathy' (pp. 73–4). Adorno was also, however, aware that songs used in this manner were also open to straightforward appropriation by the culture industry (Paddison 1996, p. 104).

As discussed briefly in chapter one, Adorno and Eisler's views on the role of music in direct political action were radically different. Eisler attempted to compose music that would be understandable to the workers and would draw their attention to their political situation and encourage them to take action to change it. By contrast, Adorno was staunchly opposed to music that was easily communicated (because it would imply an acceptance of its commodity form) and also to any form of direct political action. He argued for music to be composed in such a way that its form should reflect the oppressive nature of late capitalism, and argued against the composition of music with political content, or which incited political action.[19] The French *nouvelle vague* director Jean-Luc Godard made a similar plea for filmmaking, calling 'not for political films, but for films made politically'.[20] As Claudia Gorbman points out, (Adorno and) Eisler's prescriptions which focused on revealing the 'divergence of the media' were 'eerily prophetic of Godard' (1991, p. 281). She suggests that Godard's 'aesthetic radicalism' reveals the 'force of vision' in these prescriptions:

> Eisler states that it should be possible to 'introduce music at certain points, instead of gradually concluding the music or cautiously fading it out, to break it off abruptly' (*CF*, p. 79). When he suggests that music could be used to 'outshout' the narrative action, he presumably means having the music's volume drown out other sound and/or dominate the image. When we recall the aesthetic radicalism of these proposals as they are carried out in the cinema of Godard – consider, for example, the string quartet in *Prénom Carmen/First Name Carmen* (1984) and its fence-sitting status as either nondiegetic or inhabiting a parallel diegetic world to the main narrative – we realise what force of vision resided in this refugee in 1940s Hollywood.[21]

In the next chapter – the first of the case-studies – I argue that this 'aesthetic radicalism' takes the form of a dialectical approach to the conventions of classical Hollywood scoring. That is, by intensifying and exaggerating the application of these conventions, attention is drawn to their nature as convention, thus undermining their status as 'natural law'.

Gorbman points out that, although Adorno and Eisler illustrate their suggestions with excerpts from Eisler's scores, only one of the examples discussed was taken from a score to a Hollywood film, and that was a collaborative project with Fritz Lang and Brecht based on an explicitly political theme: *Hangmen Also Die* (1943). The other examples are drawn from Eisler's scores for European films, such as Slaten Dodow's *Kuhle Wampe* (1932), and from his two pre-Hollywood American projects: Joseph Losey's *Pete Roleum and his Cousins* (1939) and Joris Ivens's *The Four Hundred Million* (1939). Gorbman argues that Adorno and Eisler's prescriptions were simply too radical for the commercial aesthetic of classical Hollywood cinema: '[H]ow can music accomplish anti-bourgeois, anti-conventional goals in an entirely rationalized, industry? Even if the composer can get away with writing a "progressive" score, can a politically correct *part* have any progressive effect in a regressive *whole*?' (1991, p. 281).

Gorbman tests the scores Eisler produced in Hollywood against the theory of *Composing for the Films*, though most of the seven films Eisler worked on in Hollywood during 1942–47 'held some political or aesthetic interest': the directors of these films include Clifford Odets, Douglas Sirk, Jean Renoir, Edward Dmytryk.[22] She notes that Eisler orchestrated his own scores. It was relatively unusual for a studio composer to do so at this time, though on this occasion the situation proved favourable to the studios because it was cheaper (1991, p. 275). Gorbman notes that Eisler's '"sound" is distinctive' and 'elicits few stereotyped emotional associations' (p. 281). Indeed, Eisler often avoided emotional underscoring, inviting 'intellectual interpretation of the narrative action' instead (p. 282). Even in *The Spanish Main* – the most commercial and classical picture Eisler scored – Gorbman identifies moments in which alternative scoring principles are used, with music apparently working against the mood of the action depicted on screen, though such practices are usually allowable only when they are sanctioned through conventional narrative development (pp. 283–4).

In general, however, Gorbman argues that much of Eisler's music for these films conforms to the conventions of classical Hollywood scoring. His scores 'often [co-ordinate] music with picture very precisely' and his use of contemporary musical materials often reinforces mood in quite conventional ways (p. 281). The interpolation of songs does not, in general, 'carry their films out of the "realm of literal immediacy"':

> On the contrary they bring a lump to the throat, make the heart swell with uncritical emotion [as Adorno had himself hinted that they might] – not unlike the male chorus on the soundtrack as the cattle drive begins in *Red River* (1948), or the pop songs that accompany Tom Cruise's military flight training runs in *Top Gun* (1986). (Ibid., p. 280)

Similarly, Gorbman states that Eisler succumbs to the clichés of classical scoring practice in his score for *The Spanish Main* (1945): elaborate mickey-mousing and 'stinger' chords are used with little or no attempt made to counter the immediacy of these effects. Although she concedes that the Eisler 'sound' is discernible – even in *The Spanish Main* – Gorbman states that it is here 'robbed of virtually all progressive potential' (p. 284).

For Gorbman, as for Adorno and Eisler, the more commercial the film the more compromised the score: 'Fundamentally, no motion-picture music can be better than what it accompanies. Music for a trashy picture is to some extent trashy, no matter how elegantly or skilfully it has solved its problems' (Adorno and Eisler [1947] 1994, p. 116; cited in Gorbman 1991, p. 284). No matter how well motion-picture music 'rebel[s] and disavow[s] the picture that degrades it, either by ruthless opposition or by revealing exaggeration', it is still subject to neutralization through the culture industry's machinery of standardization (Adorno and Eisler 1947/1994, pp. 117, 86–7). Standardization is generated through various 'mechanisms of censorship' (which flatten out difference) and the focus on the visuals in classical filmmaking and in recording and mixing techniques, for example (pp. 86–7). The effect of the new musical materials is a case in point: music which would raise a 'hostile reaction' in the concert hall is often accepted unproblematically in the cinema (p. 87). Musical language is not in itself the answer to alternative scoring practice. Rather the 'mechanism of neutralization' must be broken (ibid.). Institutional difference offers a means by which this may be achieved.

Gorbman argues that working within the Hollywood system severely limits composers' opportunities to use the prescriptions for alternative scoring practice suggested by Adorno and Eisler. She finds such practices more congruent with those employed *outside* Hollywood cinema. Relatedly, Caryl Flinn has suggested that references to these alternative scoring practices can be identified in a number of New German Cinema films from the 1970s, in particular those directed by Rainer Werner Fassbinder and with soundtracks produced in collaboration with Peer Raben.[23] The idea that scoring practice might be considered in just such institutional terms forms the central tenet of this study.

The case-studies

The argument which is developed through the case-studies in the remaining chapters is dependent upon the notion that there was a resurgence of classical scoring in Hollywood cinema from the mid-1970s on. As a result of the ubiquity of classical scoring in high-budget Hollywood films from this period and the rising profile of these films across a number of world markets, particularly – and of interest to this study – Europe, a film's score and soundtrack offered filmmakers, their crews and composers a further opportunity by which to make clear their relationship with, or difference from, Hollywood cinema. Evidence for this argument is presented via the analysis of the scores and/or soundtracks of four films. Each of the films chosen was produced during the 1980s though two were released in 1990. Beginning with the most radical, the case-studies chart a range of relationships with classical Hollywood scoring and soundtrack practice. The first three case studies – Jean-Luc Godard's *Prénom: Carmen/First name: Carmen* (1983), Derek Jarman's *The Garden* (1990), Wim Wenders's *Der Himmel über Berlin/Wings of Desire* (1987) – are straightforwardly non-Hollywood in both their financing and (to a certain extent) their production practices. The film discussed in the final case study – David Lynch's *Wild at Heart* (1990) – was, at least partially, financed by Hollywood and used Hollywood stars.

The order in which the case studies appear in the following chapters represents a movement through non-Hollywood production toward production at the margins of Hollywood cinema; that is, from Godard through to Lynch. In line with my argument that scores and soundtracks may be usefully considered in institutional terms, I argue that this range of relationships with Hollywood cinema is reflected in the character of the scores and soundtracks analysed. For example, where my analysis of *Prénom: Carmen* demonstrates a deconstruction of classical scoring practice, I argue that analysis of the score and soundtrack to *Wild at Heart* reveals a mode of practice situated deep within classical Hollywood cinema, albeit a radically reconfigured one. For various reasons, Godard, Wenders and Lynch have all indicated that they have an ambivalent relationship with Hollywood cinema.[24] In the chapters concerned with their films I introduce and explore the nature of these relationships as evidence to support my argument.

Jean-Luc Godard is perhaps best known as one of the most significant filmmakers of the French *nouvelle vague* movement of the 1950s and 1960s. He was originally a film critic and praised the spontaneity and freshness that the Hollywood films of the studio era brought to cinema in comparison with the products of French national cinema of the period. Godard's film soundtracks are among the most interesting and innovative in Western cinema history: while there have as yet been relatively few analyses of soundtracks to films made outside Hollywood, a number of critics have analysed the soundtracks to some of Godard's films of the 1960s. In my analysis of Godard's *Prénom: Carmen* (1983), I suggest that the soundtrack to this film reveals a dialectical approach to scoring practice and soundtrack production which both utilizes and critiques classical scoring practice. The presence of a string quartet performing the fragmentary music of Beethoven's late quartets plays a pivotal role in this dialectical manoeuvre. For example, the quartet music is used to provide continuity, but this scoring practice is intensified to such an extreme that attention is drawn both to this practice as a convention and to the presence of the music. By placing the source of the film's soundtrack (the quartet) on to the image track, Godard is able to question the 'fullness' of the latter. In doing so, the (theoretical) sound–image relationship of classical Hollywood – with image and narrative foregrounded, and nondiegetic music *unheard* in the background – is deconstructed.

By contrast to Godard's films, those of British painter-turned-film-director Derek Jarman have more often been remembered more for their visuals, despite interesting collaborative work with sonic artists such as Brian Eno and Simon Fisher Turner, both of whom are particularly interested in the exploration of the boundary between music and noise. My analysis of the soundtrack to *The Garden* (1990) focuses primarily on theoretical approaches to the reception of acousmatic electroacoustic music and sound and their relationship to the ideas of 'sound-' and 'voice-off'. Through the use of out-of-sync singing, of 'real world' sounds with no visible on-screen source, of synthesized or heavily-transformed real world sounds, and the lack of lip-synchronized dialogue, I suggest that in *The Garden* Jarman, Fisher Turner and members of the film's sound team expose the potential risk, as theoretically defined, of uncoupling the unity of the sound and image track. The relative autonomy of the soundtrack in this film speaks out for a minority community consistently denied a voice by the media during the 1980s. The soundtrack to this film – and, more emphatically, that of Jarman's last completed film, *Blue* (1993) – is presented as redemptive of the image as signified by the camera.

Like Godard, Wim Wenders began his life in films as a fan and a critic. Later in his career – again, like Godard – he took up the challenge to direct in Hollywood. Unlike Godard, however, Wenders's soundtracks have frequently incorporated rock-'n'-roll and pop music rather than the classics of Western art music, in addition to originally scored music. In my analysis of *Wings of Desire* (1987) I suggest that these two elements of the soundtrack – the original score by Jürgen Knieper, and a collection of various rock and pop songs – are associated with the film's two realms: the angelic and the mortal, respectively. This relationship is defined by a connection between music and utopia, though here each central character has a different utopian dream. Further, I suggest that the film's representation of the relationship between the mortal and angelic addresses the relationship of Hollywood and European art cinema. This is achieved, at least partially, through filmmaking and scoring practice, with the mortal associated with Hollywood cinema and ocularcentrism, and the angelic associated with European art cinema and the valorization of sound over sight. Ultimately, however, neither realm (and neither cinema) is promoted over the other. Instead, *Wings of Desire* offers the possibility of a negotiation or compromise between classical scoring and alternative soundtrack and scoring practices. This chapter involves a longer contextualization of the director's relationship with Hollywood cinema because, unlike the other case studies, this analysis is based on an allegorical reading which understands the relationship between classical and alternative scoring and soundtrack practices to be thematized by the film in terms of the relationship between the film's angelic and mortal realms.

David Lynch has long been considered a contemporary soundtrack innovator.[25]

My analysis of *Wild at Heart* (1990) begins with a consideration of the ways in which music and musical performance are used and valorized in the film, and organized around the character of Sailor (who, I argue, functions as a stand-in for Lynch as controller of the soundtrack). This is followed by a discussion of the impact of technological developments on contemporary film-sound recording and playback. Due to these developments, contemporary film sound is better able to reproduce the 'reality' of the fictional world presented on screen. However, it is also now possible for films to offer moments of sonic spectacle in which these technological developments are showcased, with an audience's attention potentially diverted away from both the film's narrative and the soundtrack's confirmation of the 'reality' of the diegesis, however briefly. In *Wild at Heart* these moments of sonic spectacle reveal a network of acoustically and thematically related sounds, through which unity is generated. Whereas in *Wings of Desire* the compromise between classical and alternative scoring practices are structurally separated by the division of the film's diegetic world into two realms (angelic and mortal), in *Wild at Heart* a more integrated combination of these practices is reached. Indeed, as a result of this integration and Lynch's collaborative soundtrack production practices, and the use of scoring and soundtrack practices which draw on the conventions of the Hollywood musical, I suggest that this film fulfils the utopian potential offered by the – alienated and compartmentalized – studio production practice of the classical era.

Notes

1. Although more radical examples of alternative scoring exist in practical terms, my focus here is on theoretical approaches.
2. See, for example, Arnheim 1933, part V, and 'A New Laocoön: Artistic Composites and the Talking Film' in Arnheim [1938] 1957, pp. 199–230.
3. For example, Clair ([1929] 1985) and Cavalcanti ([1939] 1985).
4. Following 'all the unavailing attempts to tie [intertitles] into the montage composition ... such as breaking it up into phrases and even words, increasing and decreasing the size of type used ...' (Eisenstein et al. [1928] 1985, p. 84).
5. See Eisenstein 1942 and 1949.
6. An extended version of this typology can be found in the earlier essay 'Methods of Montage' (1929), published in Eisenstein 1949, pp. 72–83.
7. This point is also made by Nicholas Cook (1998, pp. 49–97). I return to this issue below.
8. This specific montage sequence was chosen for analysis in print due to its being composed of predominantly static shots, thus resulting in less of a loss in the translation from film to print media (Eisenstein 1942, p. 174).
9. Eisenstein 1942, p. 169. Nicholas Cook describes this as a 'triadic' model of cross-media relationships: 'picture and music are related not directly, but by virtue of something that they both embody' (1998, p. 57).
10. These audio–visual correspondences are presented in the form of score excerpts, frame stills and a graphical depiction of their interrelations. They can be found in Eisenstein 1942 and in Cook 1998, p. 59.

11. For a useful confutation of Prendergast's critique of Eisenstein's analysis of this sequence, see Brown 1994, pp. 135–8. Brown also highlights that 'some emotional involvement in both narrative and character' is also included, however (p. 145).

12. However, this position is much more consistent with Adorno's (rather than Eisler's) views on the matter. See Graham McCann, 'Introduction' in Adorno and Eisler [1947] 1994. p. xxviii. The role of Adorno's notion of the 'historical dialectic of musical material' in this view is discussed in more detail in Chapter 1. By contrast, Claudia Gorbman suggests the influence of Russian Formalist Shklovsky in Eisler's advocacy for twentieth-century musical idioms (1991, p. 276).

13. Adorno and Eisler [1947] 1994, pp. 38–9. '[Modern music] can be regarded as a process of rationalization in so far as every single musical element is at each moment derived from the structure of the whole. But as music becomes more pliable through its own structural principles, it also becomes more pliable for purposes of application to other media' (ibid., pp. 33–4).

14. Adorno [1949] 1973, p. 37. Of Schoenberg's freely atonal music he wrote, 'Passions are no longer simulated, but rather genuine emotions of the unconscious – of shock, or trauma – are registered without disguise through the medium of music' (pp. 37–8).

15. Adorno and Eisler [1947] 1994, p. 36. Such music has not been excluded from mainstream film scoring, even in Hollywood, though it has in general come to be associated with notions of the irrational (such as depictions of madness), or with films concerned with generating horror and/or terror.

16. 'Music, however well defined in terms of its own structure, is never sharply defined with regard to any object outside itself to which it is related by imitation or expression. Conversely, no picture, not even an abstract painting, is completely emancipated from the world of objects. ... Roughly speaking, all music, including the most "objective" and nonexpressive, belongs primarily to the sphere of subjective inwardness, whereas even the most spiritualized painting is heavily burdened with unresolved objectivity' (Adorno and Eisler [1947] 1994, pp. 70–71).

17. In such cases, both tracks must be well-integrated, which would thus involve planning each track in such a way that space is left for the other (Adorno and Eisler [1947] 1994, pp. 101-3).

18. Indeed, as discussed briefly in Chapter 1, Martin Jay (1994) suggests that a consideration of cinema sound was avoided by much Marxist-psychoanalytic film theory of the 1970s because the addition of sound to the model would have enabled the possibility of creating tension in the filmic text, such theories argued that tensions could not exist because ideology was present at the level of the apparatus.

19. Gorbman maps the aesthetic results of these different positions onto the views of Brecht on the one hand, and the Russian Formalists on the other: 'These positions, slightly at odds with each other, reflect the difference between Brecht's *Verfremdungseffekt* – the notion of breaking convention for purposes of ideological distancing – and Shklovsky's *ostranenie* or making-strange – the Russian Formalist strategy of breaking convention in order to defamiliarize, for aesthetic and not necessarily political ends' (1991, p. 276).

20. Cited by Michelson in the foreword to Godard [1972] 1986, p. viii. It should be pointed out that by asking for 'films made politically,' Godard asks for films to be made in such a way that their production practice should reflect his own radical, left-wing political views. In a broader sense, all films and cultural products are, of course, inevitably 'made politically'.

21. Gorbman 1991, p. 281. As mentioned earlier, Gorbman attributes authorship of *Composing for the Films* to Eisler.

22. Ibid., p. 275. These films were *Hangmen Also Die* (orig. story Brecht; Lang, 1943);

None But the Lonely Heart (Odets, 1944); *Jealousy* (Gustav Machaty, 1945); *The Spanish Main* (Frank Borzage, 1945); *A Scandal in Paris/Thieves' Holiday* (Sirk, 1946); *Deadline at Dawn* (Harold Clurman, 1946); *Woman on the Beach* (Renoir, 1947); *So Well Remembered* (Dmytryk, 1947).

23. Ultimately, however, Flinn suggests that references to modernist aesthetic agendas (such as *Composing for the Films*) in the soundtrack practices of Fassbinder and Raben 'provided practices to be reworked rather than retrieved' (1999, p. 177).

24. By contrast, Jarman has indicated a more straightforward dissatisfaction with mainstream filmmaking in general, though the prominence and style of musical numbers in a range of his films also suggest allusion to the Hollywood musical.

25. For example, Lynch was used in a recent advertisement for a Technics Audio-Visual Receiver which featured his face positioned at the centre of the advert, with familiar iconography from his films and the *Twin Peaks* television series merged and blurred around and into it (including the severed ear from *Blue Velvet*, the flames from *Wild at Heart*, and bits of musical score). The accompanying text reads as follows: 'Technics. The Closest You'll Get To The Sound In His Head. When David Lynch invites you to lend him your ears, ask for a receipt. The Technics AX7 AV receiver reveals the full range of the cineaste's dark arts. ... Delivering the highest sound quality home cinema experience. And permitting no escape from the sound of your dreams. Or your nightmares ...'. The advertisement appeared on the inside cover of *Sight and Sound* **10** (2), February 2000.

Chapter 4

'What is the role of the quartet?': the soundtrack to Jean-Luc Godard's *Prénom: Carmen*

Godard's essays are, like his films, a criticism of the cinema, a theory of the cinema.
Richard Roud[1]

Jean-Luc Godard is perhaps the most well-known of film soundtrack innovators, or at least the most audacious. In this chapter I focus on the use of music in Godard's 1983 film *Prénom: Carmen*: a film which makes considerable use of Beethoven string quartets and also foregrounds a song by Tom Waits. A number of critics have suggested that many, if not all, of Godard's films are about cinema. Here, I argue that *Prénom: Carmen* is a film about the conventions of classical Hollywood scoring. As discussed in the first chapter, a number of these conventions are organized around effacing the presence of music in classical cinema, making it unobtrusive by 'sneaking' it in and out under dialogue and sound effects. By contrast, in *Prénom: Carmen* attention is drawn to the conventions of classical scoring by problematizing the ability of film music to move easily across boundaries – between the diegetic and the nondiegetic, for example – and by foregrounding the manipulation and mediation of the sound recording and mixing apparatus inherent in the presence of any nondiegetic film music. With its ambiguous positioning at the margins of the film's narrative, the role of the diegetic string quartet is central to this. I set the context for the analysis of this score with a brief account of Godard's work as a critic and his relationship with Hollywood.

Cahiers du Cinéma and Hollywood

During the late 1940s and early 1950s Jean-Luc Godard – along with Truffaut, Chabrol, Rohmer and Rivette – spent much of his time at the *Cinémathèque Français* in Paris, watching repertory programmes chosen by François Langlois built predominantly around Hollywood cinema. Such programmes had been impossible during the German occupation of France during the Second World

War, but with the end of the war France was flooded with a backlog of American films. Along with the others, Godard wrote review essays for various film magazines and journals, in particular for the journal *Cahiers du Cinéma*, started by André Bazin in 1950. In *Cahiers* these critics vented their anger at the lack of innovation they found in films of the French establishment, which was, at the time, largely involved in filming adaptations of novels or stage plays. They argued that these filmed adaptations were not 'cinematic' enough, that their directors did not recognize the potential of film as a means of expression in its own right.[2] Rather, the critics located this potential in earlier or more esoteric French cinema – in the work of Max Ophuls or Robert Bresson, for example – and in some popular American cinema. The *Cahiers* critics were among the first to take this commercial cinema seriously. As Godard wrote in a 1957 review of Nicholas Ray's *Hot Blood* (1956):

> After seeing *Johnny Guitar* or *Rebel Without a Cause*, one cannot but feel that here is something which exists only in cinema, which would be nothing in a novel, the stage or anywhere else, but, which becomes fantastically beautiful on the screen. (Quoted in Hillier 1985, pp. 116–17)

In this way the *Cahiers* critics began to reformulate film theory. These changes were expressed most dramatically in the notion of film genres and the *politique des auteurs*.

During the 1950s, the *Cahiers* critics argued (somewhat polemically during this period in France) that film should be considered to offer a means of personal self-expression. Where previously the term *auteur* had been used in French film criticism to identify the author of a filmed novel or play, or the writer of a screenplay, the term began to be used to describe directors who were able to stamp their own personality or fingerprint on to a film. The valorization of the Romantic creative genius was transferred from the role of the writer to that of the director. The *politique des auteurs* was concerned with a consistency of theme and style in which the persona of the director could be detected across a number of films.[3]

While certain directors, such as Eisenstein and Welles, had long been considered *auteurs* due to the relative autonomy they enjoyed in the development of their projects, during the 1950s the *Cahiers* critics found new possibilities in the work of Hollywood studio directors such as Howard Hawks, John Ford and Vincent Minnelli, whom they also considered to be *auteurs*. As Robert Stam points out, herein lay the 'real scandal' of *auteur* theory: American cinema, 'which had classically been the diacritical "other" of French film theory, that against which it had defined itself, just as the putative "vulgarity" of American culture had long provided the diacritical counterpoint for French national identity, now became, surprisingly, the model for a new French cinema' (2000a, p. 87).

By 1959 most of these critics had directed their first feature. By the 1960s, they were looking back nostalgically to the studio era as the golden age of

American cinema. By this time, though, they believed that the evolution of *auteurs* within the Hollywood studio system occurred *despite* the studio system, rather than *because* of it.[4] As the critics' understanding of both the structures of mainstream American cinema and the constraints of the studio system grew, so their conception of the *auteur* had to change. Indeed, part of this knowledge had come from their experience of working in the European offices of the commercial film industry during this period, particularly in production and distribution departments; Godard worked for Fox for a time, for example. As John Caughie explains, the critics now suggested that 'the struggle between the desire for self-expression and the constraints of the industry could produce a tension in the films of the commercial cinema which was lacking in the "art" cinema' (1981, p. 11).

The *politique des auteurs* did not simply effect a return to a form of Romanticism. Identifying thematic and stylistic consistencies across a director's oeuvre, in the use of *mise-en-scène*, and establishing a director's persona in the first place, all involved analysing a number of films in great detail. In focusing on these elements, attention was directed away from a film's specific content. In 'On the *politique des auteurs*', originally published in *Cahiers* in 1957, Bazin stated that '[t]o a certain extent at least, the *auteur* is a subject to himself; whatever the scenario, he always tells the same story ... he has the same attitude and passes the same moral judgements on the action and on the characters' (reprinted in Hillier 1985, p. 255). In this way, recognition could be given to the fact that studio directors were rarely given the opportunity to choose their own projects. Instead, as Bazin explained:

> The *politique des auteurs* consists, in short, of choosing the personal factor in artistic creation as a standard of reference, and then of assuming that it continues and even progresses from one film to the next. It is recognized that there do exist certain important films of quality that escape this test, but these will systematically be considered inferior to those in which the personal stamp of the *auteur*, however, run-of-the-mill the scenario, can be perceived minutely   (Ibid.)

The *politique des auteurs* thus demanded that closer attention be paid to films than traditional criticism had required and also demanded knowledge of a wide range of films. In this, James Monaco (1976) detects the influence of structuralism, which dominated much French intellectual thought during this period. It is possible to argue that the focus of this criticism was the location of deep structures (in the form of a director's persona, for example) across a range of films which might otherwise appear disparate. I return to this issue in the final section of this chapter

Making films (and soundtracks) politically

Given their grounding in criticism, it is perhaps not surprising that the directors of the French New Wave made a great number of films which were implicitly about cinema in general and, frequently, Hollywood in particular. Jean-Luc Godard has continued to make such references to Hollywood explicit in his films: to genre, to the conventions of classical Hollywood filmmaking, to its economics and to its labour structures. He has worked in almost every conceivable position in relation to Hollywood. This ranges from devotion in his films of the 1950s and early-1960s – *A bout de souffle* (1959), *Une femme est une femme* (1961), *Le Mepris* (1963) – to vehement opposition as a member of the Dziga Vertov group in the late 1960s and early 1970s, to his work with video (as alternative audio-visual format) in the 1970s, followed by a return to Hollywood to direct *King Lear* (1987) for Cannon, working from an office in Francis Ford Coppola's Zoetrope Studios. Godard has also continued to make films about filmmaking in general. *Passion* (1982), for example, was accompanied by *Scénario du film Passion* which Mary Lea Bandy describes as 'a reflection upon the creative processes of filmmaking itself, on screenwriting, and the making of imagery' (1992, p. 7). Similarly, *Prénom: Carmen* is concerned explicitly with cinema, but with a cynical twist: a group of thieves devise a hoax filming which is in reality a cover for a kidnapping to raise funds for terrorism. Here Godard connects filmmaking to extortion and coercion.

In his filmmaking Godard has always been particularly concerned with signs and with the arbitrary nature of signifiers. This predisposition relates his work to that of the structuralists and, later, semiologists.[5] His Marxist-influenced aesthetic is grounded in the belief that the character of a cultural product – here, the film – is determined by the mode of production: thus, a film may be read as a sign indicating the production practices used in its development. It is for this reason that Godard calls 'not for political films, but for films made politically.'[6] In his filmmaking and his written criticism he chooses not to accept the divisions and hierarchical structures imposed by the film industry and film theory: his films often involve a juxtaposition of genres, and confuse fiction and documentary.[7]

François Musy, sound engineer on *Prénom: Carmen* and a number of the director's other films, described Godard's production practice for this soundtrack in an interview with *Cahiers du Cinéma* in 1984. Two months before shooting began Godard sent Musy a tape of the Beethoven Quartets that he wanted to use (along with Prosper Mérimée's novel, a list of scenes and a more detailed scenario). The same tape of music extracts, around which Godard interwove a narration of his plans for the film's continuity, was also sent to the actors, musicians and technicians (Musy 1984, p. 12). Such practices are rare. Musy also notes that he benefits from a good deal of dialogue with Godard before, during and after production. Rather than being part of a conventional sound team in which specialist roles are well defined and adhered to, he and Godard work as a team with each making suggestions. This collaborative production practice is also a feature of Godard's relationship with the sound-recording equipment company, Stellavox; there is the 'possibility of dialogue with the director and technicians of the company' (p. 13; author's translation). Indeed, Stellavox were happy to make adjustments to their equipment in response to Godard's and Musy's requests. Related to this non-hierarchical approach to filmmaking, Musy explains that Godard prefers to integrate the production and post-production stages of filmmaking (conventionally undertaken separately). Godard prefers to shoot and to edit the image simultaneously, and to edit and mix the sound at the same time rather than build up a soundtrack from layers distinguished by sound type, such as synchronized sound, music and ambient sound.

The concept of musical composition – in particular, orchestration – played a central role in the development of the soundtrack to *Prénom: Carmen*, according to Musy.[8] Indeed, Godard has argued that while Hamlet or Electra can exist without music, Carmen cannot.[9] Rather than the different sonic elements being faded up or introduced without drawing attention to themselves, here 'the elements are orchestrated one in relation to the others, and at times you have brutal halts, as you would in any musical composition'.[10] Further, 'it's more like a musical score in which all the sounds occur on the same level like instruments: the dialogue, the sound of the sea, the music'.[11] However, analyses of the use and function of the different soundtrack elements in Godard's films of the 1960s and of the music in *Vivre sa vie* (1962) and *Pierrot le fou* (1965) suggest that the director has used similar soundtrack and scoring practices in a number of films (Williams 1982; Brown 1994). It is worth recounting these analyses in brief here.

Vivre sa vie uses only a little over 12 minutes of music, with nondiegetic cues making up about half of that. According to composer Michel Legrand, he was asked by Godard to write a 'theme and eleven variations, because that's the way the film is constructed' (cited in Brown 1994, p. 189). However, as Royal S. Brown points out, Godard used only the opening measures of the second and third variations, repeating them throughout the film. The music became one of the elements of materials varied within the film; a material 'limited to a fragment obsessively repeated in different contexts' (p. 190). Godard divided the 12 cadenceless measures that he took from Legrand's score into three four-bar groups, each of which could be played alone, or in combination with one of the other groups. In this way, Godard used the music as a 'cinematic raw material to be juxtaposed with the other elements of the film in accordance with a logic more structural than narrative' (p. 191). Integrating his detailed study of the music and its function in the film with a more general analysis of the film's structure, Brown suggests that the film as a whole is perhaps best considered as 'a kind of macro-musical structure with its own rhythms, themes, variations, recapitulations etc.' (p. 191). This macrostructure consists of a range of different audio and visual elements, of which the nondiegetic score is only one.

In his analysis of *Pierrot le Fou*, Brown develops the idea that Godard's films are organized around musical structures. With this film, he argues, 'one begins to have the impression of a kind of serialism ... in the way the diverse component parts of the film, including its music, are *composed*': that is, non-hierarchically

(p. 209). Where classical scoring is organized hierarchically due to its subordination to the narrative (and to the dialogue as often the most important carrier of narrative information), Brown argues that Godard uses music 'in just about all the ways that music can be used in a film, any type of film' (p. 209). Furthermore, just as total serialism in music saw the serialist approach applied to rhythm and dynamics as well as pitch, so Brown argues that Godard's serialism covers several elements of filmmaking. For example, continuity editing, in which editing is subordinated to classical narrative exposition, could be described as 'hierarchized montage' (p. 209). By contrast, in *Pierrot le Fou* Godard uses non-hierarchical (or de-hierarchized) montage in which both continuity editing and non-continuity editing operate in roughly equal measure. Brown suggests that the same serialist techniques of combination also structure Godard's use of dialogue and sound, though no claims are made for the consistency of Godard's serialist approach. Indeed Brown argues that it is part serialist and part aleatoric (resulting from a combination of Brechtian aesthetics and a 'joyful improvisation in both the production and post-production phases of the filmmaking process' (pp. 210–11). Ultimately, Brown argues that in *Pierrot le fou* Godard has achieved his aim of making a film politically rather than making a political film, in the sense that the non-hierarchized politics that he wishes to express can be found expressed in material form in the structure he creates from the raw material of the filmic elements.

In 'Godard's Use of Sound', Alan Williams (1982) locates a similarly non-hierarchical approach to filmmaking. Williams argues that Godard works to keep the elements of his soundtracks separate and distinctive in order to create dialectical relationships between them in place of the 'unity' of the classical film, in which dialogue is promoted at the expense of other sound and music. For example, while Godard's soundtracks also privilege speech, dialogue is only one of many possible kinds of spoken-language modes which may be used. Others include quotation, reading aloud, interview and translation. All of these appear in Godard's films. Reading aloud from different kinds of texts – advertising, poetry, pornography – produces still more, identifiably different styles of speaking. Sometimes the sources of these voices are seen on screen, but at other times they are revealed only later in a scene or remain unseen, unreferenced within the image. In terms of the use of language in Godard's films, Williams argues that 'any one mode of functioning is merely what is being done *now* with language – replaceable by something else at almost any moment. Thus, the numerous possible linguistic options become elements in a large scale *montage* that operates in the sphere of language' (1982, p. 194). Similar effects are produced by the juxtaposition of speech by actors or characters with different accents. Williams argues that the same stylistic juxtapositions can also be found in Godard's eclectic use of music. A typical Godard soundtrack might combine works by Mozart or Beethoven with music written specifically for the film by Antoine Duhamel or George Delerue, and may also include some French 'bubblegum' pop. Such clashes of musical cultures often serve to emphasize the differences between the excerpts, both stylistically and socially.

In a similar way, in many of Godard's films, different mechanical sounds – such as construction work, pinball machines, cars, gunfire – are juxtaposed, recorded and played back at high levels, whether or not diegetic sources are presented for them. Such noisiness is often foregrounded by its abrupt juxtaposition with silence, sometimes total silence, that is, without 'room tone' or ambience.[12] While such sonic intrusions are seemingly unnoticed by the film's characters, their presence often makes it difficult for the audience to hear the characters' dialogue. In this way Godard undermines classical Hollywood's naturalized convention of placing dialogue to the fore of the sound mix, to make it audible above all else, even in situations in which – realistically speaking – it would be impossible to hear dialogue, such as during explosions. Whereas dialogue, sound and music are placed in a clear hierarchical relationship according to classical Hollywood convention, Godard's (more democratic, less hierarchical) sound-mixing practices allow each of the soundtrack elements to vie for audience attention. The sound-recording and mixing practices associated with classical Hollywood function to predigest sonic information for the audience; they tell us what is more (and less) important, narratively speaking, just as our own physiological apparatus would were we taking part in the scene in question (the 'cocktail party effect'). By contrast, Godard's sound-recording and mixing practices frequently refuse to undertake this work; he often uses omni-directional microphones, for example. Thus Williams suggests that the effect of Godard's (arguably) more 'realistic', less 'transparent' soundtracks can be considered to be the 'aural equivalent of long takes with great depth of field' (1982, p. 199).

Williams concludes that the formal organization of the constituent elements of Godard's soundtracks – too haphazard to warrant rigorous categorization – is best described as 'permutational formalism', in which the range of the different categories (or paradigmatic possibilities) which may be used is made apparent. He argues that the important role given to the soundtrack in Godard's films is due to the fact that there are comparably more distinguishable constituent categories available in the soundtrack by comparison with the image track. Thus it offers more possibilities for dialectical relations. Since this conflictual formalist play is not employed in the service of generating unity at a higher level of meaning (as was the case with Eisensteinian montage, discussed in Chapter 3) the distinctness of the individual sonic elements is preserved, allowing their sensory impact to be perceived in their own right by the audience. Furthermore, this means that the sounds also retain (and behave as signifiers of) their socio-historical associations more clearly. In this respect, Williams argues that Godard's use of sound is Brechtian. He adds that 'in eschewing Hollywood sound practices' Godard does not necessarily somehow '"deconstruct[...]" classical narrative' (1982, p. 198). This may well be true. However, as is discussed below, in *Prénom: Carmen* the classical relationship of soundtrack to image track *is* deconstructed (Wills 1986).

Prénom: Carmen

Godard's *Prénom: Carmen* features elements of Mérimée's original Carmen story as well as references to Bizet's operatic setting of Mérimée, *Carmen* (1874), and to Otto Preminger's interpretation of Bizet, *Carmen Jones* (1954).[13] Carmen X is one of a gang of criminals who are planning a kidnapping. She approaches her filmmaker uncle, Jean (played by Godard himself), for the use of his empty apartment to make a film. Unbeknown to him, the filming is a hoax, a cover for the kidnapping. Early on in the film the gang carry out a bank heist but during the chase Carmen is caught by a security guard, Joseph (José). He is instantly and magnetically attracted to her, and Carmen persuades him to run away with her and join the criminals rather than turn her in. Joseph runs away with her and is duly arrested, tried and serves a short term in prison. In a related plot-line (though at this stage we are unaware just *how* related) we are introduced to Joseph's 'special' friend Claire (Michaela),who plays second violin in the Prat Quartet. This same quartet has been booked by the criminals to perform at a hotel as the diegetic music for the hoax filming (that is, the kidnapping). At her suggestion, Claire's father has tried to help Joseph by aiding him in his search for jobs, but once released from prison Joseph returns to Carmen and a life of crime.[14] Though Carmen had waited for Joseph, she now realizes that she has lost interest in him and tells him that their affair is over. After the failed kidnapping attempt Joseph shoots Carmen.[15]

The soundtrack to *Prénom: Carmen* comprises five basic elements: dialogue, including voice-over; diegetic sound, including 'displaced' and manipulated diegetic sound; extracts from Beethoven's String Quartets Nos 9 (Op. 59, no. 3), 10 (Op. 74), 14 (Op. 131), 15 (Op. 132), and 16 (Op. 135); a Tom Waits song, 'In Ruby's Arms'; and a tape (played diegetically by Jean/Godard) of aeroplanes flying overhead combined with a one-finger rendition of 'Au Clair de la Lune' performed on a poorly tuned piano.

'What is the role of the quartet?': a locus of confusion

Not only does the film's audience see the Prat Quartet rehearsing these Beethoven Quartets throughout the film as diegetic music, it also hears many extracts of the same movements of the same quartets when the musicians are absent from the screen (see the Appendix to this chapter for a timing table which lists all music cues for the film). Despite the frequent appearance of the quartet on screen it is not until the denouement of the film – that is, the attempted kidnapping – that the quartet appear in any way related to the central narrative by more than Claire's relationship with Joseph, which is in itself presented rather vaguely.[16] (During the course of the film Joseph and Claire are seen together in only three scenes.) Thus, early on the film's audience is encouraged to ask, 'What is the role of the quartet?': a question posed later by Carmen's uncle Jean/Godard.

It would seem that the purpose of the quartet is to embody a locus of confusion: it lacks narrative motivation; and, it undermines the role(s) of music as defined by classical Hollywood scoring and exposes such scoring practices as 'conventional' rather than established by 'natural law'. The quartet achieves this not by presenting music in situations which conflict directly with classical scoring practices but by intensifying these same practices to the extent that they crack open and reveal themselves to be purely conventional. Soundtrack and image track need not coincide: they synchronize only after considerable labour on the part of filmmakers. This labour finds its (deconstructed) equivalent in the work of the quartet hired to play the music for a film that is *not* being made: the 'filmmakers' are occupied with other work, gaining funds for terrorism by orchestrating and carrying out a kidnapping. The quartet undertake a good deal of rehearsal to 'play their part' in the (hoax) filming, but this labour is wasted – it goes unrewarded – except in terms of the quality of their performance. Does this mean that we should not expect *real* art to be rewarded? Certainly the film's concluding inter-title – 'in memoriam small movies' – would corroborate this interpretation. Jean's/Godard's exchange with the leader of the quartet on their meeting at the hotel is also interesting in this respect:

Violin 1:   Ah, it's you. You know that we are not a tea dance orchestra.
Jean/Godard: Oh yes, the times are hard for blockheads like us.[17]

Writing specifically of *Prénom: Carmen*, David Wills (1986) equates the crisis that Godard creates in the dominant economy of cinematic representation with that traditionally created by the figure of Carmen in the dominant sexual economy. Through the presence of the quartet, the classical sound-image and narrative relationship is deconstructed. Wills argues that the different sonic elements of the soundtrack (including absolute silence) are organized around the *idea* of music, with the structural separation of sounds within the film likened to the scoring of music. That is, he suggests that each type of sonic element is assigned a particular voice, as with the four voices of a string quartet; for example, dialogue relates to the narrative and the central characters, sea sounds relate to the consummation of Joseph and Carmen's love.[18]

Here the making of the film is paralleled by the rehearsing of the music, and the structuration of the film is comparable with the partition or scoring of the music. It is in this sense that we might consider Godard to have found a formula for the introduction of the soundtrack into or onto the image track, as both an attempt to redress the primacy given the image, and at the same time to further, perhaps irretrievably, disturb the coherence of the image track by lodging the other of cinema within what it assumes to be its fullness. ... [I]t is done not through experimentation with the dialogue, but rather by exploiting the furthest supplement, the most dependent or repressed element of the film process, music. ... Music comes then to represent not just the whole soundtrack which in *Prénom: Carmen* is *visualised*, but its pure representationality serves to call into question, by opposition and counterpoint, the self-assurance which is assumed by the visual as signifying practice on account of the supposed naturalness of its referential process. And again this occurs as a transfer, which takes place under the cover of a diegetic ambiguity. (Wills 1986, pp. 41–2)

In this way the soundtrack to *Prénom: Carmen* performs a standard deconstructive manoeuvre upon the image track. The narrative ambiguity of the quartet is merely a cover for its real, deconstructive role: to disturb the coherence of the image track – apparently complete in its own right – by placing the soundtrack into or on to it.

Godard's filmmaking techniques refer to, conflict with and critique the screen–spectator relationship encouraged by classical Hollywood in order to reveal, and thus undermine, its ideological underpinning. Similarly, Godard's use of music in *Prénom: Carmen* reveals and undermines the conventions of classical Hollywood scoring, along with the screen–spectator relationship that they encourage. To recapitulate, classical scoring practices can be considered to affect this relationship in two ways: first, they assist with the viewing-listening subject's identification with a space within the frame, and second, they create the impression that this space is that of a single coherent subject. In terms of identification, diegetic music works to subsume the spectator-auditor into the implied space of the film's fiction by helping to define and reflect the boundaries of this world: both in the general sense of era and geographical location, and in the more particular sense of the immediate environmental conditions and acoustic constraints of this implied space. By contrast, nondiegetic music is not constrained by having to represent the spatial limitations of the implied fictional world. Rather, it occupies a mediatory space which is often perceived by the viewing-listening subject to be physically closer to them than the music sourced within the film's fiction. Through symbolic mapping, nondiegetic music can also encourage the subject's identification with spaces occupied by particular characters within the film's fiction and also with spaces attributable to individuals outside of this fictional world which may give clues to information not (yet) available to those within it.[19]

In terms of continuity, music helps to smooth over cuts and transitions on the image track.[20] In this way the spectator gains the impression of being constructed as a single coherent viewing subject rather than the fragmented subject that is actually constructed from the many disjunct spaces (points of view) which typically make up the image track. It is also for reasons of continuity that the music of the classical Hollywood film moves imperceptibly between the different levels of its musical narrating, disguising its voice as it slips in and out of the frame. For example, attention is not usually drawn to the fact that the music outside of the film's fiction – the nondiegetic music – may present more than a single position of access to knowledge (such as different characters' points of view, and those attributable only to individuals outside the constraints of the film's fiction). Related orchestration and thematic connections assist in this homogenization. The same is also true of the boundary between diegetic and nondiegetic musical voices, which is often blurred by presenting music in situations in which diegetic sources *may* exist, but where they remain unconfirmed by the image or dialogue: a car, or any room in which a radio, television or other sound-producing source might feasibly exist, or in which a live musical performance may be going on, for example.

Despite the fact that the same music is used diegetically (with the quartet present and rehearsing) and nondiegetically (with the quartet absent from the scene on screen), it is still possible to discern a distinction between these two categories of musical voice in *Prénom: Carmen*. With only one exception, when the quartet is present on screen what the spectator *sees* they also *hear*.[21] However, when the quartet is heard on the soundtrack apparently nondiegetically (and, thus, absent from the scene on screen) this same music is clearly manipulated by an external mechanical force. For example, the start and finish of excerpts are sometimes abruptly clipped mid-note.[22] Excerpts often begin or end mid-phrase, though a few feature very short, self-contained musical units which are able to stand alone as musical statements, thus making the manipulation less overt (see Example 4.1).[23] Some excerpts are continued later in a shot, having been suppressed earlier. This is achieved by one of two methods. The first involves stopping and restarting the recorded performance, as is the case with the third movement of Quartet No. 15 (Op. 132) – one extract finishes with the final crotchet of bar 29, the next starts nine seconds later from the first crotchet of bar 30.[24] The second technique involves fading down the recorded performance in the mix, leaving the tape running under the action and later fading the tape up again, as occurs with the first movement of Quartet No. 10 (Op. 74): during the extract of bars 221/4 to 238/4, bar 226 is faded down in the mix.[25]

These quartets are themselves marked by disruption and fragmentation. Godard's treatment of this music intensifies these aspects.[26] At times this external manipulation appears to maintain the musical logic of the original to some extent. The harmonic development of the original may be continued or a probable alternative provided. For example, the form of the third movement of Quartet No. 15 (Op. 132) comprises an ABABA structure, where the A section takes the form of an Adagio in the archaic Lydian mode (which Beethoven entitled 'Holy Song of Thanksgiving to the Divinity from a Convalescent, in the Lydian Mode'), and the B section the form of an Andante in the unrelated D major (which Beethoven entitled 'Feels new strength').[27] One excerpt begins in bar 25 of the 31-bar A section, only to jump seamlessly from the end of bar 31 to bar 116 – the second, rather than the first of the two Andante (B) sections.[28] On other occasions, however, musical logic plays no part: some excerpts present earlier material within a movement later within the shot. For example, an excerpt of bars 19–25 of the third movement of Quartet No. 15 is heard nine shots (and several minutes) after the excerpt which starts from bar 25 described above.[29]

There are examples of manipulation which intensify to extreme – and thus

Example 4.1   Beethoven String Quartet No. 10 (Op. 74), 1st movement, bars 1–2

break open – the convention of using music to provide continuity across otherwise disruptive cuts on the image track. Rather than sneaking in and out of the frame unnoticed, music is here often presented fairly loudly and suddenly immediately prior to an approaching cut and is then cut off abruptly afterward. Instead of functioning as a glue which sticks cuts together, as with classical scoring practices, here the manipulation of the music foregrounds the cut and paste nature of film, and thus the mediation of the apparatus.

To a certain extent, the traditional implications of the diegetic and nondiegetic categories of voice are maintained in *Prénom: Carmen* since it is still possible to attribute some degree of privileged knowledge to the nondiegetic musical voice(s). The external manipulation (of the same or similar material to that which the spectator has also seen and heard presented diegetically) which characterizes and distinguishes its nondiegetic voice(s), also implies an extradiegetic presence – someone performing the mechanical manipulation. Whereas classical Hollywood scoring effaces the mechanical element of its recording, here it is foregrounded by physical tampering with a pre-recorded soundtrack: the music's character as pre-recorded sound is emphasized.[30]

Thus, while a certain degree of difference is maintained between diegetic and nondiegetic voices in this film, considerable similarities can also be detected. For example, no distinction is made between the acoustic signature of diegetic and nondiegetic music cues. On occasion the nondiegetic music is faded low in the mix, but the quality of the recording, the implied relationship of microphone to instruments and the environmental conditions of recording do not change. There is also a unified quality to the *treatment* of both diegetic and nondiegetic music in *Prénom: Carmen*. When present on screen the quartet is always seen *rehearsing*, an act which itself performs a kind of sonic editing on the music as a result of the constant stopping and starting, repeated attempts at difficult entries, the discussion and trials of different interpretations, and so on. The manipulation exhibited by the mechanical editing of the nondiegetic voice(s) achieves a similar or related effect to this 'performed editing'.

At the denouement of the narrative – seconds before the attempted kidnapping – something disturbing happens on the soundtrack. The quartet are seen rehearsing the third movement of Quartet No. 16 (Op. 135) in the hotel dining room. Claire returns to take her seat having just met Joseph in the hallway. Before she begins to play, the sound of another quartet joins that of the quartet seen rehearsing. The spectator is simultaneously presented with movements three *and* four of the 16th Quartet (all diegetic sound is cut). Examples 4.2 and 4.3 show what is heard: bars 23–28/1 of movement three and 1–7/3 of movement four.[31] Here a nondiegetic voice is combined with a diegetic one. The sound of the nondiegetic voice (movement four) is, as would be expected, manipulated; the track is faded down during the third minim beat of bar 1, the first of bar 2, and again during the third minim beat of bar 2. However, following this the nondiegetic voice seemingly becomes diegetic: the quartet we see on screen continue *this* (the fourth) movement in their next excerpt, ten seconds later. Here then, diegetic and nondiegetic musical voices are heard simultaneously and at some point swap roles. Godard makes the distinction between these voices wholly fluid, creating an oscillation between them. How is this music to be understood? Can the characters hear it? Given the camera's close-ups of these characters, are we to assume that one of these voices is generated by the psyche of Claire, Joseph or Carmen? The soundtrack appears to construct both a diegetic and a nondiegetic space for the viewing-listening subject to occupy simultaneously. Instead of providing continuity and confirming that the space reserved for the viewing-listening subject within the frame is that of a single coherent subject, here the use of music fractures the subject, splitting it in two.

Such fluidity between diegetic and nondiegetic voices is matched by Godard's choice of Beethoven extracts to both confirm and contradict the characteristics which classically distinguish these different categories. At times the nondiegetic music appears to embody a disinterested or indifferent quality which is more often associated with the relationship between the image or narrative and diegetic music; that is, that which Michel Chion defines as anempathetic music (1994, pp. 8–9). The first bars of the first movement to Quartet No. 10 (Op. 74) which are heard on the first occasion that we see trains crossing the river at night might be given as an example of this.[32] On other occasions the 'mood' of the music seems appropriate and specific to the situation. Godard's use of the wistful lyricism of the opening to the second movement of the same quartet is a good example; it accompanies the shot in which Carmen and Joseph's eyes first meet after they have fallen down the stairs together during the bank heist.[33]

On occasion Godard moves from shots of the quartet and its diegetic music, to

Example 4.2   Beethoven String Quartet No. 16 (Op. 135), 3rd movement, bars 23–28

shots of the central narrative with the quartet cue continuing, though now manipulated, then returns to a shot of the quartet.[34] In such instances, is the implication that the nondiegetic music (heard when the quartet are absent) issues from the diegetic source (the quartet)? Is the music of the quartet somehow controlling the central narrative? The fact that comments spoken by the quartet about the music during their rehearsals frequently seem to have direct relevance to what is happening in the central narrative adds weight to this view; as when a member of the quartet states that 'It needs to be more violent', just before a return to shots of the bank robbery.[35] However, if the quartet is some kind of controlling force, why are there also a profusion of (apparently nondiegetic) musical excerpts

Example 4.3   Beethoven String Quartet No. 16 (Op. 135), 4th movement, bars 1–7

which appear indifferent to the central narrative?

Godard's choice of Beethoven's mid-to-late string quartets clearly has an effect on the reception of the film. The dramatic force, intensity, and seriousness of much of this music encourages the spectator to attempt a more serious interpretation of the film than might otherwise be the case. Indeed, on many occasions Godard has chosen particularly dramatic extracts: those defined by Joseph Kerman as 'operatic' in their gestures (1967, p. 327). One could argue that this music hails a bourgeois subject, a subject that recognizes this chamber music as the apex of serious, high art music of the Western classical tradition (and thus also to be a demonstration of wealth, intellect and a developed artistic soul).[36] Theodor Adorno considered these particular works of Beethoven's oeuvre to be perhaps the most authentic of the Western classical tradition.[37] He argued that they reveal in their ruptures and fragmentation the impossibility of the synthesis (or, identification) between subject and object (individual and society) of the time: the subject's struggle for liberation in the face of objectification (or enslavement). Perhaps Godard's choice of Beethoven should be considered to be a comment upon the objectifying industrial practices of the mass entertainment machine. It could certainly be argued that the choice of the disruptive and fragmented music of the late quartets makes reference to the highly fragmented music of classical Hollywood scores: some cues last only a matter of seconds.

The other main piece of music heard during the film, a Tom Waits song entitled 'In Ruby's Arms' is also subject to some of the same manipulation as the Beethoven excerpts. It undergoes brief moments of repetition which emphasize its recorded nature. The acoustic signature of the song changes several times; sometimes the sound is compressed, implying the diegetic source of a radio (possible in the hotel room in which the action takes place in this scene), while at other times it is not compressed and placed to the fore of the mix, suggesting a nondiegetic source. The song is also marked in other ways. First, in obvious contrast to the Beethoven it is a lyrical, melancholy pop song sung by a well-known and distinctive singer-songwriter. Second, it is the only piece of music the spectator hears in its entirety during the film. Third, as Katherine Kovacs (1990) pointed out, it defines a brief period of harmony between sound and image which is absent in much of the rest of the film. Carmen and Joseph appear to be choreographed to the music at the beginning of the track: the scene opens with the abstract image of Joseph's frustrated hand on the cold, blank and unemotional television screen; Carmen opens the curtains to the lyrics 'Morning light, across her face'. Just before the end of the song, fragments of Beethoven's String Quartet No. 16 (Op. 135) are heard and signal a return to the more frenzied action that has characterized much of the rest of the film. Kovacs argues that this song is the first and only time that the spectator hears Joseph's point of view, or his metaphorical voice.[38] If this song represents the voice of Joseph, perhaps the Beethoven should be considered to issue from Carmen's psyche?

Godard's use and manipulation of the music of Beethoven and Tom Waits in *Prénom: Carmen* does not result in the spectator losing sight (or audition) of the practices associated with classical Hollywood scoring, however. In fact, I would argue the opposite. Godard's problematization of classical scoring draws attention to these practices and forces the spectator to question the function of the film's music.

To return, then, to the issue of the quartet's lack of narrative motivation. One plausible explanation for their presence is to interpret the musicians as performers in a 'backstage' musical. Backstage musicals usually present a group of people in preparation for a performance of some kind which, more often than not, functions as the culmination of the plot. The musical numbers within the film are depicted as 'rehearsals.' Of course, each of these 'performances of rehearsals' has in reality been intricately choreographed and constructed, and has required extensive rehearsal in itself. By making the performances look easy and spontaneous, technique and hard work may be effaced, and with them the gap between producer and consumer (that is, apparatus and spectator) which may otherwise be experienced by the audience of this industrially produced mass-entertainment form as alienation from the product (or, the film).[39] In *Prénom: Carmen*, scenes of the quartet rehearsing are interspersed between and alongside those of the central narrative concerning Carmen and Joseph. In contrast to the rehearsals depicted in backstage musicals, it is unclear what the quartet are rehearsing for. During rehearsals the musicians constantly repeat difficult passages, make mistakes, criticize one another for their errors, mistimed entries and so on. These rehearsals deny the ease and spontaneity of performance that was so often implied by the backstage Hollywood musicals of the golden era, and foreground labour instead. Here, too, Godard's referencing of Hollywood undermines easy identification, and promotes confusion and hard work in its place. The presence of the quartet in *Prénom: Carmen* enables the film's music to function as a questioning, active participant in the construction of the film's viewing-listening subject.

'Qu'est-ce que c'est que cette histoire de quatuor?': 'Je t'expliquerai'[40]

Towards the end of the film, just before the attempted kidnapping, Jean/Godard asks Carmen about the role of the quartet in the (hoax) filming: 'Qu'est-ce que c'est que cette histoire de quatuor?' In this context it is interesting that he uses the word *histoire* rather than *rôle* to refer to the story, or role, of the quartet. The structuralist linguist Émile Benveniste made a distinction between *histoire* and *discours* ('story' and 'discourse') based on two systems of verb tenses. *Histoire* uses the aorist system, the temporal reference of which is to the moment of the event, rather than to the (later) moment of speech, excluding first person pronouns and deictics. *Discours* uses the perfect system of verb tenses which establish a link between the past event and the present. In a story told in the mode of *l'histoire*, the events appear to tell themselves, no one speaks for them. No clues or references are made to the mode of telling which is apparently transparent. The term *histoire* thus refers to a transparent mode of exposition in which no secondary parties play a role: events seem to tell themselves.

This mode of transparent exposition is also that which is favoured by the conventions of classical Hollywood filmmaking which stipulate that the apparatus be concealed from the spectator (despite the fact that the film's status as manufactured product is logically betrayed at every edit, and also by the ever-present boundary of the screen's edge). Theorists of suture, such as Daniel Dayan (1976) and Stephen Heath (1977–78; 1981), argue that classical editing functions in such a way that it first proposes questions and then attempts to answer them; as with, for example, the shot/reverse-shot and point/glance formats. This is done in order to conceal the film's mechanical basis and to suture the spectator into the narrative, drawing attention away from the mode of telling. Heath argues that cinematic suture is virtually identical to the operations and techniques of classical narrative filmmaking: each shot is limited, or lacking, and thus encourages the spectator to gain the knowledge that has been denied to them in that particular shot by activating their desire for the potential completeness offered by the next shot. In turn, this 'serves to deflect attention away from the level of enunciation to that of the fiction' (Silverman 1983, p. 214).[41]

In *Prénom: Carmen*, Godard denies the spectator this comfort. The film often rejects classical editing, disrupting narrative coherence and closure. The quartet plays a pivotal role in this. The spectator is encouraged to question why the quartet is seen with such frequency throughout the film since the prominence of its unmotivated presence outweighs Claire's role in the narrative. Thus, by asking about the *histoire* of the quartet, it could be argued that Godard alludes to the fact that we actually see the *discours* of the quartet, that is, the story of the quartet as told by a secondary party (*enoncé*). This is demonstrated by the manner in which the quartet are filmed rehearsing. Each of these sequences is shot from a different static camera angle, with the camera frequently located in positions which it would be difficult for a person to occupy in physical terms; the quartet are often shot from above, or from just behind a performer's elbow. Camera positions such as these emphasize the voyeuristic aspect of filmmaking, and thus reveal (rather than conceal) the presence of the apparatus: *discours*. This interpretation is consolidated by Godard's placement of the site of the film music's production – the quartet – on to the image track. The visual presence of the quartet denies the transparency (*histoire*) associated with the conventions of the classical Hollywood score, in particular the notion that nondiegetic music should sneak into and out of the soundtrack imperceptibly.

In reply to her uncle's question, Carmen replies, 'Je t'expliquerai' ('I'll tell you later'). In doing so, the reference is shifted from the structural to the post-structural through an invocation to the deferral of meaning. Carmen states that she will (forever) defer from answering this question. As Jacques Derrida argues, the meaning of a signifier is always deferred to another signifier: only mediate meanings exist and these are constantly being displaced.[42] Carmen's response to her uncle's question encapsulates the constant deferral of the potential of fullness that cinema offers (according to Stephen Heath) and makes reference to a primary means by which the viewing-listening subject is subsumed into classical narrative: continuity editing (that is, awareness of lack, negation, and limitation in terms of access to knowledge, as discussed above). We do not hear Carmen tell Jean/Godard about the quartet: this deferral is, to a large extent, the point. However, shortly afterwards the viewer is shown (rather than told) *l'histoire* of the quartet: it is to perform music in the hotel dining room for the hoax filming which is a cover for the kidnapping. *This* is the performance for which their rehearsals have been a preparation.

Laura Mulvey has said that she finds *Prénom: Carmen* to be a very moving film though not in terms of the film itself, its story, or its director (1992, p. 82). Rather, she finds it moving for its sense of looking backwards, for

> the film's situation in Godard's own history, its lapse out of self-referentiality into nostalgia. The final title, 'In Memoriam small movies,' brought back the memory of a dedication to Monogram Pictures in *A bout de souffle* (1960). There is, [in] this, a double palimpsest, one layer tracing his own early work and, deeper still, the traces of the Hollywood cinema that had been his point of departure. (Ibid.)

In relation to the film's music, Godard's decision to use Beethoven's string quartets also points to his own earlier work: the mid-to-late quartets were also featured in *Le Nouveau Monde* (1962; an episode in *Rogopag*), *Une Femme Mariée* (1964), and *Deux ou trois choses que je sais d'elle* (1966). The way that this music is used in *Prénom: Carmen* makes reference to, exaggerates, and thus undermines the conventions associated with classical Hollywood scoring. This is achieved by means of a dialectical procedure in which the quartet plays a pivotal role. Through a range of means, Godard intensifies the use of music to provide continuity to such a degree that it draws attention both to the musical cue and to the convention itself, rather than fulfilling its task: music does not creep in and out of the frame imperceptibly before and after visual cuts, but enters and exits abruptly and loudly. The fragmentary character of the late Beethoven quartets also offers, in itself, an intensification of the fragmentary nature of much classical scoring. By placing the source of the film's soundtrack (the quartet) on to, or into, the image track, Godard questions its fullness, and thus deconstructs the sound–image and narrative relationship of classical Hollywood cinema.

Notes

1. Roud, cited in Narboni and Milne [1972] 1986, p. 10.
2. See, for example, Truffaut [1954] 1976.
3. Comolli later clarified the issue thus: 'The concept of the "*auteur*" as argued by *Cahiers* was at first, I think, fairly close to that of the writer or painter: a man who controls his work in accordance with his own wishes and is himself totally immersed in it. The issue for the critics and future filmmakers of *Cahiers* was to assert that in cinema as a "collective art" artists were able to present their own "world view" and to express their personal, even private preoccupations. In short, that the individual and creator was not effaced in the collective work of creation, rather the reverse ...' (Chabrol et al. [1963–64] 1986, pp. 197–8).

4. See, in particular, the two *Cahiers* articles from the 1960s which reunited the old guard of 1950s film criticism – most of whom were now more active in production than in written criticism – Claude Chabrol, Jacques Doniol-Valcroze, Jean-Luc Godard, Pierre Kast, Luc Mollet, Jacques Rivette and François Truffaut (1963–64), 'Questions about American cinema: a discussion'; and Jean-Louis Comolli, Jean-André Fieschi, Michel Mardore, Claude Ollier and André Techiné (1965), 'Twenty Years On: A discussion about American cinema and the *politique des auteurs*'. Both articles are translated and reprinted (the first in abridged form) in Hillier 1986, pp. 172–80 and 196–209.

5. For example, in 'Towards a Political Cinema' (1950), Godard quotes the structuralist linguist Bruce Parain: 'The sign forces us to see an object through its significance' (reprinted in Narboni and Milne [1972] 1986, pp. 16–17, p. 16). Parain was later featured in Godard's *Vivre sa vie* (1963) discussing the subject of love in an intellectual conversation with Nana.

6. Godard, cited by Michelson in the new foreword to Narboni and Milne [1972] 1986, p. viii. In a broader sense, all forms of production may be considered 'political'.

7. Annette Michelson, ibid.

8. Godard said something similar in an interview with Jacques Drillon in April 1983 when he compared making a film to playing a quartet: Jean-Luc Godard, 'Faire un film comme on joue un quatuor', in Bergala 1985, p. 574.

9. Godard, cited in Bachman 1984, p. 14. Godard continues: 'This music is part of the history of Carmen; in fact, the book by Merimée was never famous until it was made famous through Bizet's putting it to music.'

10. Musy 1984, p.17: '... on orchestre des éléments les uns par rapport aux autres, et par moments tu as des arrêts brutaux comme dans n'importe quelle composition musicale' (author's translation).

11. Ibid, p. 14: '... c'est plutôt une partition musicale où tous les sons interviennent au même niveau, comme des instruments: le dialogue, une ambiance de mer, la musique' (author's translation).

12. As described by Stephen Handzo, 'room tone' is the 'distinct presence of subtle sounds created by the movement of air particles in that particular volume'. In general, a lack of room tone 'would be perceived by the audience not as silence but as the failure of the sound system'. Possible exceptions to this include moments indicating 'death, memory, a Godardian "alienation effect," etc.' (Handzo 1985, p. 395).

13 In 'Discourse and the film text: Four readings of *Carmen*', Marshall Leicester Jr (1994) provides an interesting account of discursive references in Godard's *Prénom: Carmen* and a consideration of the three other Carmen films which were produced during the same period: Carlos Saura's *Carmen* (1983); Peter Brook's *La Tragédie de Carmen* (1984); Francesco Rosi's *Carmen* (1984). Preminger's *Carmen Jones* combined Bizet's music with lyrics by Oscar Hammerstein II.

14. Though Joseph is unable to become a member of the gang because he does not have a baccalaureate!

15. It is implied, however, that Carmen survives the shooting; see Sheer 2001, p. 186.

16. Sheer states that Claire is also the daughter of the industrialist whom the gang intend to kidnap (2001, pp. 181, 187). This makes sense and further interweaves Claire's character into the film's plot.

17. Violinist 1: Ah, c'est vous. Vous savez que nous ne sommes pas un orchestre de thé dansant.
Jean/Godard: Eh oui, les temps sont durs pour des oeufs comme nous. (Author's translation.)

18. As Sheer points out, the different quartets Godard uses also fulfil a structural

function and assist in demarcating the sections of the narrative: 'Op. 59/3 belongs to the exposition: introducing the participating characters and their aims, before the real action starts (location: the mental hospital). Op. 74 is used for the robbery scene (location: the bank). Passages from Op. 131 are played while Carmen and Joseph are on their way to the apartment; Op. 132 is devoted to their love scenes (location: the uncle's seaside apartment), while excerpts from movements of Op. 135 accompany Carmen's change of heart and Joseph's growing despair and jealousy (location: Hotel Intercontinental)' (2001, p. 183).

19. Royal S. Brown points out that a good example of this can be found in Steven Spielberg's *Jaws* (1994, p. 10). On only one occasion is the audience presented with a shark attack without John Williams's ominous, nondiegetic, two-note shark theme: at the end of this sequence, the attack is revealed to be a hoax. The absence of the theme, which is heard with every other appearance of the shark, presents the audience with more information than is available to the films' characters (with the exception of the boys pretending to be a shark, of course).

20. The infamous shower scene in Hitchcock's *Psycho* (1960) offers a good example of this. Richard Maltby suggests that this scene signifies the end of classical continuity editing (1995, pp. 218–19). In one minute there are 78 shots, many of which are not connected by means of the conventional editing techniques necessary to create a safe space within the diegetic world for the spectator, such as point/glance, shot/reverse-shot. I would argue that some degree of continuity is provided by the soundtrack, however: by Janet Leigh's screams and by Bernard Herrmann's repetitive (and subsequently, predictable) string writing.

21. The exception being shot 127 (or 16/135) where the rehearsing quartet are filmed from above accompanied by the sound of seagulls and dialogue from the court scene which follows. Shot numbers and music extract numbers are from my own shot breakdown of the film, which can be found in the appendix to this chapter. The numbers in brackets which follow give the equivalent numbering of sequence/shot as they appear in the published screenplay (Godard 1984).

22. As with musical extract 41b, for example, which accompanies shots 120–121 (15/128–129).

23. Musical extract 6, which accompanies shot 31 (5/36).

24. Musical extracts 36 and 37, which accompany shots 104–105 (13a/111–112) and 107–108 (13a/114–115) respectively.

25. Musical extracts 45a and 45b, which accompany shots 165–167 (20/174–20/176).

26. Miriam Sheer states that in *Prénom: Carmen* Godard's use of the Beethoven quartets 'follows their consecutive opus numbers and movement order' and he 'never skips back to a previously quoted movement' (2001, p. 133). However, as can be seen from the timing table included in the appendix, while the *overall* chronology of the quartets is maintained, excerpts from movement four of Quartet No. 15 (Op. 132) are interspersed between extracts from movement three, disrupting this chronology (see music extracts 27–42b). As discussed above, Godard frequently disrupts the actual development of music *within* movements by presenting later excerpts earlier and vice versa.

27. These surtitles were added to the original manuscripts by Beethoven.

28. Music extract 30 which accompanies shots 89–92 (12/96–12a/99).

29. Music extract 35 which accompanies shots 101–103 (13/108–13a/110).

30. Interestingly, the presence implied by this extradiegetic persona is not in itself a performer or creator, but one who manipulates the performance of others.

31. Music extracts 54–56, which accompany shots 191–199 (21/200–21/208=206).

32. Music extract 6, which accompanies shot 31 (5/36).

33. Music extract 15, which accompanies shots 52–53 (8/57–8/58).

34. Music extracts 8–11, which accompany shots 32–38 (6/38–7/44). The first extract is diegetic, accompanying a shot of the quartet rehearsing bars 54–75/1 of the first movement of Quartet No. 10 (Op. 74). The next extract comprises bars 63/4–65/1 of the same movement heard over a shot of Joseph guarding the bank lobby. The third extract comprises bars 58/2–73/2 of the same movement though here faded down during bars 66/4–68/1 and accompanies Joseph's attempt to send away the video vendors located in the street outside and his return to the lobby. The fourth extract consists of bars 78/2–88/2 and accompanies the robbers' entry into the bank and Joseph's attempt to give chase. The last of these extracts is diegetic, accompanying a shot of the quartet rehearsing bars 54–91/2.

35. This occurs just before music extract 11 at 0.15.33.

36. Sheer also suggests that the choice of Beethoven raises the issue of class difference between Claire and Joseph (with Joseph more clearly associated with the Tom Waits track) (2001, p. 183). Of course, it is also possible that this is an ironic use of Beethoven, driven by the acknowledgement that a spectator's appreciation of such music might encourage them to undertake a more serious interpretation of the film, thus enabling Godard to appropriate and parody bourgeois perceptions of Western art music.

37. See, for example, Adorno [1949] 1973, 1976, 1982; Paddison 1993 and Davison 1994. For Adorno 'authenticity' in this sense involves a combination of the awareness of the expressive subject (composer) of his/her true freedom in society (or lack of it) and the expression of this in the musical work, but must also be held in tension with the subject's (the composer's) technical mastery of the musical material at its most advanced stage and be demonstrated in the immanent consistency of the work (or its failure to demonstrate internal consistency).

38. The song's lyrics concern a man expressing his sadness at having to leave 'Ruby'; he vows never to return. As Kovacs highlighted, 'The song involves several plays on words in English and French. Carmen, who wears red throughout the movie, is clearly meant to be the Ruby of Waits's song, which ends with the line, "I'll never kiss your lips again" – a possible allusion to the expression "lèvres de carmin" (ruby-red lips) or "peindre avec du carmin"' (1990, p. 123, n. 38).

39. See Feuer 1982; Altman 1987.

40. Jean/Godard: 'What is the role of the quartet?'
    Carmen: 'I will tell you later.' (Author's translation.)

41. See, for example, Dayan 1976; Heath 1977–78, 1981. According to Heath, the desire for completeness offered by the narrative closure at the end of a classical film is a desire that can never be fulfilled, or only superficially, if at all. Heath's theory of suture is grounded in a Lacanian view of desire, in which all desire is based on a lack, or the absence of something unattainable. It is the constant movement of displacement from one signifier to another: a constant search for ultimate meaning, which does not exist. See also Silverman 1983, pp. 149–93.

42. See, for example, Derrida [1972] 1982. Interestingly, in his comparative analysis of the four *Carmen* films that appeared in the 1983–84 period, Leicester finds a similar deferral of meaning in Godard's refusal to recognize Bizet's opera (or any other version of *Carmen*) as the original text: there is no single origin. '[Godard] concentrat[es] instead on the ways people now use what has been made of it, not how they re-enact it, but how they reconstitute it, as he himself does with the sequence *Carmen, Carmen Jones, Prénom: Carmen* in giving a new meaning and direction to "si je t'aime ..."' (1994, p. 250).

Appendix: Timing table for *Prénom: Carmen*

Shot no.	Time: hr. min. sec.	Shot no. screenplay	Description of action in shot	Music extract no.	Music extract	Significant sound effects and Bizet references	Fragment length
1	0.00.00	0/5	Cars/traffic at night				
2	0.00.12	0/6	Surtitle: PRENOM CARMEN			0.00.15 – sea and seagulls (sea faded out at 0.00.43; seagulls at 0.00.46)	
3	0.00.24	0/7	Sea				35 secs
4		0/8	Sky				
5	0.00.46	0/9	Prat Quartet – viewed over Claire's shoulder	1	0.00.46–0.01.21 Quartet No. 9 (Op. 59) Mvt 2: *Andante* bars 1-8 repeated …		
6	0.01.17	0/10	Surtitle: Cast etc.			0.01.22 – hospital sounds begin	
7	0.01.27	1/12	Nurse in corridor of hospital – 2 patients present – one is Godard who then leaves the corridor			0.01.35–01.52 patient whistles and sings melody from Habanera	
8	0.01.52	1/13	Godard leaving the corridor to walk outside				
9	0.02.03	1/14	More surtitles			0.02.05 – percussive sound of Godard tapping things begins	
10	0.02.10	1/15	Godard by his bed in the hospital				
11	0.02.34	1/16	Typewriter close-up				
12	0.02.46	1/17	More surtitles			0.02.46 - sound of Godard hitting typewriter keys	
13	0.02.51	1/18	Godard at typewriter				
14	0.03.07	1/19	Doctor and other nurses arrive for assessment of Godard				
15	0.03.21	1/20	More surtitles			0.03.21 silence 0.03.24 diegetic hospital sounds	

Shot no.	Time: hr. min. sec.	Shot no. screenplay	Description of action in shot	Music extract no.	Music extract	Significant sound effects and Bizet references	Fragment length
						continue	
16	0.03.28	1/21	Godard on bed smoking. Nurse arrives (lights off)				
	(0.04.19)						
17	0.04.39	2/22	Quartet – can see cellist (and 2nd violin) over shoulder	2a	0.04.25–0.05.29 Quartet No. 9 Mvt 2 bars 1–7/1 includes repeat at 6 and 1st time bar at 20		64 secs
					...	0.05.27 diegetic sound from next shot	
18	0.05.30	3/23	Outside: car arrives at the hospital				
19	0.05.47	3/24	Carmen runs into hospital Inside: Godard in hospital – Carmen arrives	2b	0.05.44–0.05.47 Quartet No. 9 Mvt 2 bars 13/2–14/2	diegetic sound turned off under the music	3 secs
20	0.05.57	3/25					
				3a	0.06.16–0.06.21 Quartet No. 9 Mvt 2 bars 17/1c–19/1b		5 secs
				3b	0.06.26–0.06.32 Mvt 2 (take 2nd time bar) bars 20/1c–23/1a		6 secs
21	0.06.33	3/26	Close-up of Carmen smoking			0.07.09–0.07.10 diegetic sound turned off as Carmen laughs	
22	0.07.10	3/27	Godard next to window				
23	0.08.42	3/28	Close-up of Carmen			0.09.15 piano 'Au clair de la lune'	

24	0.09.19	Close-up of Godard and ghetto-blaster			0.09.40 sound of planes added; 0.10.06–0.10.12 tape (piano & planes) turned off; 0.10.35 planes stop	25 secs
			4a	0.10.37–0.11.02 Quartet No. 9 Mvt 3 *Menuetto* (coda) bars 77–91/1; 0.10.43 piano stops		…
25	0.10.44	Quartet (all four members seen from above)				
26	0.11.02	Carmen at car with robber (Jacques)	4b	0.11.06–0.11.10 Quartet No. 9 Mvt 3, bars 93/2b–94/3		4 secs
27	0.11.15	Claire and the quartet	5	0.11.15–0.11.50 Quartet No. 9 Mvt 3, bars 88/1–26/2 of Mvt 4 *Allegro molto*		35 secs
28	0.11.51	Joseph at car, waiting for Claire with her brother				
29	0.12.20	In car with Joseph, Claire and brother				
30	0.12.23	Traffic again at night				
31	0.12.50	Train crossing river by night	6	0.12.59–0.13.01 Quartet No. 10 (Op. 74) Mvt 1 *Allegro* bars 1–2/1	0.12.49 seagulls begin; 0.12.52–0.12.59 sea; 0.13.07 seagulls stop	2 secs
32	0.13.07	Joseph working as guard at bank	7	0.13.10–0.13.19 Quartet No. 10 Mvt 1, bars 62/2–67/3		9 secs

Shot no.	Time: hr. min. sec.	Shot no. screenplay	Description of action in shot	Music extract no.	Music extract	Significant sound effects and Bizet references	Fragment length
33	0.13.24	6/38	Quartet	8	0.13.33–0.14.05 Quartet No. 10 Mvt 1, bars 54–75/1		37 secs
34	0.14.16	6/39	Joseph at bank	9	0.14.16–0.14.18 Quartet No. 10 Mvt 1, bars 63/4–65/1		2 secs
35	0.14.37	6/40	Joseph moving on the video-sellers parked in the street outside			0.14.46–0.14.49 diegetic sound turned off (faded)	
				10a	0.14.47–0.15.09 Quartet No. 10 Mvt 1, bars 58/2–73/2 (turned down bars 66/4–68/1)		22 secs
36	0.14.51	6/41	Joseph returns to the interior of the bank				
37	0.15.09	6/42	Robber enter bank and gets past Joseph				
38	0.15.19	6/43	Shot through interior window – Joseph chasing the robbers	10b	0.15.15–0.15.31 Quartet No. 10 Mvt 1, bars 78/2–88/2		16 secs
					…		
39	0.15.31	7/44	Quartet –2nd violin?	11	0.15.49–0.16.46 Quartet No. 10 Mvt 1, bars 54–91/2 (image track slightly out – late – with music)	0.16.57 diegetic sound from next shot begins	57 secs
40	0.17.01	8/45	Joseph running through a corridor				

			in the bank	0.17.07 diegetic sound from next shot begins	
41	0.17.09	8/46	Claire in the quarter	12 0.17.09–0.17.16 Quartet No. 10 Mvt 1, bars 185–188	7 secs
42	0.17.12	8/47 (47=45)	Repeated shot of Joseph running through corridor (shot 40)	diegetic sound doesn't start until 0.17.18	
43	0.17.48	8/48	Robbers	13 0.17.36–0.17.58 Quartet No. 10 Mvt 1, bars 191–206/3	22 secs
44	0.17.50	8/49	Joseph in pursuit	. . .	
45	0.17.56	8/50	Robber runs down stairs – Joseph follows	. . .	
46	0.18.04	8/51	Carmen on stairs – Joseph in pursuit	14a 0.18.04–0.18.22 Quartet No. 10 Mvt 1, bars 208–220/1 . . .	18 secs
47	0.18.21	8/52	Joseph		
48	0.18.24	8/53	Carmen on stairs	14b 0.18.24–0.18.49 Quartet No. 10 Mvt 1, bars 221/4 (last demi)–238/4 (turned down – bar 226)	25 secs
49	0.18.30	8/54	Shot looking down the stairs – Joseph falls down the stairs	. . .	
50	0.18.36	8/55	Carmen hiding in wait for Joseph – and attempts to shoot him	. . .	
51	0.18.43	8/56	Cleaner mops up blood around two of the bodies		
52	0.18.54	8/57	Carmen and Joseph fall on top of one another on the stairs		
53	0.19.04	8/58	Carmen and Joseph fighting for gun – Joseph is on top of Carmen – they kiss	15 0.19.03–0.19.07 Quartet No.10 Mvt 2 Adagio bars 1–3/2	4 secs
54	0.19.28	8/59 (59=56)	Cleaner mopping blood (repeat of shot 51)	16 0.19.18–0.19.30 Quartet No. 10 Mvt 2, bars 6–9/2	12 secs
55	0.19.38	8/60	Carmen and Joseph kissing – a robber escapes behind them	17a 0.19.42–0.20.03 Quartet No. 10	21 secs

Shot no.	Time: hr. min. sec.	Shot no. screenplay	Description of action in shot	Music extract no.	Music extract	Significant sound effects and Bizet references	Fragment length
56	0.19.50	8/61	Carmen – close-up		Mvt 2, bars 28/3–34/2		
57	0.20.04	8/62	Carmen and Joseph get-up – Joseph takes off his guard's jacket	17b	0.20.13–0.20.14 Quartet No. 10 Mvt 2, 37/1–37/2		1 sec
58	0.20.27	9/63	Hands on a steering wheel in a car in the street outside the bank	18a	0.20.26–0.20.57 Quartet No. 10 Mvt 2, bars 49/2–58/2		31 secs
59	0.20.33	9/64 (64=59=56)	Cleaner again (repeat of shot 51)		: : :		
60	0.20.40	9/65 (65=63)	Hands on steering wheel again – shot continues – driver gets out (repeat and extension of shot 58)		: : :		
61	0.20.57	9/66	Joseph and Carmen in car driving around traffic island				
62	0.21.12	9/67	Shot of gear-stick – Joseph's hands on Carmen's legs				
63	0.21.20	9/68 (68=35)	Traffic at night (repeat of shot 30)	18b	0.21.15–0.21.28 Quartet No. 10 Mvt 2, bars 64–67/2	0.21.19 seagulls 0.21.30–0.2_.36 sea	13 secs
64	0.21.36	9/69	Sea – waves breaking	19	0.21.36–0.22.24 Quartet No. 10 Mvt 2, bars 71/3–85/1 (turned	0.21.36 seagulls end	48 secs

					down during bars 74/3–75/3; 77/3–79/3; 81/3–83/3)	
65	0.22.05	9/70	Sea again – closer angle		0.21.41–0.22.04 sea 0.22.06–0.22.37 sea, shifting to diegetic traffic noise . . .	
66	0.22.32	9/71	Petrol station (shot through window)			
67	0.23.08	9/72	Man enters toilet – Joseph and Carmen enter shop and go into toilet (still tied together)		0.23.07–0.23.10 silent then fading up diegetic sound	
68	0.23.34	9/73	Shot inside men's toilet with man – Carmen uses urinal			
		20		0.23.43–0.23.45 Quartet No. 14 (Op. 131) Mvt 5 *Presto*, bars 497–498		2 secs
69	0.23.57	9/74 9/75	Man eating out of jar			
70	0.24.24	9/76	Quartet – 1st and 2nd violin			
		21		0.24.21–0.24.38 Quartet No. 14 Mvt 6 *Adagio quasi un poco andante*, bars 1-6/1		17 secs
71	0.24.42	9/77	Outside shop – Joseph releases Carmen – they run back to the car		0.24.42–0.24.45 silent – fading up diegetic sound	
		22		0.24.49–0.25.08 Quartet No. 14 Mvt 6, bars 9/2–14/1b		19 secs
72	0.24.53	10/78	Quartet – Claire miming			
73	0.25.07	10/79 (79=76)	Quartet – different angle – back to 1st and 2nd violin (repeat of shot 70)			
		23		0.25.08–0.25.31 Quartet No. 14 Mvt 6, bars 12/3–18/1a		23 secs
74	0.25.32	11/80	Sea		0.25.32–0.25.53 sea and seagulls	

Shot no.	Time: hr. min. sec.	Shot no. screenplay	Description of action in shot	Music extract no.	Music extract	Significant sound effects and Bizet references	Fragment length
75	0.25.42	11/81	Joseph and Carmen's car arrives at the coast			...	6 secs
76	0.25.53	11/82	Carmen and Joseph inside car	24	0.25.52–0.25.58 Quartet No. 14 Mvt 6 bars 20/3–22/1	0.25.58–0.25.57 sea	
77	0.26.06	11/83	Sea	25	0.26.08–0.26.38 Quartet No. 14 Mvt 7 *Allegro* bars 1–36/3 (all quiet, bars 6–8/2 & 12/4–23/3 turned down)	...	30 secs
78	0.26.39	11/84	Carmen and Joseph at car – Joseph outside – Carmen beeping horn			... 0.26.57 traffic (from sea)	
79	0.27.00	11/85	Police at petrol station, in pursuit of Joseph	26	0.27.01–0.27.17 Quartet No. 14 Mvt 7, bars 37/2–55/3 (bars 46–47 turned v. low)	0.27.10–0.27.13 no diegetic sound	16 secs
					...	0.27.13–0.27.17 sea (?)	
80	0.27.17	11/89 12/87	Carmen and Joseph at Uncle Jean's flat in Trouville				
81	0.27.56	12/88	Joseph moves into another room – Carmen joins him from the kitchen				
82	0.28.30	12/89	Police leave the petrol station	27	0.28.38–0.28.46 Quartet No. 15 (Op. 132) Mvt 3 *Molto adagio*, bars 15/3–17/2		8 secs
83	0.28.39	12/90	Carmen walking on beach				
84	0.28.47	12/91	Carmen and Joseph in flat next to window – Carmen takes off her			0.28.43–0.28.47 sea	

Shot	Time	Code	Description	Scene	Music cue	Diegetic sound	Duration
			jacket	28	0.28.49–0.28.56 Quartet No. 15 Mvt 3, bars 17/3–18/4		7 secs
85	0.29.41	12/92	Calm-sea close-up	29	0.29.41–0.30.58 Quartet No. 15 Mvt 3, bars 1/4–15/2	no diegetic sound	77 secs
86	0.30.13	12/93	Carmen and Joseph close-up		: : :	no diegetic sound 0.30.17–0.30.57 sea	
87	0.30.56	12/94	Sea		: : :		
88	0.31.00	12/95 (95=93)	Carmen & Joseph close-up (repeat of shot 86 but with diegetic sound and from earlier in shot)			0.30.58–0.30.59 silent 0.30.59–0.32.34 sea (diegetic?)	
89	0.32.25	12/96	Beach and sea – two figures walking at low tide	30	0.32.35–0.34.09 Quartet No. 15 Mvt 3, bars 25/3–31/4 then at 32 skips to second *andante* (B²), bars 116–143/1	0.32.35–0.34.07 no sea? 0.32.37–0.32.49 seagulls	94 secs
90	0.32.50	12a/97	Claire and Quartet		: : :		
91	0.33.16	12a/98	Remainder of Quartet – 2nd violin and viola or 1st and 2nd violin		: : :		
92	0.34.07	12a/99	Carmen and Joseph at window		: : :	0.34.07–0.34.13 sea (diegetic?)	
93	0.34.14	12a/100 (100=98)	Quartet (repeat of shot 91)	31	0.34.14–0.34.15 Quartet No. 15 Mvt 3, bars 149/3(8)–150/1		1 sec
94	0.34.16	12a/101 (101=99)	Carmen and Joseph at window (repeat of shot 92)			0.34.16–0.35.10 sea (diegetic?)	
95	0.34.46	12a/102	Rocks in the sea at night/dusk	32	0.34.46–0.35.00 Quartet No. 15 Mvt 3, bars 160/3 (last 2 demi.sq)–168/3 (bars 162/2–163/1 turned v. low)		14 secs
96	0.35.03	12a/103	Claire close-up (mimes correctly to another entry)	33	0.35.06–0.35.49 Quartet No. 15		43 secs

Shot no.	Time: hr. min. sec.	Shot no. screenplay	Description or action in shot	Music extract no.	Music extract	Significant sound effects and Bizet references	Fragment length
97	0.35.44	12a/104	Sea – waves breaking at night		Mvt 3, bars 166/1–174/1a	0.35.49–0.36.33 sea	
98	0.35.48	13/105	Carmen and Joseph close-up in bed				
99	0.36.06	13/106 (106=104)	Sea – waves breaking at night (repeat of shot 97)	34	0.36.07–0.36.20 Quartet No. 15 Mvt 3, bars 86/3b–88/4	(diegetic?) dialogue – v. closely miked	13 secs
						0.36.34–0.36.37 no diegetic sound under Carmen's dialogue	
						0.36.38–0.37.28 sea (diegetic?)	
100	0.36.52	13/107	Carmen and Joseph close-up in dark				
101	0.37.10	13/108	Carmen close-up (side angle)	35	0.37.19–0.37.51 Quartet No. 15 Mvt 3, bars 19/3–25/2		32 secs
102	0.37.38	13/109	Sea – waves breaking at night				
103	0.37.46	13a/110	Claire amending her quartet part		...	Quartet faded down, despite being apparently present (though unseen)	
104	0.38.08	13a/111	Dawn – Joseph outside on balcony – then enters flat and returns to Carmen on bed	36	0.38.34–0.38.40 Quartet No. 15 Mvt 3, bars 28/3–29/4	0.38.30–0.38.41 no diegetic sound	6 secs
105	0.38.35	13a/112	Calm sea and boats at dawn				
106	0.38.40	13a/113 (113=111)	Carmen and Joseph (repeat and continuation of shot 104)			0.38.42–0.39.16 sea (diegetic?)	
107	0.38.47	13a/114 (114=112)	Calm sea again at dawn (repeat and continuation of shot 105)	37	0.38.49– 0.39.03 Quartet No. 15 Mvt 3, bars 30/1–	...	14 secs
108	0.38.56	13a/115	Carmen and Joseph close-up			...	

No.	Time	Description	Music (Quartet No. 15)	Diegetic sound	Duration
109	0.39.03	(115=113=111) repeat of shots 104 & 106) 13a/116 Stormy clouds (dusk)	33/3b (demi.sq)	… …	
110	0.39.16	14/117 Carmen and Joseph in kitchen drinking tea			
111	0.40.13	14/118 Carmen & Joseph in kitchen different angle		0.39.25–0.41.00 sea – getting louder – v. loud at 0.40.56– 0.41.00 then stops	
		38a	0.41.13–0.42.25 Quartet No. 15 Mvt 3, bars 185/1b–196/3 (gradually getting quieter)	…	72 secs
112	0.41.15	14/119 Close up of Carmen ('If I love you, you're really done for')			
113	0.42.06	14/120 Joseph's hand and Carmen's genitals		0.42.07–0.42.40 sea	
114	0.42.08	15/121 Waves breaking over rocks in sea		no diegetic dialogue heard – only the sea	
115	0.42.34	15/122 Carmen talking to robber			
		38b	0.42.40–0.42.47 Quartet No. 15 Mvt 3, bars 198/4–199/4 …	0.42.48 diegetic sound added 0.42.50–0.43.34 loud seagulls	7 secs
116	0.42.56	15/123 Joseph taken by police			
		39	0.42.56–0.42.57 Quartet No. 15 Mvt 4 Alla marcia…, bars 1/3–2/2 (v. quiet)	… …	1 sec
		40	0.42.58–0.43.00 Quartet No. 15 Mvt 4, bars 3/1–3/4a	…	2 secs
117	0.43.00	15/124 Joseph put into police car 15/125		…	
118	0.43.16	15/126 Joseph put into boot of car		…	
		41a	0.43.21–0.43.25 Quartet No. 15 Mvt 3, bars 192/1–192/4	…	4 secs
119	0.43.23	15/127 Sea – waves breaking		no diegetic sound	
120	0.43.26	15/128 Jacques running to Carmen in car	41b 0.43.27–0.43.43 Quartet No. 15 Mvt 3, bars 193/1–195/3	sea (diegetic?)	16 secs
121	0.43.34	15/129 Waves breaking at night		no diegetic sound	

Shot no.	Time: hr. min. sec.	Shot no. screenplay	Description of action in shot	Music extract no.	Music extract	Significant sound effects and Bizet references	Fragment length
122	0.43.45	16/130	Joseph in court			0.44.18 diegetic sound from next shot begins (no sea sounds)	
123	0.44.21	16/131	Carmen and Joseph in kitchen – Carmen tells Joseph the kidnapping plot			0.44.43–0.44.52 diegetic sound stops – diegetic dialogue from next shot begins	
124	0.44.52	16/132	Joseph in court (Claire, etc. in background)				
125	0.45.00	16/133	Carmen and Joseph in kitchen			0.46.25 diegetic sound from next shot begins	
126	0.46.27	16/134	Joseph leaving courtroom			no diegetic sound	
127	0.46.35	16/135	Quartet			0.46.36–0.46.41 seagulls and diegetic dialogue from courtroom 0.46.42–0.46.43 silent	
128	0.46.43	16/136	Claire talking to Joseph over lunch at courtroom			0.46.44 diegetic sound begins (& something whispered)	
		16/137	(Joseph receives flower via defence counsel)				
129	0.47.46	17/138	Carmen standing at bar – robber playing pinball – returns the gun to her that she left behind (evening)			0.48.03–0.48.09 melody	

Shot	Time	Ref	Description	Cue	Music	Sound	Duration
130	0.48.08	17/139	Jacques at cafe during day – meets Uncle Jean			from Habanera whistled	
131	0.49.40	17/140	Jacques and Jean move to different table – nurse brings brioche – she remains visible in mirror behind them				
132	0.50.55	17/141	Different angle – nearer to Jean – nurse now in back right of shot				
133	0.51.19	17/142	Returns to angle from shot before last				
134	0.52.39	17/143 (143=36)	Two trains cross as they cross the river at night (repeat of shot 31)			no diegetic sound - sound from previous shot; 0.52.41 diegetic sound from next shot (pinball)	
135	0.52.45	17/144 (144=138)	Carmen at bar (repeat of shot 129) Jacques enters				
136	0.53.23	17/145	Close-up of Carmen	42a	0.53.38–0.53.45 Quartet No. 15 Mvt 3, bars 185/4b–186/4		7 secs
137	0.53.43	17/146	Video-sellers in bar – woman greeted by Carmen				
138	0.54.00	18/147	Outside bar – Carmen, Jacques – car arrives				
139	0.54.12	18/148	Back view of car – Carmen gets in – Joseph arrives – Carmen gets out	42b	0.54.05–0.54.29 Quartet No. 15 Mvt 3, bars 190/1b–193/3 … … …	0.54.29 diegetic sound stops 0.54.30 telephone ringing (sound from next shot)	24 secs
140	0.54.31	18/149	Carmen in hotel suite with Joseph				
141	0.55.13	18/150	Carmen at mirror – Joseph joins her			'If I love you that's the end of you'	

Shot no.	Time: hr. min. sec.	Shot no. screenplay	Description of action in shot	Music extract no.	Music extract	Significant sound effects and Bizet references	Fragment length
142	0.56.00	18/151	Carmen close-up				
143	0.56.38	18/152	Maid enters				
144	0.57.12	18/153	Carmen in yellow dress				
145	0.58.16	18/154	Sea – waves (as Joseph turns on TV)				
146	0.58.21	18/155	Hotel from outside – car draws up			0.58.24 sea transforms to traffic noise (diegetic)	
147	0.58.45	19/156	3 people (the victims?) in hotel hallway				
148	0.58.56	19/157	Maid makes bed				
149	0.59.36	19/158	Joseph and robbers in suite – Joseph looking for Carmen			0.59.32 'Help' shouted by robber 0.59.33–0.59.34 police siren	
150	1.00.15	19/159	Joseph by door to next room talking to Carmen inside			1.00.14–1.00.15 silent	
151	1.01.01	19/160	Carmen & Joseph and Jacques				
152	1.01.25	19/161	Carmen from different angle – on bed				
153	1.01.54	19/162	Camera fixes on Joseph's reaction as Carmen flirts with waiter				
154	1.02.26	19/163	Trains cross paths as they cross bridge		1.02.29–1.06.57 Tom Waits's 'In Ruby's arms' faded in	1.02.16–1.02.27 telephone rings loudly	268 secs
155	1.02.32	19/164	Joseph's hand on TV screen				
156	1.03.03	19/165	Joseph and television in silhouette				

Shot	Time	ID	Description	Cue	Music	Duration
157	1.03.12	19/166	Carmen			
158	1.03.39	19/167	Close-up of Carmen – Joseph stands up close to her (from kneeling)			
159	1.04.09	19/168	Carmen moves away and takes off clothes		1.04.09 music skips	
160	1.04.54	19/169	Carmen moves into next room – Joseph chases her		1.04.54 music skips	
161	1.05.11	19/170	Carmen and Joseph enter next room		1.05.13 music skips	
162	1.06.17	19/171	Carmen on bed – Joseph enters	43	1.06.18–1.06.34 Quartet No. 16 Op. 135 Mvt 1, bars 176–185/1a	16 secs
				44a	1.06.41–1.06.42 Quartet No. 16 Mvt 1, bars 185/1b–185/2a	1 sec
				44b	1.06.51–1.06.57 Quartet No. 16 Mvt 1, bars 191–194 …	6 secs
163	1.06.55	19/172	Claire in quartet			
164	1.06.59	19/173	Trains in daylight			
165	1.07.07	20/174	Joseph enters shower room	45a	1.07.09–1.07.12 Quartet No. 16 (Op. 135) Mvt 2 Vivace bars 20/2–26/1	3 secs
166	1.07.14	20/175	Joseph in hotel suite	45b	1.07.30–1.07.35 Quartet No. 16 Mvt 2 bars 62 (1st time bar at 67–18)–24/1 (louder than dialogue)	5 secs
167	1.07.32	20/176	Carmen & Jacques and Uncle Jean (nurse?)			
168	1.07.39	20/177	Different angle of previous shot – includes Joseph			
169	1.09.24	20/178	Policemen on phone in hotel lobby			

'What is the role of the quartet?'

Shot no.	Time hr. min. sec.	Shot no. screenplay	Description of action in shot	Music extract no.	Music extract	Significant sound effects and Bizet references	Fragment length
170	1.09.32	20/179	Carmen enters next room – Joseph and waiter follow	46a	1.09.28–1.09.32 Quartet No. 16 Mvt 2 bars 27/2–36/1 (?)	1.09.28–1.09.32 no diegetic sound	4 secs
171	1.09.45	20/180	Carmen makes advances to waiter	46b	1.09.44–1.10.39 Quartet No. 16 Mvt 2, bars 62 (2nd time bar at 67)–177/1		55 secs
172	1.10.09	20/181	Chandeliers being cleaned		: : :	no diegetic sound – sound from next shot	
173	1.10.10	20/182	Carmen enters shower room – Joseph pushes waiter away and follows her		: : :		
174	1.10.17	20/183	Carmen close-up		: : :		
175	1.10.21	20/184	Carmen & Joseph in shower – Joseph masturbating			1.10.25–1.10.39 no diegetic sound	
176	1.10.51	20/185	Carmen leaves shower and crawls across floor – Joseph joins her	47	1.10.50–1.11.06 Quartet No. 16 Mvt 2, bars 195–225/3	(1.10.53 shower turned off)	16 secs
					: : :	1.11.06 sound of water running continues	
177	1.11.11	20/186	Carmen & Joseph in bedroom	48	1.11.10–1.11.21 Quartet No. 16 Mvt 2, bars 254/2 (taking 2nd time bar at 269)–end of mvt		11 secs
178	1.11.16	20/187	Carmen close-up		: : :		

Shot	Timecode	Shot ID	Description	Cue	Music	Duration
179	1.11.19	21/188	Car outside hotel		. . .	
180	1.11.27	21/189	Dining room in hotel – quartet rehearsing – Carmen, Uncle Jean and Jacques enter	49	1.11.34–1.12.08 Quartet No. 16 Mvt 3 (*Lento assai . . .*), bars 1–5/2a	34 secs
181	1.12.17	21/190	Extras are seated by Uncle Jean	50a	1.12.18–1.12.51 Quartet No. 16 Mvt 3, bars 3–7/1c (continues?)	33 secs
182	1.12.53	21/191	Chandeliers being cleaned		. . .	
183	1.13.06	21/192	Uncle Jean and ghetto-blaster	50b	1.12.56–1.13.06 Quartet No. 16 Mvt 3, bars 9–11/2a	10 secs
184	1.13.15	21/193	Quartet and victim	51	1.13.14–1.13.20 Quartet No. 16 Mvt 3, bars 14/1b–15/1a	3 secs
185	1.13.37	21/194	Uncle Jean and ghetto-blaster (repeat of shot 183)			
		(194=192)		52	1.13.39–1.14.02 Quartet No. 16 Mvt 3, bars 14/1c–17/2a	23 secs
186	1.13.46	21/195	Close-up of Carmen		. . .	
187	1.13.54	21/196	Victim looks at Carmen		. . .	
188	1.13.56	21/197	Carmen close-up (repeat of shot 186)		. . .	
		(197=195)				
189	1.14.03	21/198	Claire gets up to leave quartet			
190	1.14.04	21/199	Policemen on phone (repeat of shot 169)	53	1.14.05–1.14.10 Quartet No. 16 Mvt 3, bars 18/1a–18/2b	5 secs
		(199=178)				
191	1.14.11	21/200	Jacques and Joseph clash	54	1.14.17–1.14.56 Quartet No. 16 Mvt 3, bars 23–28/2a	39 secs
192	1.14.21	21/201	Chandeliers through balcony railings			

Shot no.	Time: hr. min. sec.	Shot no. screenplay	Description of action in shot	Music extract no.	Music extract	Significant sound effects and Bizet references	Fragment length
						1.14.23–1.14.31 industrial background noise starts	
193	1.14.29	21/202	Uncle Jean and Quartet – Claire returns		…	1.14.36–1.15.10 no diegetic sound	33 secs
194	1.14.41	21/203	Claire	55	1.14.36–1.15.09 Quartet No. 16 Mvt 4, (*Grave* . . .) bars 1/1–7/3 (turned down 1/3–2/1 and 2/3)		
195	1.14.55	21/204	Joseph appears at door		…		
196	1.14.55	21/205	Close-up of Joseph		…		
197	1.15.07	21/206	Close-up of Carmen		…		
198	1.15.15	21/207	Uncle Jean and nurse				
199	1.15.21	21/208 (208=206)	Carmen close-up (repeat of shot 197)	56	1.15.17–1.15.27 Quartet No. 16 Mvt 4, bars 11–12/3a (pause)		10 secs
200	1.15.29	21/209 (209=207)	Uncle Jean and nurse (repeat of shot 198)		…	1.15.23–1.15.27 no diegetic sound	
201	1.16.02	21/210 (210=203)	Claire crying (repeat and continuation of shot 194)	57a	1.15.37–1.15.57 Quartet No. 16 Mvt 4, bars 12/3b–38/1	Nurse to Uncle Jean as music stops: 'The perfect harmony of several voices impedes their individual progress'	20 secs
202	1.16.08	21/211 (211=196)	Victims leaving (repeat of shot 187)	57b	1.16.02–1.16.11 Quartet No. 16 Mvt 4, bars 45–58/1		9 secs

Shot	Time	Ref	Action	Cue	Music	Sound notes	Duration
203	1.16.11	21/212	Carmen & robber – Joseph cries	57c	1.16.23–1.16.29 Quartet No. 16 Mvt 4, bars 72/3–80/1		6 secs
204	1.16.28	21/213	Uncle Jean and victims	57d	1.16.34–1.16.42 Quartet No. 16 Mvt 4, bars 17/2–26/4		8 secs
205	1.16.33	21/214	Robbers and Uncle Jean				
206	1.16.43	21/215	Nurse	57e	1.16.43–1.16.51 Quartet No. 16 Mvt 4, bars 28/1–38/1	1.16.42–1.16.43 silence no diegetic sound??	8 secs
207	1.16.51	21/216	Carmen getting gun – pulls it on Joseph then leaves – policemen arrive			1.17.05–1.17.16 sounds from dining room (diegetic?)	
208	1.17.15	21/217	Massacre	58	1.17.45–1.18.55 Quartet No. 16 Mvt 4, bars 136/3–173/3a	1.17.17 shooting begins 1.17.31–1.17.35 sounds from dining room (diegetic?)	70 secs
209	1.17.57	21/218	Chandeliers	⋮	⋮		
210	1.17.58	21/219	Stairs	⋮	⋮		
211	1.18.02	21/220	Carmen and victim – Joseph arrives	⋮	⋮		
212	1.18.08	21/221	Policemen	⋮	⋮		
213	1.18.10	21/222	Joseph and Carmen – shot fired	⋮	⋮		
214	1.18.18	21/223 (223=221)	Policemen (repeat of shot 212)	⋮	⋮		
215	1.18.26	21/224	Joseph and Carmen – Joseph shoots Carmen	⋮	⋮		
216	1.18.47	21/225	Chandeliers through balcony	⋮	⋮		
217	1.18.49	21/226	Chandelier	⋮	⋮	1.18.49–1.19.44 sounds of dining room – diegetic	

Shot no.	Time: hr. min. sec.	Shot no. screenplay	Description of action in shot	Music extract no.	Music extract	Significant sound effects and Bizet references	Fragment length
218	1.18.52	21/227	Waiter approaches Carmen		⋮	1.19.11–1.19.27 industrial background noise added again	
219	1.19.08	21/228	Carmen on ground				
220	1.19.27		Waiter				25 secs
221	1.19.45	21/229	Sea – calm	59	1.19.35–1.20.00 Quartet No. 16 Mvt 4, bars 249-end of mvt		
222	1.19.49	21/230	Surtitle		⋮	1.19.47–1.19.54 sea	
223	1.19.51	21/231 (31=229)	Sea – calm		⋮		
	1.19.57	21/232	Surtitle		⋮		

Chapter 5

Playing in Jarman's *Garden*: sound, performance and images of persecution

The focus of this chapter is the soundtrack to Derek Jarman's *The Garden* (1990). Much of the film was shot in and around the garden that Jarman created in the inhospitable environment of Dungeness beach – the largest area of estuarine shingle in Europe – under the shadow of a nuclear power station.[1] After an introductory film-within-a-film sequence (based on the fall from grace in the Garden of Eden), we see a shot of Jarman falling asleep at his desk, with the suggestion that the film which follows is a dream sequence. The central (though nonlinear) narrative is based loosely on the story of the Passion, though the traditional figure of Jesus is substituted with a gay couple on several occasions: in this way the suffering of Jesus is equated with that of homosexuals, with particular focus on their suffering since the AIDS crisis.[2] The film combines documentary footage shot on Super-8mm – inexpensive, lightweight cameras – over the previous three years with sequences shot on video and film, and also uses shot repetition, filters, and time-lapse photography. While it is a serious and, at times, harrowing film it also has moments of humour and is ultimately optimistic in its outlook. Through an investigation of the film's sound–image relationship, a consideration of acousmatic sound and music, and the film's sung performances, I suggest that a gap is exposed between sound and image. I argue that this creates a space in which the soundtrack is able to speak its own voice, liberated from slavery to the image. In the analysis which follows, I suggest that *The Garden* presents a damning criticism – embodied in the form of the image and the camera – of the renewed vigour demonstrated by the British tabloid press in their persecution of homosexuals since the AIDS crisis. In this film the soundtrack embodies redemption.

Derek Jarman

Jarman trained as a painter and theatre set designer at the Slade School of Art in London. He first worked in film when he was employed as a set designer on Ken Russell's big-budget production *The Devils* in 1970. At around the same time Jarman began to film his friends with a Super-8mm camera, just as his father had filmed Derek and his sister during their childhood.[3] Even when he began to make feature films, Jarman continued to shoot footage with Super-8mm cameras. He also continued to paint, create installation art, make short films, work on set designs, write books, and design and shoot pop music videos. Indeed, Jarman did not think of himself as a filmmaker per se, but as an artist, or painter, who happened to make some films. This can be seen perhaps most obviously in the tableaux that are featured in his films, particularly in *The Garden* (1990) and in his poetic portrait of the life of the late-sixteenth- to early-seventeenth-century Italian painter, *Caravaggio* (1986). Indeed, critics highlight that Jarman's painterly aesthetic and work in set design infused the style of his filmmaking:

> His strong sense of artifice and emphasis on set design or *mise en scène*, together with a frontality and system of textural and colour effects which are painterly, find no real equivalent in British cinema. Equally there is a crudity, a brittle edge which some have identified as amateurishness (or incompetence) that gives his films a fresh quality. (O'Pray 1996, p. 10)

His relative inexperience of mainstream film form enabled him to try things which the Establishment rarely attempted, such as 'putting amateurs in leading roles, mixing genres, as well as using music, dance and poetry with audacity and nerve' (ibid.). This naivety also led to a particularly collaborative mode of production.[4]

Despite a renewed interest in his paintings since the mid-1980s, Jarman continues to be best known as an openly gay British filmmaker who often made films that depicted gay love, or reclaimed history for the homosexual community.[5] In December 1986 he discovered that he was HIV-positive. From that point on he became something of an ambassador for those who were HIV-positive or had developed AIDS, speaking openly to the liberal media about his condition in a way that had never previously been undertaken by someone in a position of (cultural) power infected with the virus.

Liberating the soundtrack

As discussed in Chapter 1, until relatively recently film theory defiantly maintained a camera-oriented visual bias, theorizing the soundtrack only as a redundant adjunct to the image, which functions in its service but adds little or nothing to it. From the late 1970s this prioritization of image over sound began to be questioned. For example, in 'Moving Lips: Cinema as Ventriloquism', Rick Altman (1980b) reversed the prioritization of image over sound completely. In a deconstructive manoeuvre, Altman theorized the soundtrack as a ventriloquist and the image as its dummy: by moving the lips of the image track, the soundtrack creates the illusion that the image produces the film's sound in order to conceal the soundtrack's absence from the image. The soundtrack allows this illusion of subservience to the image in order to conceal its predominance *over* the image. The purpose of this reversal was to demonstrate that neither the soundtrack nor the image track is in practice prioritized over the other: both are necessary in order to confirm the truth of the other.

Work such as Altman's has sought to redress the theoretical balance in favour of the soundtrack in recognition of the vital role it plays in proposing and confirming the reality of the film's diegetic world. It is the synchronization of sound to image – best exemplified by lip-synchronization in on-screen dialogue – that convinces us of the reality of the film's fictional world, for instance. As Mary Ann Doane points out, however, such re-evaluations of the role of the soundtrack also incur the revelation of the soundtrack's potential to expose the diegesis as a false reality, thus in turn disclosing the material heterogeneity within film as a medium – that is, sound *and* image (1980, p. 35, 40). The camera works to perpetuate the myth that sound issues from the image (by behaving as though it must always move to identify the source of a sound, for example) in order to mask the film's material sound/image split (and, thus, the technologically and mechanically generated nature of the film). While sound- and image tracks are usually unified in classical cinema, they can clearly also be combined in more antagonistic and divergent ways which demonstrate the schism that persists between them. For example, while on the one hand the presentation of off-screen sound can be said to confirm the continuity of diegetic space by denying the limitations of the frame, on the other, such sounds always entail the risk of threatening a film's unity of discourse. Classical cinema contains this risk by making reference to the existence of these sounds within the diegesis (ibid., p. 41). The basis of this 'tension of the unknown' inherent in sounds that lack the visual confirmation of their sources in the image derives from the physical differences between light and sound: unlike light, sound can travel around corners (Altman 1980b, p. 74). I want to suggest that this risk – of threatening the classical film's unity of discourse – is precisely the resource that the soundtrack offers to Jarman in *The Garden*.

Authorship of the soundtrack to *The Garden* belongs to a number of individuals who worked collaboratively to produce it. They include Derek Jarman, Simon Fisher-Turner (composer of original music), Dean Broderick (string arrangements and arranger of Roger Edens's 'Think Pink'), Nigel Holland (sound editor), Marvin Black (sound engineer), Gary Desmond (sound recordist), Richard Fettes (assistant sound editor), Bill Garlick and Beryl Mortimer (foley artists). I mention this not to diminish Fisher-Turner's responsibility as composer of the soundtrack's original music, but to highlight the collaborative character of the production of this soundtrack, particularly the contribution of the sound team in developing much of the electroacoustic acousmatic music.[6]

The soundtrack for *The Garden* comprises original and pre-composed music, sound effects and voice-over. There is little on-screen dialogue in this film: what conversation there is, is shown as mute. Lip-synchronization does occur elsewhere during the film, but only intermittently and only in non-spoken vocalizations, such as laughing, screaming and singing. Jarman's rejection of on-screen dialogue results in the loss of the primary technique by which a film promotes an illusory unity of discourse.

Early in the film we are presented with a scene which not only reveals the soundtrack's potential to liberate itself from the tyranny of the image, but also allows the image to seek to reassert this containment. The scene in question is the attack on Mary (Tilda Swinton) by masked photographers, which occurs about 12 minutes into the film (Illusion 5.1). It features a small group of paparazzi-like photographers dressed in black and wearing (terrorist) balaclavas to cover their faces. The scene begins with the photographers shouting instructions for poses to Mary, who holds the baby Jesus in her arms. The photographers quickly become more aggressive, first toward each other, then toward their subject. Mary sets the child down and tries to walk away from them. The photographers try to obstruct her escape, and as she persists they begin to chase after her. At the end of the scene we see Mary successfully fight off the photographers as they attack her and brawl together on the beach. This chase and attack on Mary is intercut with short, peaceful shots of the baby in close-up, playing with a plastic windmill in Jarman's Dungeness garden. A sonic elision connects the child's gurgles with his mother's acoustically distorted screams.

During this sequence – produced predominantly by the film's sound team – the soundtrack features birdsong, music, diegetic sound, and the manipulation of diegetic and real-world sounds which have no visible on-screen sources. Even before the images of the sequence appear on screen, the clicking of camera shutters can be heard on the soundtrack. During the sequence this (apparently) diegetic sound is manipulated by means of compression, distortion and looping. The new sounds that result, though different from the original camera sounds, retain a strong enough similarity to them that they may be heard as generated by the same on-screen source. When the sounds of non-visible sources – a helicopter, the firing of machine guns, and a noisy mechanical printer – are heard, however, the manipulated sounds of the cameras retrospectively take on a mediatory role. Despite the fact that these sounds have no apparent source within the fictional world of the film, and thus represent a threat to its unity (and subsequently, its reality), these manipulated sounds provide a 'sonic bridge' between the unseen real-world sounds and the sound of the cameras (which are rooted in the image). In this way the image provides a possible source for the unseen sounds and attempts to contain the threat they pose.

The sounds of helicopters and machine guns clearly present codes associated with surveillance: chase, persecution, violence, terrorism and the armed forces. Because these sounds are presented at the same time as images which show the photographers' aggression toward, and subsequent pursuit and attacking of Mary, their meaning in this context is confirmed – they serve to associate these codes of persecution with the camera itself. The implication that these sounds are actually

Illustration 5.1   The photographers (*The Garden*)
Photo: Liam Daniel, courtesy Basilisk Communications Ltd

generated by the cameras makes their incorporation surreptitious. This sequence presents materially what retheorization of the soundtrack can mean for film: it suggests that the soundtrack and image track need not coincide, and thus reveals the material heterogeneity of the medium. In this sequence, however, the danger to the singular 'truth' of the image brought about by the liberation of the soundtrack is concealed by implying that the liberated sounds are actually sourced in the image track after all.

In broad terms the liberation of the soundtrack is effected in three different ways in the course of the film: first, through the presentation of real-world sounds without visible sources, as demonstrated by the camera-shutter sequence; second, through the use of certain kinds of electroacoustic acousmatic music on the soundtrack; and third, through out-of-sync singing directly to the camera. The first and second of these routes to soundtrack liberation are closely related, since sounds with unseen sources can also be defined as acousmatic. The next section is concerned with the acousmatic listening situation, and explores the means by which it represents a liberatory potential for the soundtrack.

Acousmatic listening

The term *acousmatic* dates back to ancient Greece. During his lectures, Pythagoras concealed himself from his students by means of a curtain. He did this in order to assist his students in focusing their attention on his words rather than other less important sensory information, such as the necessary mediation of the body in speech. In a broader sense the term defines any listening situation in which the sources of the sounds are withheld or concealed from the sight of the auditor. The term was introduced into music theory in the 1960s by composer and theorist Pierre Schaeffer and his colleagues. Due to the profusion of radios, tape recordings, vinyl records, and so on, the acousmatic listening situation was, by then, ubiquitous.

While Schaeffer himself realized that the Pythagorean curtain would not be enough to discourage the instinctive curiosity that auditors have about a sound's source and/or cause, he argued that the acousmatic listening situation made favourable the potential for 'reduced listening' ('l'écoute reduite') (1967, p. 93). This involved discarding any knowledge of a sound's source and any symbolic meanings such sounds may have, and listening to the sound as an object in itself ('l'objet sonore'). Schaeffer's goal was to create a new musical language from sound, a task which resulted in the development of *musique concrète* – music built from altered and reorganized natural (real-world) sounds.[7] He saw advances in audio technology and the potential for the acousmatic listening situation that they enabled as a means for developing subjects' listening skills and, thus, their awareness of the music in all sound. John Dack (1994) suggests that it was probably as a result of his dealings with sound and sound effects as a radiophonic artist, rather than through music per se, that Schaeffer came to argue that it was possible for real-world sounds to transcend their causal origins and symbolic meanings and be listened to as 'sounding objects' ('les objets sonores').

Schaeffer began to investigate the relationship between a listening subject and the object of its perception under the acousmatic listening situation offered by radio and sound recording. He found that auditors were not particularly unsettled by listening to traditional music on the radio or a recording if they were familiar with the musical instruments of that culture.[8] Sounds used in radiophonic art heard under the same acousmatic conditions were less easily recognized due to the manipulation to which they were subject: mixing, amplification, juxtaposition and filtering, for example. From listening to these recorded and transformed real-world sounds in the studio, and by the isolating effects of recording very short fragments of sound and listening to them repeatedly, Schaeffer suggested that they could function beyond mere sound *effects*. He proposed that a wholly different experience could be created for the listener than that elicited by traditional musical instruments (with their easily recognizable sources) in terms of the relationship between a subject and a sound. In suppressing the support that vision gives to the identification of sound's sources, the acousmatic listening situation has the potential to cause the listener to misrecognize such sources. It also makes listening to sounds as sounding objects in their own right easier; that is, in terms of disregarding their sources and symbolic meanings.

Advances in sound-recording technology made it possible to isolate very short sequences or segments of sound by recording them and looping them together – either by means of a physical loop of tape, or, now, digitally – thus facilitating repeated listening. Repeated listening to a sounding object fixed by recording reveals that listening is not static and fixed but dynamic: repeated listening allows the focus of a listener's attention to be drawn to different aspects of a sounding object at different times. This potential, together with the juxtapositions made possible by radiophonic art, means that even quite prosaic sounds can be, in a sense, 'renewed', revealing new, multiple meanings.

The acousmatic listening situation covers a potentially huge range of sounds: from the presentation of real-world sounds, the sources of which are concealed from sight (as in the camera-shutter sequence), to that of wholly synthesized sounds. Following Luke Windsor, I shall use the term *acousmatic music* to define 'music that is recorded and then diffused without combination with live electronics or live performers; it exists only on tape (whether analog or digital) or as a fixed set of instructions to a computer'.[9] This definition also covers a potentially large range of electroacoustic music, from those works that present a montage of minimally transformed real-world sounds to those that present only wholly synthesized sounds. The soundtrack to *The Garden* uses both transformed-but-recognizable real-world sounds (for example, fingers around the rims of wineglasses, the slowed-down sounds of rocks hitting concrete, flares, manipulated camera-shutter sounds) and sounds that have been generated wholly by synthesis (such as the pulsating harmonic sound of the film's opening credit sequence, and the sound that succeeds it, which is focused on a single pitch). At times both types are combined with sounds produced by traditional musical instruments.

When transformed-but-recognizable real-world sounds are presented in *The Garden*, the original sources of the sounds are usually seen on screen simultaneously, thus assisting spectators with source recognition. With sounds which are less recognizably real-world derived, the image works to propose feasible source objects in an attempt to conceal their acousmatic character. This is particularly true of their first presentation on the soundtrack. For example, the second sustained acousmatic sound used in the film – which I will refer to as sound B – is presented in sync with a close-up of a six-spot lighting rig, the implication being that the sound issues from the rig. Seconds later, a repetitive rhythmic pulsing that could be the sound of a heartbeat is heard. Its very first rhythms are heard in sync with the impact of droplets of water dripping onto a phallic rock located within the image. The liberatory potential of the soundtrack is contained by the image in a manner similar to the way in which the (unseen) real-world sounds presented during the camera-shutter sequence are contained. After their first appearance on the soundtrack, however, examples of acousmatic sound and music often recur during the film without visual reference to plausible sources.

The recognition and differentiation of sounds is made more difficult again by the close sonic relationship between several of the sustained acousmatic sounds, which are often heard layered on top of one another. For example, just under six minutes into the film we are presented with an image of a chair burning on a bonfire on Dungeness beach in front of the power station. The soundtrack at this point comprises the diegetic sound of the burning chair, sound B (heard earlier in connection with the lighting rig) and a new electroacoustic sound (sound C). This last sound is perhaps best described in terms of an oscillatory motion: it is repetitive – a sound that fades in, is sustained, and fades out again at regular intervals. It has a high proportion of broadband noise within it and so also bears a strong resemblance to the sound of the flares (signal lights) and of the sea, both of which are frequently seen and heard during the film. About 15 seconds after the first presentation of this sound we see the image of a radar tracking device for the first time. Its motion matches that described by sound C closely enough to imply that the sound's source has now been located by the camera. With the visual presentation of the tracking device, however, a louder, pitched sound is superimposed on top of sound C. This sound (sound D) also matches the oscillatory motion of the tracking device, but is only heard when the tracking device is seen on screen. The image moves between shots of a boy playing near a washing line and the radar tracking device, combining diegetic sound (the boy hitting the washing with some bracken from the beach) with sound B and the pitched sound (D) associated with the tracking device. The diegetic sound and

**Illustration 5.2   The source of the oscillatory wine glass sound (*The Garden*)
Photo: Liam Daniel, courtesy Basilisk Communications Ltd**

sound D are faded out when a shot of a table in Jarman's garden is seen, followed by a shot of another table (that of the Last Supper) around which women in black are seated, moving their fingers around the rims of wineglasses (Illustration 5.2). The sound created by this action (which is first heard in sync with the appearance of its apparent source) bears a strong resemblance to both sound B and sound D, but is also related to sound C by virtue of its oscillatory motion. The sound of waves lapping against the shore is also heard, while the image includes the superimposition of a boat sailing on the sea in the background, behind the table.[10] Here, then, similarities between sounds work against attempts to locate feasible source objects within the image.

While Schaeffer's concept of reduced listening (mentioned above) may be a useful tool in terms of compositional technique and the development of new musical languages, it does not provide an accurate account of listeners' actual experience of acousmatic sound and music. Drawing on psychoacoustics and ecological psychology, several more recent theorists of listening argue that acousmatic sound and music is not only potentially threatening to the image because it denies sound–image unity, but also because listeners are predisposed to search out and identify the sources of sounds presented to them, both in terms of general perception and musical listening, and are thus unable to separate a sound from its source.[11] What happens when this natural inclination is frustrated? Such matters are of central importance with acousmatic music. Wholly synthesized, or maximally transformed real-world sounds that display behaviours not reminiscent of any real-world sounds may confound a listener's natural predisposition to locate and identify these sounds' sources.

Luke Windsor (1995) suggests that a descriptive theory of acousmatic music which takes into account a listener's perceptual response to everyday sounds offers a more accurate representation of a subject's understanding of this music. Windsor argues that an ecological approach to perception, which assumes a direct and dynamic relationship between a subject and its environment, is appropriate to the task,[12] He extends and reinterprets the ecological position to include socially and culturally defined phenomena as environmental materials directly perceivable by an organism.

Ecological psychology proposes that perception is unmediated by mental representations of the external world. It describes a direct relationship between the receiver and her/his environment, in which the environment is structured and organisms are directly sensitive to this structure. Organisms' perceptual systems evolve to pick up information which will increase their chances of survival. The dynamic relationship between the organism and its environment 'is seen to provide the grounds for the direct perception of meaning' (Windsor 1995, p. 58). Gibson defines this direct perception of meaning as 'affordance'. That is, certain objects and events 'afford' certain possibilities for action; for example, a chair affords being sat upon. Affordances differ according to the organism and are also dynamic in terms of individual perceptual development. Thus, affordance describes the 'relationship between a particular environmental structure and a particular organism's needs and capacities' (ibid.).

Windsor argues that, in terms of acousmatic music, events, rather than sounds, should be considered to be the primary units of auditory perception. Thus, in terms of describing musical structure, pertinence would be defined by the events perceived in the acoustic structure of the music rather than by more abstract musical categories such as rhythm.[13] Windsor and the other authors cited above dispute the possibility of a mode of listening in which the auditor is wholly freed from her/his natural predisposition to search out and identify sounds in terms of the events (and thus also sources) that cause them. The pull of this hard-wired inclination is too strong to ignore completely. Thus, if an auditor is unable to identify the event that caused a particular sound, the implication is that he/she will feel some degree of discomfort.

Smalley (1994) proposes that without the presence of 'gesture' in music (and thus, at some level, the mediation of the human body), listeners are alienated. The development of electroacoustic acousmatic music has, for the first time in history, resulted in a music in which the obligation of bodily mediation is undone. Before this situation arose, the presence of the human body, whether as sounding body in itself or as mediating agency, was mandatory in the realization of all instrumental and vocal music. Smalley argues that behind the causality of human gesture inherent in traditional musical performance lie, first, a more general sense of physical gesture and 'its proprioceptive tensions' and, second, 'a deeper, psychological experience of gesture' (p. 39). In order to describe the different strengths of the relationship between acts of human gesture and sounds in music (acousmatic or traditional) Smalley creates the concept of gestural surrogacy.

First order surrogacy describes instrumental gestures that 'stand-in-for' non-musical, physical gestures. For example, the bowing of a stringed instrument implies the necessity of a physical gesture in order to produce the sound. The possibility of *second order surrogacy* is a result of the development of electroacoustic music techniques, in which traces of human gesture are maintained by sound alone. At the far end of the spectrum lies *remote order surrogacy*, in which links between sources/causes and sounds have been severed, as in the case of maximally transformed real-world sounds and wholly synthesized sounds in acousmatic music: access to gesture is not mediated by (and cannot be located in) the timbre of the sound. Here, gestures are maintained only in terms of their translation into the energy/motion field, which may then be interpreted in terms of psychological states or gestures, though neither a specific gesture type nor source can be identified. When all reference to gesture has been dissipated – whether that be actual bodily gesture, a more general sense of gesture, or psychological gesture – there is nothing for the listener to grasp: '[listeners] may feel as if "observing" invisible phenomena displayed on a screen or in a space' (Smalley 1992, p. 525). Thus, the presence of the human trace in music through history still weighs heavily on musical listening.

Conventional nondiegetic film music that uses recognizable musical instruments does not threaten the reality of the diegesis in the way that electroacoustic acousmatic music does because, on the one hand, its presence is conventional, and on the other, listeners recognize the mediation of the human body in its production. In the case of the transformed real-world sounds and wholly synthesized sounds on the soundtrack to *The Garden*, spectators tend to accept the false yet 'feasible' real-world sources proposed by the image. As a result, they are protected from the potential danger posed by the presence of acousmatic music and sound.

I suggested above that the presentation of sounds while concealing or withholding their sources has the potential to destabilize the dogma of the image in film theory's model of the sound–image and –narrative relationship of the classical Hollywood film. Part of this relationship involves convincing the audience of the 'reality' of the filmic diegesis. If sound does not confirm the veridicality of the image by being visibly synchronous with it, it holds the potential to undermine the image as the most truthful source of knowledge. Although, to a certain extent, all film sound and music falls into the category of the acousmatic – not only is it distributed by loudspeakers situated behind the screen and at various points around the auditorium, much of it is also recorded separately from the image, with the soundtrack only synchronized to the image at a fairly late stage in post-production in many cases – classical film sound usually denies its acousmatic character: to do otherwise would be to admit the separately manufactured nature of the sound–image complex in film, and thus deny the 'reality' of the diegetic world, revealing its mechanical, technological origin.

In *The Garden* the image works to present feasible real-world source objects for the electroacoustic acousmatic music, and also offers a number of synchronized sound sequences, in order to conceal the separately manufactured nature of the soundtrack. Cracks are left to gape unfilled, however: there is a profusion of acousmatic music which is only accompanied by the appearance of a feasible real-world source at its first presentation on the soundtrack; there is a lack of on-screen dialogue; and there are a number of out-of-sync sung performances. The remainder of this chapter addresses the film's several (apparently) live sung performances and explains how Jarman's referencing of Stanley Donen's 1956 film musical *Funny Face* assists in presenting a reappraisal of the camera and, consequently, the image.

Singing in *The Garden*

There are three occasions when characters are seen to sing whole songs or song verses within the screen's frame. Two of these sung performances – 'God Rest Ye Merry Gentlemen' and the excerpt from 'La donna e mobile' (from Verdi's opera

Rigoletto) – continue the action of the central narrative, which is, as mentioned above, concerned broadly with the story of the Passion.[14] They are sung a cappella by the policemen and are directed to the gay couple (who share the role of Jesus with a more traditional, bearded, robe-wearing performer). The policemen do not actively engage or address the camera. The spectator is constituted as one who overhears the performance.

The other sung performance in the film – 'Think Pink' by Roger Edens – occupies a more ambiguous position in relation to the central narrative;[15] it disrupts rather than furthers the film's narrative exposition. The song is sung by Jessica Martin, who does not appear in any other role during the film. The gay couple appear in the frame with her for a few seconds, wearing pink suits and cradling a baby, but the song is sung *on behalf of* or *with* the couple, rather than *to* them. It is addressed, instead – with Jessica Martin's look – to the camera and spectator, and is accompanied by a (nondiegetic) chamber orchestra and chorus, who perform Dean Broderick's arrangement of the song from *Funny Face*.

It is useful to consider these three performances as falling into the following two groups: performance as spectacle and performance as denial, with the former exemplified by 'Think Pink' and the latter by the policemen's singing. In performance as denial a negative function of performance is foregrounded, in particular its use as a mechanism for shutting out an unwanted relationship with the external world, thus creating an invisible barrier around the performer. Performance in this context is marked by the performer's unwillingness and consequent inability to hear anything but her- or himself. It is often used to indicate fear and/or obstinacy and impertinence on the part of the protagonist. Comparable examples can be found in both opera and film; for instance, Bizet's *Carmen* (1874) and Tom Shadyac's *Liar, Liar* (1997). When Captain Zuninga attempts to question Carmen about the fight at the factory, not only does she not answer his questions, she refuses to acknowledge that she has heard them by starting to sing a song instead: 'Tra-la-la-la-la-la-la-la.' When, in *Liar, Liar*, Jim Carrey's lawyer character realizes he is unable to tell lies anymore, he places his hands over his ears and begins to sing loudly to facilitate an escape from his offices without destroying his career. Similarly, the policemen's singing in *The Garden* is a defence mechanism – protecting them from any response the couple might make – but also an attempt to threaten and humiliate through the use of their voices and music as weapons. Furthermore, on both occasions when the policemen sing, the gay couple are unable to respond. On the first occasion – 'God Rest Ye Merry Gentlemen' – they are asleep (Illustration 5.3); on the second – 'La donna e mobile' – they have been bound and gagged, then tarred and feathered (Illustration 5.4). It is as though the policemen need to make doubly sure that they can protect themselves from the couple's reply. The couple's fate is thus decided by the media's vehement desire to prevent them from speaking: to make them die in silence.[16]

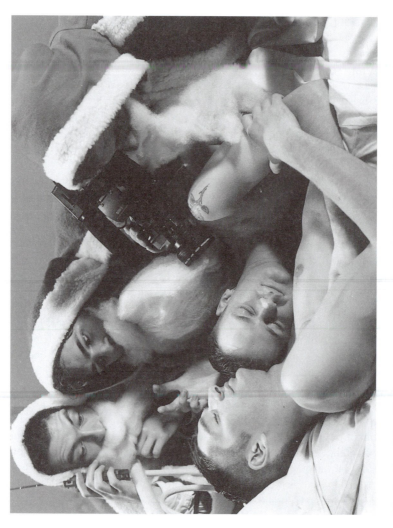

Illustration 5.3 'God rest ye merry gentlemen' (*The Garden*)
Photo: Liam Daniel, courtesy Basilisk Communications Ltd

Illustration 5.4 'La donna e mobile' (*The Garden*)
Photo: Liam Daniel, courtesy Basilisk Communications Ltd

'Think Pink': Performance as spectacle

During the sequence in Stanley Donen's *Funny Face* in which 'Think Pink' originally features, Miss Prescott (Kay Thompson) is complaining about the as yet unissued next edition of *Quality Magazine*, which 'doesn't speak'. As she does so – 'd for dreary, d for dull and for depressing, dismal, and deadly' – she places in her mouth a cigarette, which is subsequently lit by one of her fussing editorial assistants who strikes the match on a piece of pink card. Suddenly Miss Prescott alights on the theme that the issue lacks: 'Pink!' (Cue song). The song's lyrics take the form of an editorial – 'Letty, take an editorial!' – which is itself a call to women everywhere to ditch every other available colour in favour of pink. Pink suits every occasion, activity, time of day and social class. Miss Prescott even suggests that readers should 'try pink shampoo' and 'pink toothpaste too'. The first segment of the song is sung by Kay Thompson, who sings to the camera, addressing the internal audience formed by her entourage. The final section (a return to the music of the first) is sung and danced to camera by Kay Thompson and her entourage (augmented by a number of painters and decorators). The middle segment of the song is sung by a chorus of unseen female singers (who appear, in retrospect, to be Miss Prescott's editorial assistants). It is accompanied by a sequence of shots of photo-shoot material that have been edited together into a collection, and which will provide the photographs for the 'pink' feature. The sequence uses images which have been generated by state-of-the-art trick-shot filmmaking.[17]

In *The Garden's* version of 'Think Pink' (Illustration 5.5) the apparent lip-synchronization is clearly and deliberately out-of-sync at certain points, perhaps indicating nostalgia for the earlier, more innocent time of the Hollywood musical. To a certain extent this performance acknowledges the artifice of its construction, both in terms of the poor lip-synchronization and the address of Jessica Martin's performance directly into the camera.[18] As Jane Feuer (1982) has pointed out, the direct address to camera is a means used by both the film musical and the avant-garde to achieve radically different ends: in the latter it is a technique of modernist alienation, in the former it encourages audience identification. Feuer argues that it is the tradition of its particular contextualization which decides the resulting effect. Direct address in the film musical encourages identification due to the genre's evolution from earlier models of live entertainment such as the music hall, and the subsequent incorporation of its forerunner's live audience into the frame (though over time the presence of this internal audience on screen became redundant due to its conventionalization). As a modernist technique of the avant-garde, the direct address works against identification. It generates alienation and distance instead through the audience's recognition of both the presence of the apparatus, and of the film as product created with an audience in mind.

It is perhaps a result of Jarman's partial, yet uneasy, alignment with both of

Illustration 5.5   'Think Pink' (*The Garden*)
Photo: Liam Daniel, courtesy Basilisk Communications Ltd

these traditions that 'Think Pink' functions to encourage identification to a certain degree, while also incorporating a distancing effect. The spectator is constituted as the live audience of both a spontaneous musical performance and a technologically generated, materially heterogeneous filmic discourse. It is in this gap exposed between sound and image, manifested at the material level in the out-of-sync singing to camera, that a space is created for the soundtrack to speak its own voice.

The act of recontextualizing 'Think Pink' by performing it in *The Garden* appropriates the song as an anthem for gay liberation: footage from marches and demonstrations for this cause are projected onto the blue-screen behind Jessica Martin; relatedly, Broderick's arrangement of the song foregrounds elements of military music, such as the use of snare and bass drums in march rhythms and trumpet fanfares. There is subtle and camp humour, resulting primarily from the irony created by transplanting the song wholesale from the context of a 1950s fashion magazine's call to action to that of a Jarman film concerned with issues that include the persecution of homosexuals. The line 'Who cares if the new look has no bust' is a case in point, since, in this context 'thinking pink' distinctly implies a 'lack' in that department! More interesting, however, in terms of this recontextualization, is Jarman's reappraisal of the camera as representative of the media.

Donen's film is set in the world of fashion photography. Several of its musical numbers – including 'Funny Face' and 'Bonjour Paris' – allude to this world in their use of state-of-the-art camera trickery (the film won an Oscar for its photography). *Funny Face* makes reference to its photographic heritage and fetishizes the camera. Jarman also references this heritage in *The Garden*, not by using state-of-the-art technology, but rather through the use of the relatively low-fi Super-8mm camera and its characteristic facilities, such as mobility. This camera, launched by Kodak in 1965 and widely available, was marketed as a home-movie camera. It was smaller, cheaper and easier to use than its competitors, and included features such as an automatic light meter. Jarman exploited such ease-of-use features for other, more creative purposes, producing blurred, grainy, dream-like images. Furthermore, by purporting to use a soundtrack recorded at the same time as these images, Jarman placed the camera *itself* on to the soundtrack in *The Garden* – the sounds of both stills cameras and the Super-8mm are featured prominently. So, *The Garden* also references its photographic heritage, but does so without idolizing the camera. Whereas in *Funny Face*, Dick Avery's (Fred Astaire's) camera was necessary to transform Jo Stockton (Audrey Hepburn) from an 'ugly duckling' into an object of desire – to liberate her latent beauty – in *The Garden* cameras become the tools of aggression and invasion. This transformation is also exemplified by the sound team's foregrounding of these sounds in the mix and the manipulation of their diegetic sounds.

This reappraisal of the camera both portrays the renewed vigour of tabloid journalism's persecution of homosexuality since the AIDS crisis and also comments upon the photographic and cinematic representation of homosexuals and people with AIDS: it suggests that the British media are unable to present a positive picture – in both senses of both terms – of the person with AIDS that is not invasive and aggressive. As Paul Julian Smith asks: 'How can film represent an invisible virus whose transmission cannot be seen and whose carriers have been subject to hostile surveillance and revelation?' (1993, p. 18). By referencing *Funny Face,* Jarman is able to demonstrate how the role of the camera had changed from that of a liberating force, to a tool of surveillance, disclosure and persecution. In light of this reassessment, the camera could not then be used to present the testimony of those who are HIV-positive.

It is possible to intepret the final film Jarman completed before his death, *Blue* (1993), as a logical step forward from *The Garden,* in particular in terms of the relationship between sound and image. *Blue* grew out of a fascination with the work of painter Yves Klein, especially his *Symphonie Monotone.*[19] O'Pray describes the first presentation of what was later to be developed into the film:

> At a special AIDS benefit screening of *The Garden* at the London Lumière cinema on 6 January 1991, Jarman and Tilda Swinton put on a pre-screening event entitled 'Symphonie Monotone'. They sat at a table on stage creating sounds by running their moistened fingers around the rim of wine glasses, as in the Last Supper sequence of *The Garden,* and recited passages from various writers on the theme of 'blue'. On the cinema screen was projected a 35mm film of a detail from an Yves Klein blue painting shot at the Tate Gallery. At various points slide images were projected on to the blue field. Sitting on the floor before the stage was a group of musicians led by Simon [Fisher-] Turner playing gentle, almost hippie-style music. Now and then the young boy actor from *The Garden* would run out into the audience with small blue and gold painted stones which he gave to individuals. The whole performance lasted about an hour and was mesmeric, a reminder of the range of Jarman's reference points.[20]

The narrative of *Blue* traces the onset of Jarman's blindness. The image presented by the film remains the same throughout: a blue screen, created by film-processing techniques. *Blue* confirms the acousmatic character of film sound by filling the screen with the colour blue, preventing any attempt to propose that the source of the film's soundtrack lies within the image. In this way, *Blue* offers the total liberation of the soundtrack, presented as a potential in *The Garden.* Similarly, in John Greyson's AIDS film musical *Zero Patience* (1993) – made in the same year as *Blue* – an attempt is made to recuperate the voice of the person with AIDS, as well as that of the disease itself, in the form of (soprano) Miss HIV.[21]

In *The Garden,* the soundtrack bears witness to the media's aggression toward and persecution of those with AIDS, linking the camera directly to codes of persecution. Attempts are made to liberate the soundtrack from the image through the use of acousmatic electroacoustic music and sound, but the threat of these efforts is contained and denied by the image through the proposal of feasible real-world sources on the first appearance of each new sound, for example. Jarman also proposes that the Establishment – in the form of the Church, law enforcement agencies, and so on – is unable to hear the voices either of people with AIDS or of homosexuals because it is itself making too much noise in self-defence. Nevertheless, *The Garden* is not without hope, for it highlights the potential of the soundtrack as a liberating force, able to undermine the dogma of the camera, and thus the image.

In its possible liberation from the image, the soundtrack of *The Garden* presents the potential for the reparation of these communities' voices – a potential that is more fully offered by *Blue*.[22] Furthermore, this liberation from the image happens not only in the recontextualization of 'Think Pink,' but also in a number of other sequences in the film. For instance, in one musical interlude (a caricature which draws on the aesthetic of television commercials) a character addresses the camera directly and introduces what he calls 'credit card day', a day in celebration of consumerism.[23] The music of this sequence is ironic: it is emphatically tonal and orchestrated in a somewhat saccharine manner with a generous helping of harp glissandi. This sequence both identifies the spectator as part of a live audience of a spontaneous performance and simultaneously alienates him/her from the diegetic world by revealing the filmmaking apparatus. Furthermore, the sound is out-of-sync with the image, which results in the rupture of the sound–image unity proposed by classical Hollywood cinema. Another example of this occurs in the performance of a flamenco dance, throughout which the sound is slightly out-of-sync with the image, and in which the performer addresses the camera directly.[24]

In *The Garden*, Jarman, Fisher-Turner and Broderick, together with various members of the sound team (notably Holland, Black and Fettes) demonstrate that the soundtrack and image track of a film need not be unified. Liberated from the image, the soundtrack is able to speak for a minority community which has suffered much through the hostile surveillance and revelations of the tabloid media.

Notes

1. Dungeness is situated on the south Kent coast. Jarman made a home there in a beachcomber cottage (Prospect Cottage) in the late 1980s. The garden he created there has become infamous, and something of a source of pilgrimage since Jarman's death. See Jarman and Sooley 1996.
2. There are also sections that deal briefly with Christ's early life, though in a contemporary setting: one with Madonna and child, and another with a young boy and a man, which Michael O'Pray suggests might portray the young Jesus and Joseph (1996, p. 11).
3. Some of these home movies appeared in later Jarman features, including *The Last of England* (1987), and also in a music video made for Wang Chung's 'Dance Hall

Daze' (1983).

4. As Chris Lippard suggests: 'Although his own expertise developed over the course of his career, he continued to rely on the skill of his collaborators both behind and in front of the camera, thus drawing out ideas that might otherwise have remained unspoken' (1996, p. 3).

5. As Michael O'Pray points out, however, it should also be noted that 'Jarman's films have often been problematic for the gay press. His sado-masochistic rendering of homosexuality was seen as a narrow view of homosexual relations and he was never a gay filmmaker in the sense of being a balanced spokesman for gay issues' (1996, p. 11).

6. I am very grateful to James Mackay (producer of *The Garden*) for discussing the genesis of the soundtrack with me in some detail (personal communication, 19 November 2002). See also Young 1996 for more discussion of the collaborative working practices of Simon Fisher-Turner and Derek Jarman on this film.

7. Schaeffer's work was radically different from the German school of electroacoustic and electronic music which was based in studios at Cologne. There his contemporaries, such as Karlheinz Stockhausen, were interested primarily in composing music from sounds that they had created ab initio.

8. Though this is less true of some twentieth- and twenty-first-century music that involves extended techniques of playing, for example. Here, listeners' expectations of what an instrument can do – the range of sounds by which it is recognized – are manipulated, often making recognition of the sound's source very difficult.

9. Windsor 1995, p. 5. See also Windsor 2000 for a summary of the ideas presented in Windsor 1995.

10. This backdrop was shot on video and matted in; see O'Pray 1996, p. 179.

11. Christianne Ten Hoopen states that '[w]e are naturally inclined (like animals) to relate sounds we perceive to what might have caused them, especially with sounds unfamiliar to us or when sounds occur in unexpected circumstances' (1994, p. 61). Similarly, Trevor Wishart argues that 'studies of behaviour and aural physiology would suggest that our mental apparatus is predisposed to allocate sounds to their sources' (1985, p. 70). On the bonding of sources with sounds, Denis Smalley states that we have a 'natural tendency to relate sounds to supposed sources and causes, and relate sounds to each other because they appear to have shared or associated origins' (1994, p. 37).

12. For a Gibsonian view of ecological approaches to perception, see Gibson 1966 and 1979.

13. Though Windsor also warns against neglecting musical context.

14. These performances take place at approximately 46 and 57 minutes into the film, respectively.

15. This performance occurs approximately 28 minutes into the film.

16. This phrasing is a reference to the refrain from Michael Gough's final voice-over in *The Garden*: 'They die so silently . . . you die so silently . . . we die so silently . . . I die so silently.'

17. This segment of the song (and the first part of the final section) is absent in Jarman's version; a short transition passage is added in its stead.

18. The out-of-sync character of this performance was the result of contingent factors which affected the production of the sequence. Having watched a video of *Funny Face* during the production period, Jarman wanted to record the 'Think Pink' sequence with Jessica Martin the next day. Martin's vocals were recorded to the original arrangement of the Edens song from the soundtrack album of the film. However, the production budget was not large enough to cover the copyright costs

to use the arrangement of the song as it appeared in *Funny Face*. The film's producer, James Mackay, bought use of the melody alone and asked Dean Broderick to rearrange the accompaniment. Broderick recorded this arrangement in the studio to fit with Martin's already-recorded vocal line. When Martin came to record her visual performance in front of the blue-screen, she mimed to her own already recorded version of the vocals here accompanied by Broderick's arrangement of the music. (Personal communication from Mackay, 19 November, 2002.)

19.   According to the exhibition catalogue *Yves Klein 1928–1962: A Retrospective* (Institute for the Arts, Rice University, Houston in association with The Arts Publisher, Inc.; New York, 1982) the score for Klein's *Symphonie Monotone* – and its other basic form, *Symphonie Monotone-Silence* – dates from 1947, although recorded performances did not take place until *c*. 1960 (p. 348). 'The exhibited score directs that a D-major triad be sounded by twenty voices and thirty-two instruments for five to seven minutes, followed by forty-four seconds of absolute silence. There is evidence that a musician, Pierre Henry, scored this work for Klein. The two basic forms of the piece – the *Monotone-Silence Symphony* and the *Monotone Symphony* – are orchestrated with various numbers of instruments and voices' (p. 348).

20.   O'Pray 1996, p. 201. The fact that this event took place before an AIDS benefit screening of *The Garden* strengthens the connection between the two films which I suggest here. Though Jarman made *Edward II* (1991) and *Wittgenstein* (1992) between *The Garden* and *Blue*, both of the former films were commissions: *Edward II* for the BBC, and *Wittgenstein* for Bandung (for Channel 4), with extra finance from the British Film Institute. Jarman spent several years raising the funds to make *The Garden*. The film and radio play of *Blue* were finally made for Channel 4 and BBC Radio 3, though Jarman had developed the project over several years.

21.   See Pearl 2000.

22.   The idea that *Blue* presents a liberation of the film soundtrack is further supported by the fact that Fisher-Turner and a small band of musicians who had played on the original film soundtrack later performed live performances based on the film. These performances incorporated live music, recorded music and sound mixed live with the use of record decks and samplers, voice-overs by Derek Jarman among others, and also featured live projections of sequences of Super-8mm film. The results were recorded and released on an album, *Live Blue Roma* (Mute CDSTUMM149), which Mark Kermode described as a 'film soundtrack-as-rock-concert-album in which the sounds are culled, not from a movie, but from a live concert' (1995, p. 71).

23.   This sequence occurs approximately 20 minutes into the film.

24.   This sequence occurs approximately 32 minutes into the film.

Chapter 6

Music to desire by: the soundtrack to Wim Wenders's *Der Himmel über Berlin*

This chapter is concerned with the soundtrack to Wim Wenders's 1987 film *Der Himmel über Berlin* (with the English title *Wings of Desire*). An international co-production, set in Berlin, this film is a meditation on such issues as identity, history, Germany, memory, storytelling, displacement and desire.[1] In this chapter I argue that, as with many other films directed by Wenders, *Wings of Desire* also offers a self-reflexive contemplation on the nature of cinema, more particularly, on the relationship between Hollywood and European art-house cinema. Indeed, in order to understand Wenders's filmmaking, Timothy Corrigan suggests that it must be considered in terms of its dialogic relationship with Hollywood:

> While other directors share, willingly or not, Wenders' obsession with the social, artistic, and psychological presence of the American cinema within the German consciousness and theatres, few locate it so effectively and so regularly as the centre and persistent background for the argument of their films. (1994, p. 19)

I argue that the same is true of the score and soundtrack to *Wings of Desire*.

In the film different kinds of music are used to represent the ontological difference between the two realms depicted in the diegesis – the angelic and the mortal. Each of these musical languages also has a utopian function for a different subject: the film's music reflects the divergent utopian desires of the characters, director and audience. By means of an allegorical reading, I suggest that rock music is representative not only of the mortal realm but also of the potency of the Hollywood production-distribution system. By contrast, Western art music is associated with the angelic realm and the relative impotence of filmmaking outside Hollywood. The angel Damiel dreams of becoming mortal so that he can be present in the 'here and now' and have a story of his own, instead of cataloguing someone else's. However, in achieving this utopian dream Damiel loses his angelic privileges, such as the ability to walk through walls, and to over-see and overhear everything. If the allegorical reading is accepted, then Wenders valorizes the potency that Hollywood offers the non-Hollywood director, represented by mortal life in this film. However, working in Hollywood also incurs the loss of apparent omniscience which Wenders implies is granted to filmmaking outside of the Hollywood production system – that is, the opportunity to follow a single artistic vision without challenge – here represented by the angelic realm. *Wings of Desire* implies a link between classical Hollywood filmmaking and ocularcentrism on the one hand, and between alternative filmmaking practices and the valorization of listening over seeing, on the other. Ultimately, however, I argue that the soundtrack and scoring practices used in this film negotiate a compromise between classical and alternative scoring practices.

I begin the chapter by presenting an overview of Wenders's ambivalent relationship with American popular culture – in particular, rock music and classical cinema – as presented in his critical writing and his films. In particular, I trace the production history of the film Wenders directed in Hollywood, *Hammett* (1982), since *Wings of Desire* can be read as a response to this experience, on some level. This is followed by an introduction to Caryl Flinn's notion of film music as utopian, and the analysis of the score and soundtrack to *Wings of Desire*.

Wenders and Hollywood

> The Yanks have even colonized our subconscious.
> Said by a character in *Im Lauf der Zeit* (*Kings of the Road*) (Wenders, 1976)

Born in Germany shortly after the German surrender to Allied troops in 1945, Wenders grew up in a country occupied by American forces. During the mid-1960s he moved to Paris to become a painter, but soon became hooked on films, seeing 'three or four films a day, and at weekends up to seven' (Wenders 1989, p. vii). He began to make notes on the films that he saw, and was particularly interested in many of the same directors and genres as the critics of *Cahiers du Cinéma*: the Western, John Ford, Nicholas Ray, Douglas Sirk, Sam Fuller, Alfred Hitchcock, and indeed also the French filmmakers of the New Wave, such as François Truffaut and Jean-Luc Godard. When he returned to Germany and became one of the first students at the Munich *Hochschule für Fernsehen und Film* he continued to write about films and became a critic for *Filmkritik*.[2] Thus, as with so many of the directors of the French New Wave, Wim Wenders began his career in film as a critic with a particular admiration for American cinema of the 1940s and 1950s.

Wenders was drawn to what he saw as the 'tenderness' of the camera in Hollywood cinema of this period, and to a sense of physicality and experienced duration this cinema could express.[3] In this way, cinema could offer a redemption of sight, or ways of seeing. In many ways this has become the main focus of his aesthetic. He calls filmmaking a 'heroic' act which records and temporarily halts the 'gradual destruction of the world of appearances': 'The camera is a weapon against the tragedy of things, against their disappearing.'[4] He cites film theorist Béla Balázs: 'The possibility and the purpose of films is to show everything the way it is.'[5] In his filmmaking, he aspires to the innocent 'curiosity and lack of prejudice' that he attributes to children's perception.[6] Wenders has written of his unease with the relationship between images and stories.[7] In order to function as part of a story, images have to be 'forced' or manipulated. This can lead to 'narrative art', but more often, does not; instead, 'life' is sucked out of the images in question. Although he accepts the need for story structure in his films (and indeed as important to survival), it is clear that Wenders would rather show a series of images, leaving the connections to be made by the viewer; in a number of his early shorts he used a static camera, with a single focus and no imposition of narrative.[8]

Writing in 1970, Wenders draws attention to those instances in cinema which offer the same directness and concreteness of perception which elude Damiel until his fall to earth:

> There are some moments in films that are suddenly so unexpectedly direct and overwhelmingly concrete that you hold your breath or sit up or put your hand to your mouth. ... For a moment the film was a smell, a taste in the mouth, a tingle in the hands, a draught felt through a wet shirt, a children's book that you haven't seen since you were five years old, a blink of the eye.[9]

This ideal of pure perception hints at a kind of latent body-memory which bypasses conceptual thought. In his essays of the late 1960s and early 1970s, Wenders suggests that American rock and roll is able to generate this kind of perception more often than films.[10] Indeed, he argues that film should aspire to rock music of this period:

> The new thing about this music: it was pure pleasure.
> No cultural knowledge was required,
> only some sort of present, physical,
> simple and direct experience. That was new to me.[11]

In his youth Wenders considered rock and roll to be 'the only alternative to Beethoven ... because I was very insecure then about all culture that was offered to me, because I thought it was all fascism, pure fascism; and the only thing I was secure with from the beginning and felt had nothing to do with fascism was rock music.'[12] As with many other young people in Germany at this time, rock offered Wenders the possibility of self-expression and identity formation. While Nazi associations permeated the official *Kultur* of Austro-German art music, rock music was young enough to have avoided exploitation in this way. New German Cinema faced similar problems with the past. As Kolker and Beicken highlight in their study of Wenders's films:

> While the French used American film to do battle against the deadened images and petrified narratives of the [French] post-war Cinema of Quality, the Germans had no body of images and narratives to struggle against. More accurately, the images

they had were so inextricably tied to the past as to be useless to the imagination. (1993, p. 29)

Such images included those of the Nazi propaganda machine. Germany had grown suspicious of its sounds and images, turning to and 'swallow[ing] up all the foreign images it could, as long as they distracted it from itself'.[13] Wenders argues that no other country had experienced 'such a loss of faith in its own images, stories and myths as we have'.[14] To the filmmakers of the New German Cinema, American cinema thus offered a means of redeeming sight and the image.

The first generation of German filmmakers to challenge the old and search for these new images took radically Modernist approaches to filmmaking.[15] Filmmakers such as Alexander Kluge and Jean-Marie Straub sought to undermine cinematic conventions through direct confrontation and attempted to fight the passive consumption of films by making intellectually demanding works. Though these films were influential in the development of New German Cinema, they were not commercial and failed to gain a large audience. By contrast, Wenders and the otherwise eclectic collection of filmmakers which made up New German Cinema were united by a single goal: to re-establish that trust between the German public and the image, which Nazi propaganda had obliterated. Thus, instead of directly opposing the conventions of classical Hollywood cinema, the directors of the New German Cinema worked *with* them (though often in widely differing ways) in order to reach as large an audience as possible.[16] They drew heavily on the genres that Hollywood had perfected: the thriller, the road movie, the detective story, for example. American cinema of the 1940s and 1950s offered New German Cinema something to emulate, in order to encourage German audiences back into the cinemas to see films made in Germany about Germany. Certain elements of American cinema, in particular its distribution system, were considered deeply problematic by these filmmakers, however.

During 1966 Wenders worked in the administration offices of United Artists in Düsseldorf. He wrote a short essay about his experiences there: 'Despising What You Sell' (1969) (reprinted in Wenders 1989, pp. 36–7). Here Wenders expresses his anger at an industry which appeared to despise both its goods and its customers. Films were discussed 'as if they were new potatoes or meat prices' (p. 36), and chains of cinemas could pick and choose their films, but small suburban cinema-owners were forced to 'book films and carry out contracts that guaranteed bankruptcy' (ibid.). Wenders found the same to be true of the films themselves: 'The films I saw ... were almost always a continuation of what I had experienced during the day in the distribution office. And vice versa: the distribution system was only an extension of the films that kept it going. From production to distribution, the same violence was at work' (p. 37). As a result, with the notable exception of *Hammett* (discussed in more detail below) Wenders has worked hard to produce and distribute his own films independently.[17]

Although Wenders sees America as a country in love with images, he believes that this proliferation of images is damaging to (cinematic) vision. Recent Hollywood films no longer desire to tell stories or have something to say. Instead they 'ambush ... daze ... blind' and take their form from commercials: '*advertising* is easy: you don't have to have anything to say as long as what is said and shown sounds good and looks impressive' (p. 138). Such films tell viewers exactly what they must see, and in doing so, perform an act of violence.[18] Indeed, he argues that, '[o]nly European cinema is capable of maintaining dignity and morality in a savage cacophony of images, is capable of stemming the avalanche that's heading our way'.[19] While the filmmakers of the New German Cinema found an efficient means of storytelling, corporeal qualities and the possibility of reaching a large audience in golden age Hollywood cinema, it was also important for them to distance themselves from this cinema in some way.[20] The extent to which New German Cinema achieved this can be measured by the success of a number of these films, such as Wenders's 1977 film *Der amerikanische Freund* (*The American Friend*), in both America *and* Germany. In an ironic twist, some of these films were *so* well-received in America that their directors were invited to work in Hollywood. Indeed, this happened to Wenders. After seeing *The American Friend* Francis Ford Coppola invited him to direct a film in Hollywood at his own American Zoetrope Studios. Wenders's film had featured his favourite maverick American film directors – Samuel Fuller, Nicolas Ray and Dennis Hopper – and provided a commentary on the ambivalent relationship that Wenders had developed toward America and Hollywood. These directors (and others such as John Ford) represented a tension that Wenders believed was possible within the Hollywood system. Perhaps that is why he agreed to make Coppola's film about the author of hard-boiled detective stories, Dashiell Hammett. However, from the first tests to release, *Hammett* took four years to make. The experience left Wenders somewhat damaged.

When Wenders entered the Hollywood industry with *Hammett* he became part of a system in which the distribution of his work – and the potential to reach a large audience – was more or less guaranteed. He was also guaranteed a sizeable budget, though he was not able to find out how much of it he was using. The production system planned and scheduled the shooting of every scene, and thus took away the autonomy Wenders had enjoyed as an independent producer of his own work. Wenders believes that the film was ruined by over-preparation. First there had been a radio version scripted by Tom Pope, which Wenders had directed and which starred Sam Shepard and Gene Hackman. This had then been made into a storyboard, which was in turn made into a video, accompanied by the radio-track. By the time the video was complete Wenders says that they were 'completely fed up with the film'. At which point Coppola scrapped the script they had been using and told them to start again from scratch.

In the event I made two *Hammetts*. First I filmed and edited a version by Dennis

O'Flaherty – he was the third scriptwriter we used. There was only the ending still to do, less than ten minutes. And then Francis Ford [Coppola] said once more: we'll start again, hire a new scriptwriter and he can use some of the existing scenes. And that's what happened. The next writer, Ross Thomas, retained about four or five scenes and re-wrote everything else. I re-shot the film in just four weeks. In the final edit, we used about 30 percent of the original version and 70 percent of the new one.[21]

Wenders made three films which were direct responses to his experience in Hollywood. Two were documentaries – *Reverse Angle: NYC March '82* (1982), *Chambre 666* (1982) – and the third was a fiction film written and directed by Wenders – *Der Stand Der Dinge* (*Hammett: The State of Things*) (1982). This latter film retold his experience of the making of *Hammett* through the eyes of a fictional filmmaker, Friedrich.[22] However, rather than offering a simple denunciation of Hollywood, the film implies that some kind of compromise between art and commerce must be met in order to assure the survival of other, more personal, or subjective cinemas. Kolker and Beicken interpret the film as 'a cry of anger at an unresponsive industry and at an artistic temperament that cannot yield to that industry', and suggest that it is the most 'insightful film about filmmaking since Godard's *Contempt* [*Le Mepris*]' (1993, p. 95).

The first part of the film follows a director, Friedrich, and a film crew as they make 'The Survivors' on location. The second section shows the crew stranded in their hotel in Portugal as they await the money needed to finish the film.[23] The producer (Gordon) returns to Los Angeles, seemingly to find the necessary finance. The final part of the film follows Friedrich's search for Gordon in Los Angeles, after he has realized that he and his film have been abandoned. *The State of Things* avoids all the conventional narrative elements that Coppola and *Hammett*'s financiers persuaded Wenders to adopt in his reshoot of the latter film. According to Wenders, originally *Hammett* had used mainly long shots, which gave the film a slow, even meditative pace. At the studio's request he reshot the film so that it could be cut to a 'tempo ... to American taste'.[24] By contrast, *The State of Things* used mainly single (that is, few reverse) shots filmed in black and white, avoided linear narrative, and had a predominantly slow tempo, particularly in the middle section of the film, during which the crew wait in their hotel.

Friedrich is depicted as an aesthetic purist, who wants to avoid the manipulation of storytelling, but rather than celebrating this, the film rebukes his character for the uncompromising stand that he takes: Friedrich appears cold and distant in relation to the film's other characters. In particular, in contrast to Friedrich, Gordon (the producer) is depicted as 'a witty and spirited character, a storyteller, and indeed more streetwise and full of life than anyone in Wenders's films' (Kolker and Beicken 1993, p. 105). Ultimately, Friedrich's unwillingness to compromise aesthetically and his 'feign[ing] ignorance of cinema's economic realities' leads to the downfall of both characters (ibid.).

Wenders does not attack Hollywood indiscriminately, however. Rather, as

Kolker and Beicken point out, his view is suggestive of the Frankfurt School's deeply pessimistic view of the all-powerful culture industry. However, as a film director who valorizes both American cinema and popular music yet seeks to 'desire to protect cinema from the subversive powers of the culture industry', this is an awkward position for him to assume. They explain:

> For Wenders, the choice (in retrospect) was clear. He needed a way to condemn and compromise, to rail against the fascism hidden in the spirit of commercial filmmaking and continue to be a commercial filmmaker at the same time. He had to accommodate both Friedrich, who, like himself, was insisting upon just and valid images, and Gordon, who, like Francis Coppola, is driven to make commercially viable film. (Kolker and Beicken 1993, pp. 109–10)

Although Roger Cook states that 'by contrast to *The State of Things*, *Wings of Desire* is not, of course, about the filmmaking process' (1997, p. 163), I suggest that Wenders's *Wings of Desire* may indeed, on one level at least, be read as an allegory of the director's ambivalence toward Hollywood.[25] The soundtrack and score play an important role in this.

Wings of Desire

The film's narrative is concerned with two angels, Damiel and Cassiel, who observe people living and working in Berlin in the mid-1980s. We follow the angels as they float all over the city: in and out of apartments, vehicles, a film set. Neither the Berlin Wall nor the human body are experienced as boundaries by the angels: they walk through the Wall and have unlimited access to their charges' thoughts. In this sense they have a kind of omniscience. However, sensuality proves to be a very real barrier to them. Damiel has grown tired of being able only to watch and catalogue the sensuous experiences and feelings of mortals. He longs to experience them for himself. He becomes drawn to Marion, a lonely trapeze artist working in a circus, who yearns to find an identity and to be loved. The actor Peter Falk (playing 'himself') is also in Berlin, making a film about the Second World War. Falk happens to be an ex-angel and attempts to recruit Damiel to mortality when he senses the angel watching over him at a refreshments stand. He tells him that he wishes he could see him and tell him how great mortal life is. Shortly after this experience Damiel tells Cassiel the sensory experiences he would like to have on his first day as a mortal. As he does so he starts to leave visible footprints in the ground and is fleshed out in colour film: at this moment, Damiel descends from eternity to mortal life. He goes in search of Peter Falk in order to reveal himself and gain knowledge about human life, but Falk tells him that he has to find out for himself: 'That's the fun of it!' Damiel searches for Marion, only to find that the circus has left Berlin. He refuses to give up hope of finding her and later returns to the Esplanade, the music venue where he had previously watched her dance and where the band who recorded the song he heard her sing along to are playing (Nick Cave and the Bad Seeds, also playing 'themselves'). Damiel and Marion are finally united at the bar.[26]

Wenders portrays neither the angelic nor the mortal realm as idyllic, choosing, rather, to depict both ambivalently. On the one hand, despite the angels' ability to over-see and overhear everything, they are unable to affect the lives of the Berliners that they watch over; they are omniscient yet simultaneously impotent. On the other hand, despite the possibilities that a place in space, time and causality offers to the film's humans, the mortal world can be a lonely place. The mortal realm is the focus of angel Damiel's utopian dream, however: a dream that offers an impossible, irrecoverable, lost plenitude of existence in the here and now. Subsequently, we see his utopian dream become a reality. By contrast, for the lost and lonely Marion the role of trapeze artist in the circus offers the utopian promise of identity and rootedness that she lacks (and which may be read as being the utopian desire of all humanity). However, Marion's utopia slips from her grasp at the moment that she finally attains it, since the circus closes before the end of the season. In *Wings of Desire* apparently impossible utopian futures are attained, while other, seemingly achievable ones are consigned to history and memory.

Wenders uses both black-and-white and colour film: the angelic realm – when we see what the angels see – is signified by the use of black-and-white film; the mortal realm by colour.[27] When we see in black-and-white it can be assumed that the sounds heard are those audible by – often only by – the angels. Interestingly, the first time that we see in colour is the first time that Marion – the film's female protagonist – is presented.[28] As with the introduction of sound, the initial use of colour in the history of cinema was, paradoxically, associated with fantasy rather than reality. As Steve Neale points out, '[c]olour was a *problem* for realism because it could distract the eye' (1985, p. 145). As a result its use was restricted to particular genres, such as the musical and the costume romance. Colour was also used creatively, in terms of the sensory pleasure it gave, in the presentation of the female star: 'The female body both bridges the ideological gap between nature and cultural artifice while simultaneously marking and focusing the scopophilic pleasure involved in and engaged by the use of colour in film' (ibid., p. 152). Perhaps this momentary depiction of the female body in colour in an otherwise angelic black-and-white realm is Wenders's own playful homage to, and reversal of, the original 'fantastical' role of colour film in cinema history: given that the angelic is here depicted as 'realistic', and the mortal realm as Damiel's own fantastical utopia.[29]

In *The State of Things*, the director Friedrich's decision to use black-and-white film is portrayed as signifying an aesthetic stance against the high production values (and high economic cost) of commercial – and thus, colour – cinema. A conversation between an actor and the film's cinematographer, Joe, played by Henri Alekan – the cinematographer of *Wings of Desire* and, many years before, of Jean Cocteau's *La Belle et la Bête* (1946) – calls attention to the notion that while life itself may be in colour, black-and-white is more 'realistic'. As mentioned above, this view was (or is) historically mediated by the fact that until the 1950s colour was used only for particular genres. However, it might also be argued that the sensory pleasure of this initial momentary use of colour leads the spectator-auditor to follow Damiel in his desire for the (colour) mortal realm.

On a more general level, each of the angels can also be seen as an identificatory figure for the film's viewers. This identification occurs not only physically, as we see and hear as though through their eyes and ears for much of the film, but also symbolically, as we watch people's lives unfold on screen before us. As a cinema audience we too are impotent in our inability to affect the existence of the characters that we see and hear though our privileged access to their circumstances, thoughts and feelings may drive us to desire to do so.

Film music and utopia

The first part of my score and soundtrack analysis draws on Caryl Flinn's *Strains of Utopia: Gender, Nostalgia, and Hollywood Film Music* (1992), in particular, her argument that we have come to think of film music as aligned with an ideal of unity, associated with a plenitude which lies outside of history and society. Flinn offers a number of different reasons for this, such as classical criticism's (negative) idealization of film music as abstract and non-representational; film composers' own such idealized claims for music; film music's association with nostalgia for a better time, now long past, as a result of classical criticism's view of the musical language used; and the studio composers' Romantic dreams of authorship and status as independent creators. Thus we have come to associate film music with the traditional view of utopia as proposed by Thomas More: that is, as an impossible no-place which cannot be represented. Such conceptions of utopia are 'obsessively marked by escape, excess, and as something beyond discourse' (Flinn 1992, p. 92).

Flinn highlights that notions of utopia are historically constructed: 'utopia' is not a stable concept. Following Adorno and Horkheimer's ([1944] 1979) critique of the culture industry and, more recently, the work of film and popular culture theorist Richard Dyer (1977), she argues that some utopias are constructed in order to perpetuate the status quo. These idealized utopias are usually unrealizable and offer only temporary escape from reality rather than changing the nature of that reality. For Adorno (see pp. 24-28 above), utopian promise which succumbs to the identity-thinking characteristic of commodity culture (through the construction of false utopias) results in the perpetuation of dominant ideologies, which amounts to false consciousness. However, other utopias are based not on impossible, idealized situations that will never be achieved, but on the goal of changing the nature of the status quo instead. Adorno argued that such utopian promise is possible but can only ever be expressed or recognized in a negative sense.[30] Music's nature as 'non-conceptual cognition' (or non-representational sign) makes it the art that has the potential to approach most fully Adorno's programme of non-identity thinking and, thus, also, the art that has the potential to present authentic – rather than false – utopias. However, while some music may be able to assist us in our realization of the *dys*topian nature of late capitalist society and activate nostalgia for a lost totality, Flinn emphasizes Adorno's position which states that it cannot restore that (utopian) plenitude. For Adorno, a positive view of the future could only be projected in terms of a negative view of the present. However, not all change-inspiring utopias are necessarily progressive, as Flinn makes clear (following Jameson 1971) in her example of the regressive Fascist vision of the 1930s (1992, pp. 105–6).

As was mentioned in Chapter 1, Flinn argues that a society's utopian thoughts reveal what that society currently believes to be missing or deficient within it. She turns to Adorno and the mystical Marxist Ernst Bloch in order to re-establish this link between utopia and socio-historical reality which she argues is missing from traditional accounts of utopia such as More's.[31] However, whereas Adorno argued that utopia is 'fleeting and partial', can only be glimpsed momentarily and thus remains an 'unstatable' notion, Flinn suggests that it is not unstatable because it signifies non-representationally (and thus lies outside of linguistic discourse) but because utopian signs are necessarily partial and require interpretation.[32]

Flinn also relates utopia's representational deficiency to Dyer's assertion that we can only ever glimpse what utopia might feel like, rather than how it is organized. Thus, utopian signs (in music) may be non-representational not because *music* is but because all utopian signs are. Bloch, too, argued that music is a good medium for the presentation of utopian signs for this reason; he proposed that such partial signs offer strategies by which the future may be altered. Both Bloch and Adorno argued that music is rooted in the age of its production. However, while Adorno believed that music presents this relationship with society in mediated form, Bloch asserted that music is also estranged from the age of its production. Furthermore, *contra* Adorno, Bloch considered music to be capable of offering a restorative potential in an active and material sense. Thus, Flinn argues that while appearing not to, music does actually respond to the 'needs of its time' (1992, p. 96). For Bloch, the utopian function of music is found in *future traces* (alternative semiotic fields or non-representational signs) involving *cultural surplus* (which allows art to outlive its immediate socio-historical and aesthetic contexts). Music has the potential to offer us a consciousness of a possible utopian future in the world of the 'not-yet-conscious':

> Every great work of art, above and beyond its manifest content, is carried out according to a *latency of the page to come*, or in other words, in the light of the content of a future which has not yet come into being, and indeed of some ultimate resolution as yet unknown.[33]

In her assertion that future traces may advocate regressive or negative utopias – that is, not just authentic or politically progressive utopias – Flinn's theory offers a powerful corrective to Bloch's. Utopias which promote change are not necessarily more authentic or positive than those that do not. Flinn argues that classical film music holds within it partial future traces, which we – as critics – can then interpret; our interpretations are dependent upon our own subjectivity, gender and the perceived lacks of our cultural and historical present. In doing so Flinn's model shifts the socio-historical grounding of utopian signs from the material itself (as Bloch argued) to the moment of interpretation: from the object's cultural and historical present, to the subject's.

My analysis of *Wings of Desire*'s soundtrack and score involves a move back to the materialism of Bloch's partial future traces but also draws on Adorno's and Flinn's qualitative correctives to Bloch's theory. For Adorno, a utopian promise for the future can only be expressed in terms of the dystopian nature of the present.[34] For Flinn, utopian signs as partial future traces may be positive or negative, and utopias which advocate change are not necessarily more authentic or politically progressive than those that do not.

The score

Broadly speaking, the soundtrack to *Wings of Desire* comprises three different kinds of music: Western art music,[35] rock music and circus music.[36] Each of the different kinds of music becomes associated with a different realm or space, through the image: the art music is associated with the angels, rock music with the mortal realm and circus music with the circus (also part of the mortal realm). The art music is the only category of music presented nondiegetically during the film; all rock and circus music is seen to be performed or played back diegetically on radios or records, or as live performance. Just as the angels are unseen by the Berliners, so nondiegetic music has no apparent source within the fictional world of the film. As (usually) the final element added to a film nondiegetic music has the temporal freedom to access the film's narrative structure and is able to draw upon that knowledge to warn its viewers of what is to come or, equally, to deceive. In *Wings of Desire* this omniscience of nondiegetic musical voices is associated not only with the angels' privileged access to knowledge but also with their impotence, which results from their inability to be present 'here and now'. The angels exist in the *temps mort* of eternity and are unable to intervene in or affect the mortal world. Rather than being omniscient (or omni-present), Wenders's angels signify omni-absence.

On one level, then, the different kinds of music used in this film function as representations of the ontological status of the characters in the two realms – the nondiegetic art music represents the angelic, the diegetic rock and circus music the mortal. On another level, each of these categories (and also a further subdivision of the art music category) represents a utopian function for a different subject. However, some of these musical utopias have a dual status: on the one hand they represent a particular subject's utopian vision, and on the other they reveal the dystopian nature of the subject's present situation. Such conflicts are revealed by drawing on the different means by which music signifies: harmonic and stylistic references, orchestration and temporality. The most complex kind of music, in this respect, is the art music composed for the film by Jürgen Knieper (who has written music for several of Wenders's films).

The art music

Stylistically speaking, most of the art music is modal, usually in the minor modes (a small proportion is quasi-atonal – I return to this below).[37] Modal harmony can operate as a signifier of the historical period before the development of tonal functional harmony in the seventeenth century. I would argue that this aspect of the art music – its modal harmony – functions as a depiction of the angels' utopian vision of a time long past in which they were able to intervene in the mortal world; nostalgia for a time when they could assist and affect the lives of mortals.[38] However, the orchestration and performance style of much of this music could operate as a stylistic marker for a much later historical period – the Romantic era. This is also the period of music associated most closely with classical Hollywood film music. If Flinn's view is accepted, then this musical signification to the Romantic era can be considered to have a utopian function for the film's audience, offering an ideal of unity, associated with a plenitude which lies outside of history and society.

In addition to these two different historical signifiers of the film's art music, there is a third, which is related to the listener's experience of temporality as created by this music. Both the rock and the circus music are built from tonal functional harmony, as a result of which they construct a sense of forward propulsion, of linear temporality. With functional harmony (in both major and minor keys) an inherent necessity emerges from the tonal language: a particular progression of chords implies a particular continuation, for instance, a dissonant chord must eventually be resolved to a consonance.[39] Our familiarity with the way that this kind of harmonic language works – expectation, deferral, resolution – generates a form of forward propulsion that is absent, or different, in music which is not tonal. The modal art music – associated with the angelic realm, and performed nondiegetically – creates a sense of static temporality rather than a sense of forward propulsion: modal harmony tends to create a less dynamic experience of temporality than that which results from tonal functional harmony. The static quality of Knieper's music is emphasized by the particular way in which he uses this harmonic language (discussed below). I would suggest that the impression of stasis created by this music, when considered in comparison with the dynamism of the mortal realm's tonal functional harmony and its connection with Damiel's descent into mortality (discussed below), represents the predicament in which the angels find themselves. It represents an authentic utopian function in the Adornian sense – that is, it reveals the dystopian nature of angelic reality. On the one hand, the original historical context of modal harmony as musical material represents the angels' utopian vision of a lost time in which they were able to intervene in mortal life, by making reference to a time long past. On the other, the static quality of the temporality created by this music represents their actual 'impotent' status, that is, the dystopian reality of their world when judged in comparison with mortality.

As I mentioned above, Knieper's music for *Wings of Desire* falls into two categories: quasi-modal music, which combines Eastern European tonalities and Orthodox Christian sacred music;[40] and a quasi-atonal style which is reminiscent of music of the early period of the Second Viennese School of composition, though this latter style appears in only two cues. In fact, both of these styles of composition dissolve the linear temporality of functional harmony, but do so by opposing means. The quasi-atonal style denies the sensuous 'pull' of dissonance through the sheer abundance of dissonance – there are so many dissonant notes that the necessity of their resolution is nullified. By contrast, the modal music does not possess the tonal directedness of functional harmony since it is not structured according to the intervallic relationships that 'pull' sensuously toward more stable degrees of the scale.[41]

The opening credits music, during which we first see the angels watching the Berliners ('The Sky over Berlin' cue[42]), comprises music from both modal and quasi-atonal categories. (See Illustration 6.1.) It begins with a harmonically unstable introduction performed by a string trio. This is replaced, after a minute and a half, by a drone of open fifths on a synth-pad (which plays back a sampled sound at different pitches) above which a solo cello gradually builds an arpeggiated melody that climbs, then falls with resignation. The cello melody is ornamented and quasi-modal. The drone then moves to a minor chord[42] over which voices sing suspensions to 'ah' and the cello melody returns with a similarly climbing melody (this time doubled, two octaves higher, by a violin). The cue ends with the return of the earlier drone's open fifths; the voices' suspension resolves, and the cello plays a brief postlude. Several of the other cues which are associated with the angels share features with this cue. For example, the music heard when we see angels in the library ('The Cathedral of Books' cue) also features a drone of open fifths: first on a synth-pad, then further emphasized by intoned whispers of readers' thoughts at the same pitches.[44] To this ground a mixed choir adds suspensions over each of the drone pitches (the tonic and the fifth) at a distance of a semitone and a tone which subsequently resolve. Towards the end of this sequence the choir sing slow repeated notes at a major third above the tonic, then falling to the minor third. The overall effect hints at modal scales (particularly due to the open fifths and flattened second).

Illustration 6.1   The angel Damiel (*Wings of Desire*). © Road Movies Filmproduktion GmbH, 1987; reproduced by permission

This is followed by a melancholy melody in the Dorian mode, sung by a mixed choir in unison, which also emphasizes the importance of the drone pitches by returning either to the tonic or the dominant at the end of each phrase.[45] While the drone of fifths is absent in the music we hear as we watch Damiel soothe the victim of a road accident awaiting death (the 'Dying of the Bridge' [*sic*] cue) and as Cassiel and Damiel listen compassionately to the internal monologues of an old man – 'Homer' – both in the library and again at Potsdamer Platz (the 'Potsdamer Square' cue), the melodies of both cues are centred around the interval of the perfect fifth. In the latter cue the melody is fairly conventional and set in the minor. However, its harp accompaniment – an arpeggiated chord built on the third of the scale – is harmonically ambiguous, and lacks a satisfying resolution.[46] The melody and accompaniment of the 'Dying of the Bridge' cue are also emphatically minor in nature but, here too, with the second and seventh scale steps flattened.[47] These alterations remove the 'pull' to resolve to the tonic which is expected with diatonic harmony.

The music heard during Damiel and Cassiel's discussion about mortal history (the 'Glacial Valley' cue) is related to the third section of the opening credits music ('The Sky Over Berlin'), in which voices enter and the drone moves to a minor harmony. The 'Glacial Valley' cue begins in $C^\sharp$ minor, with a second inversion tonic chord (Ic). This moves to the dominant chord with an unresolved suspension (V^4); thus the leading note does not appear. This returns to the second inversion of the tonic chord (Ic), which then moves to the tonic major chord in first inversion ($Ib^{\sharp 3}$), before returning once again to the second inversion tonic minor chord (Ic). This movement from tonic minor to major and then back to minor is particularly unexpected, both because the major third arrives in the bass, forming a false relation with the $E_\natural$ in the previous bar, and because part of the melodic line ($G^\sharp$ – F^x – $E^\sharp$) is suggestive of $E^\sharp$ minor (Example 6.1). Thus, the function of the progression is ambiguous and the sensuous pull of the leading note is absent. This section is then broken off and replaced by a string trio playing a chorale. While remaining fundamentally modal/altered minor in nature – and also related to the third movement of Beethoven's String Quartet Op. 132 (subtitled 'The Hymn of Thanks from a Convalescent to the Deity in the Lydian Tonality') – this section of the cue's music aspires more to the diatonic harmony of a major key. The chorale is also related to the music heard as we watch Cassiel as he sits in the back of an old Mercedes en route to the film set (the 'Old Mercedes' cue). Here again though, the music of this cue is quasi-modal rather than diatonic.

There is a scene in which Cassiel flies through Berlin at night.[49] We see what he sees: people sleeping rough, dysfunctional family situations and so on. The music heard during this scene (the 'Paranoid Angel' cue) is suggestive of Second Viennese School string chamber music writing – though more banal. It sounds like a grotesque parody of a stylized form of nineteenth-century salon music. Later in the scene, shots of Berlin in the mid-1980s are intercut with flashes of

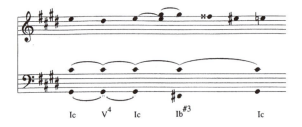

Example 6.1   Pitch structure of opening of 'Glacial Valley' cue

documentary footage of the city on fire at the end of the Second World War; the introductory cello melody of the 'Dying of the Bridge' is heard again. In comparison with the rest of the nondiegetic music, the quasi-atonal segment of this ('Paranoid Angel') cue and the opening to the first cue add a sense of foreboding to the angelic realm, with which it is associated, when compared with the tonal functional harmony of the diegetic music. Perhaps this signifies 'a storm blowing in from paradise'.[50] The angels are powerless to change the situation of mortals; 'progress' moves them ever onward. That we hear a *major* chord when Damiel begins to materialize as a mortal next to the Berlin Wall – at which point he is filmed in colour and begins to leave footprints – strengthens this interpretation in that it signifies a move to functional harmony and to the temporality of forward propulsion that it generates.[51] The major chord represents Damiel's transition into the mortal world, in this film signified not only by colour but also by functional harmony.

That Wenders chose to associate his impotent angels with the tradition of autonomous Western art music (in contrast to the film's circus and rock music) is perhaps not surprising. Adorno's view of music's apparent autonomy suggests that it has social function precisely because of its apparent functionlessness.[52] The more art becomes autonomous, the more it is able to criticize the social world but the less it is able to impact upon, or relate directly to it, and thus it becomes more powerless. Paradoxically, it is only as a result of withdrawing from society and existing separately from it that music can reveal the truth about society. The angels' predicament (and that of authentic, avant-garde music) embodies the dialectical double edge of the Modernist agenda. In their separation from society the angels are able to contemplate it in its entirety but are unable to have an effect upon it. Wenders's depiction of the angels thus adopts a Modernist (rather than Romantic) view of society; a view supported by the fact that *Wings of Desire* is littered with references to Modernism.[53]

However, despite the fact that certain aspects of the film assume a Modernist stance, the film's music does not. For, if the music were also to espouse a Modernist viewpoint then it would be required to be composed in accordance with the historical progression of musical materials as set forth by the Modernist agenda.[54] That is, the music would be critical of the materials handed down to it by the previous generation. Instead, the simple, static quality of the film's nondiegetic music evokes the genre of music perhaps best described as the 'new simplicity' or 'new spiritualism' suggestive of works by composers such as Arvo Pärt and John Tavener. Such music seems backward-looking, perhaps even regressive when considered in terms of the Modernist agenda. David Clarke (1993) highlights the quandary that the musical establishment has found itself in with regard to Pärt's music. On the one hand this music 're-opens the communication channels, offering tonal purity and simplicity of design' (p. 680); it offers solace from the alienating complexity of Modern music. As such, it presents a means by which the deep wounds inflicted on music by Modernism may be 'patched up' (ibid.); however, in doing so it denies the possibility of 'true' resolution to the crisis thrown up by Modernity. Or rather, it does if musicology continues to subscribe to the Modernist agenda.

It could be argued, that the contradiction between the Modernist elements of *Wings of Desire* and the style of art music used is inescapable today. For, it may be that it is now impossible to compose in an authentically Modern musical style, in the Adornian sense. Indeed, Croft (1997) has argued that it is now impossible to produce Modernist art in the Adornian sense because all assumptions about art have already been broken down, as John Cage's *4'33"* exemplifies. Instead, in order to be critical today, works must adopt elements of previous styles and critically reconstruct them. Despite the fact that Knieper's music makes reference (albeit briefly) to the material of Viennese Modernism in the form of a quasi-atonal style, it does not critically reconstruct the style; it is pastiche. Clarke suggests that such a reconstructive moment can, however, be located in Pärt's music.

Since the mid-1970s Pärt has been using diatonic harmony as the mainstay of his musical material. Focusing on the 'tintinnabuli' style of Pärt's compositions – 'the ubiquitous unfolding of note patterns drawn from the prevailing tonic triad' – and his use of techniques developed in medieval and early Renaissance music, Clarke argues that complex textures can and do result from these apparently simple materials and procedures (1993, p. 680). He suggests that Pärt's treatment of the historical material of tonality can be considered critical of itself to the extent that '[it resists] participation in [its] associated system of meaning – such as functional harmony or unfolding musical argument – through a number of devices, among them mensuration canon, isorhythm, quasi-serial manipulation or permutation of note sequences, and principles of strict symmetry' (p. 682). These techniques 'defamiliarise the ... domain of the diatonic' (ibid.). Pärt's works resist modulation and renounce thematic development 'on all but the most local level' (ibid.):

> The overall tendency ... is towards temporal stasis: where each moment in the piece exists only for itself rather than as part of a kinetic progression towards the next; where the whole is a harmonious juxtaposition of such moments and is equally reflected in them at every stage. (ibid.)

Pärt's inability to 'fit' is a result of 'mis-reading the music purely in Modernist terms' (p. 683). It might be better to read this music's 'denial of the dynamics of musical development and its associated dissolution of linear temporality' as directing our attention elsewhere – to the sensuousness of sound itself, and to the passing of time (p. 683).[55] Such a view corroborates my interpretation of Knieper's 'Pärt-like' music, which expresses the dystopian nature of the angels' situation – their inability to have stories or teleologies of their own, to take part in linear temporality.[56]

The circus music

The circus music has a utopian function for Marion dreaming of the circus.[57] We hear Laurent Petitgand's circus music when Marion rehearses and performs her act.[58] This music combines chromaticism and tonal harmony; much use is made of the minor third, but it is mixed with both a major and minor sixth.[59] The slippery nature of its harmony is further emphasized by the chromatic and modal scalic movement of the melody instruments in unison – a cliché of circus music. The music is performed (diegetically) by an ensemble comprising accordion, saxophones, drum kit and keyboard. This instrumentation, in combination with the use of chromaticism and the film's location in Berlin, also suggests a relation to cabaret and decadence.

When her utopian dream – an identity as a trapeze artist – is shattered Marion turns to rock music for cathartic consolation: we see her play records and dance to live performances at the Esplanade. Damiel watches, unmoved by the music that he is unable to feel but moved by its effect on Marion. Through dancing she is able, temporarily at least, to create a space or identity for herself in which to exist. For Damiel, the angel dissatisfied with his lot, rock music embodies the utopian promise of the sensual mortal world.

The rock music

Marion listens to a Nick Cave LP (*Your Funeral, My Trial*) in her caravan and hums along to the track, 'The Carny' (illustration 6.2).[60] The lyric to this song tells the story of a circus performer ('the Carny') who disappeared some weeks previously ('no-one saw the Carny go'). The company are moving on. With no sign of him they shoot his horse – 'Sorrow' – and bury him in a shallow grave. But then it starts to rain and the dwarves that dug the grave – Moses and Noah – regret not burying Sorrow more deeply! As the rain continues it washes away the Carny's caravan that the company had left behind. Nothing remains of the Carny or his belongings, he has simply vanished into thin air.[61] Clearly there is a correlation here with Marion's feeling of identity-loss as the Circus Alekan prepares to leave, taking with it her utopian dream of an identity as a trapeze artist. The song opens with a wailing harmonica line as the waltz accompaniment

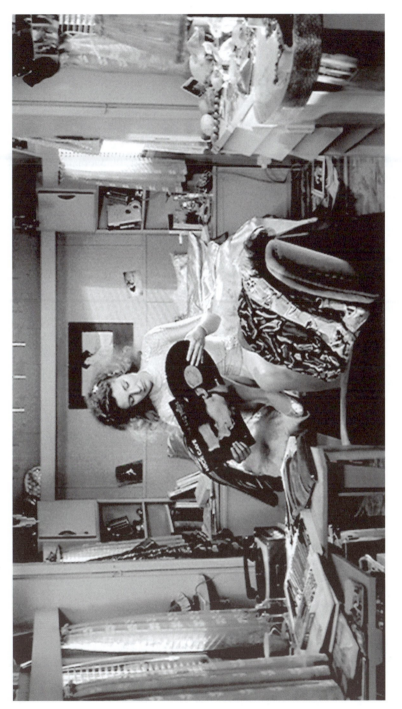

Illustration 6.2 Marion turns to rock music (*Wings of Desire*). © Road Movies Filmproduktion GmbH, 1987; reproduced by permission

fades in (as though the circus are on the move). It is in triple time – another circus music cliché – and shares more than a passing resemblance to Petitgand's circus music: in terms of instrumentation (the presence of an accordion), subject matter (the circus), and the clichéd chromatic passages that slide around in the song's inner voices (here on a synthesizer, in Petitgand's music on saxophone).

When Damiel first watches Marion at the Esplanade he sees her dance to 'Six Bells Chime' performed live by Crime and the City Solution.[62] The next time we see Marion at the Esplanade she is dancing to a live performance of Nick Cave's 'The Carny'. This song is followed by a performance of 'From Her to Eternity' which concerns a man's desire for, and desire to comfort, the woman who lives in the flat above him. He can hear her crying ('it is the most melancholy sound [he's] ever heard') and tries to catch her tears in his mouth as they fall through the floor. At this point in the song Marion looks unsettled and moves away from the band into the next-door bar. The song ends when Marion and Damiel finally meet for the first time in the flesh.[63]

Laurie Anderson's 'Angel Fragments' track is also apparently diegetic (the headphones of a man's personal stereo are shown several times). A synth-pad, here playing back a sampled voice at different pitches, presents an arpeggiated accompaniment figure. More synthesized keyboard sounds present fragments of melody repetitively, forming an ostinato in an irregular metre. Anderson sings a fragile line made up of cries and gasps. The harmony of this track is centred around open fifths, and implies a minor key. The music conveys a desperation and vulnerability that the earlier tracks do not. Interestingly it shares some qualities with the nondiegetic music heard as we watch the angels listen to Berliners in the library ('The Cathedral of Books' cue). This connection further emphasizes the angels' impotence since the track is heard as we watch Cassiel fail to stop a man commit suicide by throwing himself from the top of the Mercedes building.[64]

During the course of the film, Damiel gradually takes on a more central role, with rock music replacing art music as representative of his utopian dream. This supersession of one conception of musical utopia by another also reflects Wenders's own feelings about music mentioned earlier: Western art music is for Wenders forever tainted by its appropriation by the Nazis. Unable to understand most of the (English) lyrics when he was first exposed to rock and roll as a teenager, such songs took on an abstract sensuous form for him. That Wenders associates rock and roll with the creation of his own identity further emphasizes the link to the Romantic aesthetic which also argues for music's existential function.[65] In his writing, Wenders retains the Romantic mystification of music as non-representational signifier, something that cannot be stated in words, but substitutes Austro-German art music with rock music, a musical style young enough to have avoided Nazi exploitation.

Rock music continues to play a major role in virtually all of Wenders's films, with the significant exceptions of his commissions, *Hammett* and *The Scarlet Letter* (1973). However, although Wenders has a strong desire to put pop and rock

Illustration 6.3 Cassiel and Nick Cave on stage at the Esplanade (*Wings of Desire*). © Road Movies Filmproduktion GmbH, 1987; reproduced by permission

music on film, he wants to avoid *fixing* the meanings of the songs with images, which is why he frequently films his characters listening to records (*Kings of the Road*, *Wings of Desire*), or jukeboxes (*The American Friend*), or attending live performances (*Wings of Desire*). He argues that pop videos limit the imagination of the listener:

> The great thing about rock and roll, in my view, is that when you hear a piece of music over a period of time, in the summer or during the winter, you begin to form images in your own head that correspond to the music. It's like everyone creates their own videoclip for a song. That then becomes a kind of collective dream. In the case of the Beatles' song, *Nowhere Man* or whatever, there existed a kind of world-wide videoclip, but only in the minds of the listeners. That was wonderful and creative. Today each song already comes with its own dream.[66]

Wenders wants to avoid this imposition of meaning and aspires to create 'open' films instead, in which the viewer can 'generate their own set of film images' for a particular song.[67] This is the reason he gives for incorporating Nick Cave and the Bad Seeds into the narrative of the film. (Illustration 6.3.)

Clearly Wenders's view of rock music is idealistic and Romantic, and this appears to be supported by the narrative of *Wings of Desire*. When Damiel falls to earth and is unable to find Marion because the circus has moved on, it is rock music that is responsible for uniting them, in the form of a poster for a gig by Nick Cave and the Bad Seeds. However, further analysis reveals that Wenders creates a complex interplay between Damiel's utopian dream as represented by rock music, and his angelic nature. As I mentioned above, we watch Damiel watch Marion turn to rock music for catharsis. On another occasion, we see Damiel's own confusion over his motivation – his desire to touch, and thereby reassure Marion, also driven by his desire to provide the love that she longs for. Just for an instant we sense a different, more intrusive element to his 'super-vision'. This occurs when Marion listens to 'The Carny' on the record player in her caravan.[68] The combination of Damiel's choreographed movements and the camera's framing of him encourages us to question our perception of his character. We see Damiel in mid close-up begin walking towards Marion in synchrony with the (diegetic) music. His head and shoulders fill the shot as he moves in toward her. Through this *mise-en-scène* it is suggested that Marion is unable to escape from Damiel. No other such synchronized movements of angels to music (diegetic or otherwise) occur during the film. Furthermore, the fact that this music has a 'real world' rather than an 'ethereal world' source tends to conceal the more sinister truth of this moment, implying that the music's relationship to the image is coincidental, rather than specific and intended, as one would usually expect of nondiegetic music. The angels' watch over mortals is benevolent when uncomplicated by desire. Here we see Damiel appear to abuse his angelic privileges, which conflicts with our perception of his compassionate, sex-less, angelic nature; he becomes a peeping Tom rather than a compassionate guardian. During this brief moment Damiel becomes threatening and intrusive, and, for an instant, the controlling power inherent in the angel's unreturned gaze is made apparent.

I have argued that the ontological status of the film's music represents the ontological status of the two worlds depicted in the film: the nondiegetic art music representative of the angelic realm, and the diegetic rock and circus music representative of the mortal realm. I have also suggested that Wenders and his musical collaborators draw on the notion of classical Hollywood film music as an embodiment of utopian promise, but offer a more complex and ambivalent conception of music as utopian, as Flinn's study suggests is possible. On one level, Wenders simply substitutes one kind of musical utopia (classical Hollywood's late Romantic one) with another (rock and roll) during the course of the film, but closer analysis reveals that this supersession is more complicated. Each kind of music has a utopian function for a different subject: the circus music for Marion, as representative of her dreamed-of identity as a trapeze artist; rock music for Damiel, as representative of the potency and the sensory physicality of mortal life and all that goes with it; the art music for the angels, as representative of a time long past when mortals were able to hear the angels and be affected by them.[69] I have also argued that the utopian function of the art music has a dual status: in comparison with the linear temporality created by the tonal functional harmony of the rock and circus music, the art music's harmony generates a static temporality. In retrospect, given Damiel's fall and its association with tonal harmony, I have interpreted this lack of forward propulsion as being representative of the actual dystopian status of the angels, powerless to interject or affect the mortal world. This aspect of the art music thus presents an authentic utopia in the Adornian sense in that it presents the negative character of the present situation rather than a positive view of the future. However, I have also suggested that the utopian function of the rock music is not as straightforward as it first appears, due to the scene in Marion's caravan described above.

In the final section of this chapter, I argue that the rock music – as representative of Damiel's utopian dream – presents an allegory of the potency and efficacy which Wenders associates with the Hollywood system of production and distribution (though not unproblematically so). The static quality of the art music – as representative of the dystopian status of the angelic realm – thus presents an allegory of the relative impotence of some aspects of filmmaking outside Hollywood. In this reading the angels stand in for Wenders as non-Hollywood film director: although he has an omniscient viewpoint in the sense that he has much more control over the production and distribution of his films by choosing to work outside Hollywood, he is unable really to interject, to make a difference on a grand scale or reach a large audience. In order to achieve that,

Wenders would have to 'descend', as Damiel does – that is, accept a position within Hollywood – and thus lose his privileges, as Damiel does, and indeed as Wenders did when he made *Hammett* for Francis Ford Coppola.

Hollywood, sight and sound

Classical Hollywood cinema is dominated by sight, in terms of the framing and editing conventions of shot/reverse-shot and point-glance sequences with eyeline matching, for example. By contrast, as discussed in the previous chapter, the conventions of classical Hollywood sound are limited by the frame of the image: that which enters the frame from beyond its limits or from an unseen or unknown source can be considered to destabilize and thus threaten the image.[70] Roger Cook (1997) has argued that during the first half of *Wings of Desire* the viewer is frustrated in her/his desire for narrative as constructed by classical continuity editing. This is due to the many lengthy, mobile camera shots which, it is implied, form the point-of-view of the angels, and which are completed by very few reverse shots because only children are able to see the angels.[71] The second half of the film uses more conventional classical continuity editing techniques which, Cook argues, correspond with the more classical love-story narrative of this part of the film. Furthermore, Damiel's longing for a story, his desire for a history of his own and to be situated in the present, is matched by the audience's desire for narrative, for storytelling. As Damiel attains his goal so do we: the long single takes of the first part of the film are replaced by classical continuity editing which sutures viewers into the film's narrative.[72] Cook's interpretation of the film's shift from one style of filmmaking to another endorses the idea that Damiel's fall – from omniscient, though ineffectual angel to sensorily potent mortal – provides an allegory of entry into Hollywood.

The soundtrack to the second half of the film is also significantly different to that presented in the first part – dominated by the angels – where the film's soundtrack is focused upon their listening to, or overhearing the inner voices of the Berliners, to which we too are given access. These voices express thoughts: no lip-synchronization confirms their on-screen sources. This contributes to the dream-like, fantastical atmosphere presented during the first part of the film. After Damiel falls, this is gradually replaced by the lip-synchronized dialogue associated with more classical conventions. Similarly, in the first part of the film there is more of the nondiegetic music associated with the angels. By the film's last half-hour this has been replaced almost totally by rock music presented diegetically. With Damiel's descent into mortality the reverie of the angelic realm, of sound without seen source, is replaced by the ocularcentrism of the conventions of the classical Hollywood film.

During the first part of the film we see the angels as impotent despite their compassion for mortals. However, Damiel wants to desire and we learn that his desire-to-desire can be achieved by his being inserted into the (ocularcentric and colour) Hollywood system (here, mortality) which is represented by Peter Falk, apparently playing himself. As mentioned earlier, Peter Falk plays an ex-angel ('Peter Falk'), who now engages in the here and now of mortal life, thus (or by means of) entering the ocularcentric Hollywood system, both metaphorically and literally: Falk is, of course, a famous Hollywood film and American television actor. It is 'Falk' the ex-angel who senses Damiel's presence (though he is unable to see him) and encourages him to become part of the sensual (ocularcentric) world, telling him 'how good it is to taste hot coffee', for instance. Damiel doesn't realise until after he has become mortal that 'Falk' was previously an angel himself. Is it stretching things too far to read 'Falk' as standing for the coaxing Coppola who encouraged Wenders to direct *Hammett* for him in Hollywood?[73]

If we read *Wings of Desire*'s two realms allegorically in relation to Wenders's feelings about the institutional production choice facing directors – Hollywood or non-Hollywood – it would seem that no compromise exists. Given that the film's ending is optimistic for Damiel's future, it suggests that Wenders has made his decision (Hollywood), although Cassiel looks on with apprehension – a monochromic insert in an otherwise colour image. The film ends happily after Marion and Damiel's first meeting, with mortality and the ocularcentrism of classical Hollywood cinema valorized, though not unproblematically so. Ultimately, neither realm is promoted above the other. While Damiel falls and experiences sensuality and Marion finds love and support, the mortal realm continues to be a lonely place. With its fluid camerawork, beautiful black-and-white cinematography and unseen heavenly choruses, the angelic realm seems dream-like, though the angels' apparent privileges – to be simultaneously 'everywhere' for 'everyone' – offer little real comfort.

As mentioned above, the focus on the angels' overhearing in the first part of the film, and the abundance of unconfirmed sound sources that it brings with it (through the lack of lip-synchronization), assists in creating a dream-like atmosphere. The nondiegetic music (with *its* unconfirmed visible source) is also associated with the angels. These elements of the soundtrack are further linked through the use of voices with unseen sources; the whispered internal voices are pitched during some of the library sequence and subsequently begin to sing on 'ah'. Although the nondiegetic music conforms to classical scoring practices in some respects, the connection of this music with the angels' overhearing – do the angels hear this music too? – foregrounds the notion of source, and thus leads to a questioning of the conventional positioning of this musical voice. By contrast, in the second half of the film, the prioritization of sound over sight is replaced by more classical soundtrack conventions, with the shift to lip-synchronized dialogue, for example. The move away from (the here problematized) nondiegetic music to diegetic music, the source of which is confirmed by the image, works to re-establish the ocularcentrism of classical cinema, though here without classical scoring.

Writing about Wenders's oeuvre in general, Thomas Elsaesser has argued that it is not so much that Wenders is ambivalent over whether to make commercial or independent cinema, but that he feels both 'an attraction and revulsion more comparable to the probing of a wound that absorbs one's distracted attention' (1997, p. 243). Whether or not one accepts the suggestion that the different ontological realms depicted in this film may be considered representative of this institutional distinction, the probing of this wound has, in *Wings of Desire*, produced a rich and interesting soundtrack and score in which a compromise between classical and alternative scoring practices is negotiated.

Notes

1. The film was produced by Road Movies (Berlin) and Argos Films (Paris) in association with Westdeutscher Rundfunk.
2. A number of Wenders's essays and reviews have been reprinted and published in three volumes: Wenders 1989, 1991 and 1997.
3. For example, in a review of Walsh's *The Tall Men* (1955) written in 1969, Wenders writes of one scene: 'The shot is so wide you can't tell the details apart any more, but it's precisely because of this that the spectator feels as though he is physically experiencing the whole thing' ('Three Rivals: *The Tall Men*', reprinted in Wenders 1989, pp. 21–3, p. 22). On the film's sense of 'slowness' he writes: 'Slowness in this Western ... means no action is worth so little that you could speed it up, shorten it or even leave it out to make way for another, more exciting or more important one. And because all the images are of equal value there is no suspense to suggest peaks and pauses, but only a constant feeling of tension, to present all the physical and psychological events as clearly and as comprehensively as possible, and in the right order too, so that can be "experienced"' (ibid.).
4. See 'Why do you make films? Reply to a questionnaire' (1987), reprinted in Wenders 1991, pp. 1–2, p. 2. In an interview conducted in 1991 Wenders points out that *Wings of Desire* has itself become something of a historical document: 'Starting with the bridge where the motocyclist dies. That's gone. The place where we had the circus is now a park. No need to mention Potsdamer Platz. Or the Wall either. The whole film suddenly turned into an archive for things that aren't around anymore' ('A step ahead of the times: Conversation about photography, painting and film with Paul Püschel and Jan Thorn-Prikker', reprinted in Wenders 1997, pp. 131–9, p. 133).
5. Wenders, 'The American Friend', reprinted in Wenders 1991, pp. 18-20, p. 19.
6. Wenders, 'Perceiving Movement: in conversation with Taja Gut' (1988), reprinted in Wenders 1997, pp. 27–43, p. 43.
7. Wenders, 'Impossible Stories' (1982), reprinted in Wenders 1991, p. 53; also in Cook and Gemünden 1997.
8. Such as *Schauplätze* (1967), in which Wenders filmed a street from a high window for ten minutes.
9. Wenders, in 'Van Morrison' (1970), reprinted in Wenders 1989, pp. 52–4, pp. 52–3.
10. 'Music from America is more and more replacing the sensuality that the films have lost: the merging of blues and rock and country music has produced something that can be no longer experienced only with the ears, but which is visible, and forms images, in space and time' ('Emotion Pictures: Slowly rockin' on' (1970), reprinted

in Wenders 1989, pp. 49–51, pp. 49–50).

11. Wenders, 'America' (1984), reprinted in Wenders 1989, p. 125.

12. Quoted in Jan Dawson, 'An interview with Wim Wenders', in her *Wim Wenders*, trans. Carla Wartenberg (New York: Zoetrope, 1976), p. 12; cited in Kolker and Beicken 1993, p. 12.

13. Wenders, 'That's Entertainment: Hitler', reprinted in Wenders 1989, pp. 93–9, p. 94.

14. Ibid., p. 94. '[N]ever before and in no other country have images and language been treated with such a complete lack of conscience as here; never before in no other place have they been so degraded to impart nothing but lies' (p. 95).

15. Twenty-six German filmmakers wrote and signed the Oberhausen manifesto in 1962. The group has come to be known as 'Young German Film'; their title reflects their attacks on 'Opas Kino' (grandpa's film). It is regarded by many as the starting point of New German Cinema.

16. 'Because the way of telling a story, the language of the American cinema is still valuable ... I mean, for me, there is no other language, no other film language'. (Wenders, in Dawson, 'An interview with Wim Wenders', p. 9; cited in Cook and Gemünden 1997, p. 12.

17. Initially Wenders produced his films through the *Filmverlag der Autoren*, developed with other New German Cinema filmmakers, then later with his own Road Movies production company (co-owned with poet, novelist and screenwriter Peter Handke).

18. Wenders, 'Perceiving movement: Conversation with Taja Gut' (1988), reprinted in Wenders 1997, pp. 27–43, p. 31.

19. Wenders, 'Not alone in a big house' (1988), reprinted in Wenders 1997, p. 147.

20. In describing the influence of the Japanese director Yasuhiro Ozu on his work, Wenders states: 'The importance of Ozu for me ... was to see that somebody whose cinema was also completed developed out of the American cinema, had managed nevertheless to change it into a completely personal vision.' Wenders, in Dawson, 'An interview with Wim Wenders'; partially reprinted in Cook and Gemünden 1997, pp. 60–61, p. 60.

21. Wenders, 'Le Souffle de L'Ange' (1987), reprinted in Wenders 1991, pp. 89–113, p. 101.

22. I have as yet been unable to locate a copy of this film. Thus, for the discussion of *The State of Things* which follows I am indebted to Kolker and Beicken 1993, pp. 87–113.

23. Interestingly, Wenders decided to make a film on the subject when he was approached for film stock by an actress who was part of a film crew (directed by Raul Ruiz) who were, in reality, stranded on location in Portugal, having run out of production money. Wenders kept the entire crew of the film on in order to make his own film about their situation. See Kolker and Beicken 1993, pp. 95–113.

24. Wenders in Michel Ciment (1982), 'Entretien avec Wim Wenders', *Positif*, no. 261, November, pp. 17–23, pp. 21–2; cited in Kolker and Beicken 1993, p. 99.

25. Further, in an essay by Thomas Elsaesser, part of which concerns Wenders's 'weav[ing of] Hollywood ... into the fabric of each of his films' (1997, p. 242), *Wings of Desire* is conspicuous in its absence from the discussion.

26. Although the love story forms the main narrative thread running through much of the film, there is a profusion of other fragments involving other characters, notably Cassiel and Homer, which I do not have the space to discuss here. As Kolker and Beicken suggest, '... Homer is the representative and bearer of collective memory, the spirit of history. He is also the spirit of Berlin, who laments the vanishing of the city in the war and the cycle of aggression and destruction created by humans throughout time' (1993, pp. 150–51).

27. An earlier angel film – Powell and Pressburger's *A Matter of Life and Death* (1946)

– also signified heaven with black-and-white film, and presented 'real life' in Technicolor.

28.   This occurs approximately 24 minutes into the film.

29.   Although Damiel does not see Marion in colour, the fact that we – the audience – do has an effect on how we believe Damiel sees her: as a fantastical vision.

30.   See for example, 'Society', pp. 225–6 in *Aesthetic Theory* ([1970] 1997), particularly p. 233: 'The iridescence that emanates from artworks, which today taboo all affirmation, is the appearance of the affirmative *ineffable*, the emergence of the nonexisting as if it did exist. Its claim to existence flickers out in aesthetic semblance; yet what does not exist, by appearing, is promised. The constellation of the existing and nonexisting is the utopic figure of art. Although it is compelled toward absolute negativity, it is precisely by virtue of this negativity that is not absolutely negative.'

31.   Flinn (1992) draws substantially on Bloch's theories of utopia as set out in *Geist der Utopie* and *Das Prinzip Hoffnung*. The latter of these is translated as Bloch 1986. The large section concerning music in the former is translated in Bloch 1985, pp. 1–139.

32.   Flinn seems to argue this point *contra* Adorno, whereas the necessity for interpretation (at immanent, sociological, and philosophical-historical levels) is central to Adornian aesthetics (see Paddison 1993, p. 59–64) and is particularly true of what Adorno calls art's *promesse de bonheur*, its riddle character. See Paddison 1993, pp. 74–8, for a consideration of Bloch's influence on Adorno in terms of notions of utopia.

33.   Bloch, *Geist der Utopie*; cited in Flinn 1992, p. 97; emphasis original. However, Flinn criticizes Bloch for his belief that 'utopian meaning is fixed within the trace itself, that its significance is somehow immanent, already there in the text and not shaped by reading' (p. 103). She accuses Bloch (and others) of failing to recognize the importance of the subject's role in the interpretation of utopian traces. But, alongside Buhler and Neumeyer (1994), I would argue that the interpreting subject is actually built into Bloch's theory. As Buhler and Neumeyer point out '[f]or Bloch, coming to understand the trace involves shifting one's interpretative stance so that what had once seemed an enigmatic, or even unremarkable, facet of the material object suddenly realises unforeseen utopian potential':

> If the utopian meaning is in a certain sense always already fixed within the trace, it is not so much because 'its significance is ... already there in the text' but even more so because this meaning (that is, its interpretative potential) is always already present as a potential of our own enigmatic self. The utopian meaning must be a potential of our own self before it can be deposited (even by the unconscious) in the material dimension ... Materiality thus functions as a strange mirror in which we can at times catch glimpses of a future, utopian self, a self that has been forged in the smithy of our unconscious and that now stalks the realm of what Bloch calls the 'not-yet-conscious.' The not-yet-conscious, Bloch writes, 'is a place where one has never been before, although it is still native to us' (1994, p. 374).

Instead, Flinn 'divest[s] utopia of its material dimension' (ibid.) and places it wholly with the interpretative subject. In so doing, she virtually severs the connection between music and its socio-historical context that she has worked so hard to make.

34.   Such a view is not completely pessimistic, however, since a dystopian view may involve the possibility of something better, whether it is expressible or not.

35.   I am not using the term 'art music' in order to valorize this kind of music, but simply

to point to the canon of the Western classical tradition of music and its concomitant association with music as notated (though this is an increasingly problematic assumption to make at the start of the twenty-first century), and as an opposition to the categories of rock and circus music presented in the film, the performance traditions of both of which are founded on oral, rather than notated traditions.

36.   At one point the circus performers sing a folk song which, because it is performed diegetically and also shares harmonic characteristics with the circus music, I have placed in the same category.

37.   Some of this music is not in fact modal in the strict sense, but presents altered minor diatonic harmony. However, this harmonic language shares a number of features with modal harmony, particularly its avoidance of tone relations that 'pull' sensuously toward other, more stable, tones (through pitch alteration). I return to this issue below.

38.   Indeed, in the sequel to *Wings of Desire* – *Faraway, So Close* (1993) – Cassiel explicitly admits such a utopian dream. He complains that the angels are not relevant to humans anymore, that they can't know how to help them unless they understand what it is like to be a mortal now. However, such a plea could also be interpreted as false, since this justification can serve to conceal Cassiel's own desire to become mortal.

39.   See, for example, Kramer 1988 and Meyer 1967.

40.   Henceforth I will use the term 'modal' to cover both modal and quasi-modal music.

41.   The same effect is achieved by the flattening of certain scale degrees of tonal functional harmony, in what I refer to as quasi-modal music.

42.   The cue titles given here are taken from the CD soundtrack album of the film, *Wings of Desire: a film by Wim Wenders*', CD IONIC 2 (Mute Records).

43.   This chord is in second inversion, the tonic of the drone falling a tone.

44.   This sequence occurs approximately 17 minutes into the film.

45.   The Dorian mode is given below:

46.   The melody is clearly in A minor. The harp accompaniment centres around a major chord built on the third of the scale: C–E–G. However, the tonic – A – is also present, which creates a tension between two closely related keys: the harmony could be C major (with an added sixth) or A minor (with a flattened seventh) in first inversion.

47.   This sequence occurs approximately 35 minutes into the film.

48.   This sequence occurs approximately just over an hour into the film.

49.   This sequence occurs approximately one hour and six minutes into the film.

50.   Benjamin [1955] 1992, p. 249. Benjamin's 'Theses on the Philosophy of History, No. IX', from which this line is quoted, refers to Paul Klee's painting 'Angelus Novus' (1920). We overhear one of the mortals in the library reading about this painting. Benjamin describes this angel thus: 'His face is turned toward the past. Where we perceive a chain of events, he sees only one single catastrophe which keeps piling wreckage upon wreckage and hurls it in front of his feet. The angel would like to stay, awaken the dead, and make whole what has been smashed. But a storm is blowing from Paradise; it has got caught in his wings with such violence that the angel can no longer close them. This storm irresistibly propels him into the future to which his back is turned, while the pile of debris before him grows skyward. This storm is what we call progress' (p. 249). See Cook (1997) for a consideration of the role that Benjamin's text plays in the film's meditation on German history.

51.   That the modal and quasi-modal cues also contain discordant suspensions does not

undermine this argument because these progressions are not subject to the same syntagmatic functions as are those of diatonicism.

52. Adorno [1970] 1997, pp. 225-8.
53. 'Images of modernity infiltrate the film, in the architecture of Berlin – so much a part of the film's *mise-en-scène* – and through small references: in the library sequence the pen that is taken by Damiel is from a music student, who is copying a letter by the modernist composer Alban Berg; lying on top of one of the opened scores is Theodor W. Adorno's book on Berg; in the library one also sees German avant-garde composer Hans Werner Henze's score *Das Ende einer Welt (The End of the World)*, which happens to be close to the title of Wenders' next film, *Bis ans Ender der Welt (Until the End of the World)*' (Kolker and Beicken 1993, note on p. 151).
54. See Adorno [1949] 1973, pp. 32–7.
55. However, a Modernist would probably suggest that such aesthetic solace simply provides escapism *from* a controlling leisure industry, provided *by* a controlling leisure industry. Ultimately Pärt's music cannot be recuperated by a Modernist aesthetic.
56. Interestingly, in their critique of Flinn's *Strains of Utopia*, Buhler and Neumeyer make a case for film music that is similar to that which Clarke makes for Pärt's music. They suggest that film music may offer us the opportunity to hear the music that Modernism repressed, that it may 'preserve those remnants of musical culture that modernism has cast aside in the ruthless pursuit of its historical dialectic' (p. 385). They argue that Modernism criticizes film music for not progressing according to the historical dialectic of musical materials, and thus dismisses it as artistically unworthy (so leaving it to the same fate as Pärt's music). Thus, it may be that Modernist musicology's rebuttal of both film music and of Arvo Pärt's music may be an attempt to conceal the challenge to its hegemony which such music poses.
57. The music is also related to the French folk music which Marion and the bandleader (Petitgand) sing together after the circus's final performance. The sequence occurs approximately one hour and 14 minutes into the film.
58. One such sequence occurs approximately one hour and nine minutes into the film.
59. Since Bizet's *Carmen* at least, chromaticism has been associated with sensuality and seduction; see, for example, McClary 1992. It could be argued that this further emphasizes the link between such music and the sensuality that Damiel desires.
60. *Your Funeral, My Trial* by Nick Cave and the Bad Seeds (Mute Records CDSTUMM34).
61. Given the presence of angels in this film, Wenders's decision to use Nick Cave is interesting; the lyrics to many of Cave's songs contain biblical references, in particular the spectre of Old Testament fate. See Sean O'Hagan's sleevenotes to *The Best of Nick Cave and the Bad Seeds* LCDMUTEL4.
62. This sequence occurs approximately one hour and 16 minutes into the film.
63. Some commentators (and indeed Wenders himself) have noted that the song might more aptly be entitled 'From Eternity to Her'. Murphie 1996, p. 32; Wenders cited in the inner sleevenotes of Connoisseur Video's release of *Wings of Desire* CR003.
64. This sequence occurs approximately one hour and four minutes into the film.
65. Kolker and Beicken (1993) point out that proponents of early German Romanticism, such as Wackenroder, provide a historical precedent to Wenders's existential belief in music.
66. Wenders, in Reinhold Rauh, 'Ein Gespräch mit Wim Wenders', in his *Wim Wenders und seine Filme* (Munich: Heyne 1990), pp. 237–64; cited in Cook and Gemünden 1997, p. 81.
67. Ibid., p. 82.
68. This sequence occurs approximately 28 minutes into the film.

69. Indeed, that each of these different kinds of music functions as utopian for a different subject could be seen to add weight to Flinn's argument that the promise of utopia is more dependent upon the nature of the subjectivity in question than future traces in the musical material.

70. See, for example, Altman 1980b and Doane 1980. However, as these authors also point out, sound that is sourced by objects that exist or events that occur only outside of the image is also necessary in order to encourage the film's viewer to believe that the diegetic world extends beyond the frame of the image.

71. The opening moments of the film provide an exception to this rule, but this is necessary in order to establish the relationship between children and the angels (Cook 1997, p. 168).

72. Though Damiel and Marion's direct to-camera shots which occur during their meeting, provide a notable exception to this.

73. Interestingly, in 1974 Coppola made a film about surveillance in general and 'listening in' unnoticed in particular – *The Conversation*. However, in Coppola's film it is not angels who overhear, but a sound engineer who specializes in surveillance (played by Gene Hackman). Hired by a faceless corporation, the sound engineer uses cutting-edge sound-recording technology to 'listen in' on a young couple.

Chapter 7

'People call me a director, but I really think of myself as a sound-man':[1] David Lynch's *Wild at Heart*

Unlike the films discussed in the other case-studies, David Lynch's *Wild at Heart* (1990) was financed, at least partially, by Hollywood (through Polygram Filmed Entertainment). Lynch's relationship with Hollywood is complicated. A number of his films have been financed by Hollywood.[2] Films such as *Wild at Heart* exhibit the high production value gloss of Hollywood cinema and use Hollywood stars. Yet Lynch is considered to be a cult figure, existing on the margins of Hollywood. While the narratives of his films offer the most obvious explanation for this, in this chapter I explore how his work as a 'sound-man' functions in relation to classical scoring and soundtrack practice. Rather than working in accordance with the highly compartmentalized classical Hollywood model of production practice – with its institutionalized separation of sound and music production (Belton 1985a, p. 70) – Lynch operates according to a highly collaborative mode of soundtrack production practice.

In *Wild at Heart* this collaborative production practice is thematized through the character of Sailor (as temporary member of the band and controller of the soundtrack), and is materialized in the soundtrack in terms of the integration of the different sonic elements and the highly interconnected structures of thematic and acoustic relationships created between sonic signifiers. The potential for such soundtracks is inherent in developments in contemporary sound technology. The same developments enable moments of sonic spectacle in Hollywood blockbusters which also serve to exemplify high production values. The soundtracks to Lynch's films go further than these, however. I argue that this is due to Lynch's collaborative mode of production, which while rooted in classical Hollywood production practice – in the utopian potential that the vertically integrated 'all under one roof' Hollywood studio structure *could* have supported – offers a radical reconfiguration of it.

Wild at Heart[3]

Two young lovers – Sailor Ripley (Nicolas Cage) and Lula Fortune (Laura Dern) – are on the run from Lula's mother, Marietta (Diane Ladd). Marietta wants Lula returned to her 'safety' and also wants Sailor killed, because she believes that he knows that she and her lover, Marcello Santos (J. E. Freeman) – for whom Sailor used to drive – had murdered Marietta's husband, by setting fire to him. Lula does not know any of this. Marietta hires Bobby Ray Lemon to kill Sailor. Sailor defends himself but kills Lemon in the process (his act of self-defence well exceeds what is necessary to stop the attack – we see him literally beat Lemon's brains out). Sailor is sent to Pee Dee Correctional Facility on a manslaughter charge.

Lula waits for her man and, against her mother's wishes, collects him on his release. To escape Marietta, Sailor decides to break parole and drive with Lula from the East Coast to California. First, Marietta sends her current boyfriend, private detective Johnnie Farragut (Harry Dean Stanton), after them. She then calls in Santos to kill Sailor. Santos suggests that he take the opportunity to kill Farragut too (before the detective finds out about the drug-dealing racket he and Marietta are involved in together). Marietta tells him *not* to kill Farragut, but Santos puts a contract out on him anyway. The contract on Farragut is passed to Juana and Reggie who kill him as part of a masochistic sexual ritual with voodoo overtones. Worried that Marietta may have put a contract out on him, Sailor detours to Big Tuna in Texas to ask an old colleague, Perdita (Isabella Rosselini). Although the contract has been passed to her boyfriend, Bobby Peru (Willem Dafoe), Perdita lies to Sailor and tells him that she has not heard of a contract on him.

While Lula and Sailor are stuck in Big Tuna without money, Lula finds out that she is pregnant. Peru persuades Sailor to take part in a bank heist, during which he plans to shoot Sailor. The heist goes wrong, however, and Peru is killed Sailor is sent back to prison for six years. Once again, Lula waits for her man and collects him on his release, this time accompanied by their five-year-old son, Pace. Sailor decides that his family would be better off without him, however, and after giving Pace some man-to-man advice he starts walking back to the depot. He is surrounded by a street gang, whom he provokes verbally. After the gang knock him unconscious, Sailor is visited by Glinda, the 'good witch' (from *The Wizard of Oz*), who calls on him not to turn away from love. On recovering consciousness he thanks the gang for helping him to see the truth, turns heel and runs after Lula. He finds Lula and Pace stuck in a traffic jam, beckons Lula from her seat onto the bonnet of the car and they are reunited.

Wild at Heart is primarily concerned with the passion and power of Lula and Sailor's love for one another. It is this force which enables them to overcome the seemingly insurmountable obstacles put in their way by Marietta. Music is one of the primary means by which the power of their love is expressed. This occurs through both musical codes – in particular, through the music of Richard Strauss and the speed metal band, Powermad – through the valorization of musical performance and in Lula and Sailor's active and bodily response to musical performance.[4]

'Up in Flames': music in *Wild at Heart*[5]

From the opening credits sequence it is clear that the use of music is central to *Wild at Heart*. The sequence is ignited into life by a match. The greatly magnified close-up of the flame seen on screen is paired with an intensely reverberant and heavily amplified 'aural close-up' of the combustion produced by it on the soundtrack. As this sound begins to diminish, the lush romanticism of the orchestral introduction to 'Im Abendrot' from Richard Strauss's *Vier letze Lieder* (*Four Last Songs*, 1948) begins – quietly at first – with a winding line played by the upper wind and strings (Example 7.1). On screen, as the music gradually begins to swell, the names of Nicolas Cage and Laura Dern appear on intertitles. With that – and by now the music is really building – the words 'Wild at Heart' speed towards the front of the screen space one after another from a point on an illusory horizon, growing in size as they do so. The motion of the words is synchronized to the sound of a flame burning – here too, heavily amplified, but without the sound created by the friction of the strike which produces the flame; an explosion without the bang. The amplitude of the sound is linked proportionally to the size of the words (that is, as the words speed toward the front of the screen, increasing in size, so the sound gets louder). Immediately each word has reached the front of the screen space, the sound – now very loud indeed – stops abruptly. At this point, huge swirls of flames engulf the screen. At times, the sound of this great fire threatens to drown out the music, but ultimately a balance is maintained. Just as the names of the actors playing the roles of Sailor and Lula are connected in the credits by a single flame, so the bond between their characters in the film becomes associated with the representations of power and strength of both the music and the flames in this sequence.[6]

The *Four Last Songs* were the final works Strauss completed before his death in 1949. The texts and mood of the songs present a serene acceptance of death as a stage on a path towards eternity. 'Im Abendrot' ('At Dusk'), the last of the four, is written in a major key and regularly affirms its tonality. The music opens with a tonic chord played from which the upper wind and strings begin a long descent with a meandering line that, owing partly to the use of drone-like pedals as accompaniment, fails to establish the rhythmic emphasis of a regular metre. The absence of movement in the opening bar (the chord) also contributes to this lack of metre and to the quality of timelessness or free-falling which results. This is further compounded by the abundance of notes tied across bar lines, which creates a general sense of delay in the teleology of the lines. The impression of a

Example 7.1 Richard Strauss, 'Im Abendrot' from *Four Last Songs*, bars 1–22. Reproduced by permission of Boosey & Hawkes Music Publishers Ltd

Example 7.1   Cont

Example 7.1   Concluded

suspension of metre during the introduction to the song invites the listener to be suspended alongside the music in its ethereal descent. The happy resignation of the teleology of the descending lines of the upper wind and strings is confirmed by the reaffirmation of the tonic chord (E♭) on reaching this destination (bar 20). Michel Chion describes the opening of this music as having an 'extraordinary sense of notes bursting into flower'; a description which captures well its joyous, passionate, and yet also enduring nature (1995, p. 134).

The Strauss extract is first presented nondiegetically with the engulfing flames of the opening credits, then later, again nondiegetically, with Sailor and Lula's silent proclamations of love under a red evening sky (literally *Abendrot*).[7] It is also heard as we watch Lula despair at the prospect of losing Sailor to 'black angel' Bobby Peru.[8] Finally, it accompanies Sailor's realization that he 'should not turn away from love' following his visitation by Glinda, the 'good witch'.[9] The strength and passion of Lula and Sailor's love are not only expressed in the lush neo-Romanticism of the orchestral introduction to Strauss's 'Im Abendrot', however: they are also present in the speed metal track 'Slaughterhouse' by Powermad. This latter song is a loud and grandiose piece of rock music that builds in strength through a combination of the emphatic repetition and variation of thematic figures and percussive interruption of these figures.[10] Chion suggests that these two very different pieces of music actually provide 'two expressions of the same power of love (the accent should fall on the word "power")'.[11] The slow, bombastic introduction to the Powermad track is first presented when Sailor defends both himself and Lula from Bobby Ray Lemon's threats in the opening scene. It is next heard when we see Lula and Sailor making love for the first time after he has been released from Pee Dee.[12] Its next appearance starts with the second, quicker semiquaver section of the song when Lula and Sailor dance to the band as Powermad perform the song at the Hurricane Club.[13] Later, the slow introduction is heard again as we see Marietta's flashback to the scene of Bobby Ray Lemon's death, with Sailor (literally) pointing the/his finger towards her,[14] and as we watch Sailor and Lula having sex.[15] The last time Powermad is heard – and here again it is the fast section of the song – is when Lula can find only misery on the car radio. She pulls the car off the road and screams at Sailor to find some music. He stumbles across 'Slaughterhouse' as he twists the dial and the two of them dance frantically at the roadside until they are breathless.[16] After Lula and Sailor come upon the fatal car crash – following which their situation deteriorates further – the Powermad song is never heard again. It is certainly possible to read its absence as signifying the absence of Lula and Sailor's physical relationship, until they are reunited at the end of the film.

In contrast to Chion, Martha P. Nochimson (1997) argues that, following the conventions of the Hollywood musical, Lynch makes a distinction between popular culture and high art, aligning the former with 'spontaneity and direct contact with the audience', and the latter with negative associations. She suggests that this is proved by associating the violence of Santos and Mr Reindeer with 'sickeningly sweet renditions' of Western art music, while Sailor and Lula are aligned with categories of popular music such as rock and jazz (p. 230, n. 10). While popular culture is certainly celebrated in *Wild at Heart*, Nochimson's interpretation of the film's music ignores the use of 'Im Abendrot': one of the most important elements in the film, and one of the two most striking pieces of music used.

Sailor and Lula are portrayed as more receptive to music than any other characters in the film: whether speed metal or 1950s piano jazz, it makes them dance. The exception here is Mr Reindeer who, as Nochimson points out, is also associated with music: a simpering, solitary high-register violin melody with barely audible accompaniment. Mr Reindeer does not dance, however, though he watches others dance – usually virtually naked women in his employment. We see no evidence that music has any physical or emotional impact upon him. Mr Reindeer's association with art music is a superficial one which is not grounded in feelings, but instead functions as a signifier of bourgeois musical taste. Sailor and Lula, on the other hand, gain release from the evils of the world through music and their bodily response to it. The clearest example of this occurs at the end of a day's driving on the open road, as mentioned above. Lula is unable to find any music on the radio: the only stations she can find recount stories of sexual abuse, violence, and so on. Shots of Lula's despair at having to listen to this 'crap' (as she looks in disbelief at the radio) are intercut with shots of the radio in extreme close-up as she twists the dial erratically. Of the four shots of the radio in close-up, two linger on the radio alone with Lula's hand absent: are we to infer that the radio itself is a force of evil, polluting the air with tales of destructive acts? Lula pulls the car off the road aghast: 'Holy shit! There's not a livin' fuckin' thing ...' When Sailor asks 'What's wrong, peanut?', she climbs out of the car screaming 'I can't take no more o' this radio. I never heard so much shit in all my life! Sailor Ripley, you get me some music on that radio this instant. I mean it.' As Sailor starts to fiddle with the radio dial, the words 'sexual assault', 'mutilations' and 'rape' are picked out from the different stations. As soon as there is a cut to a shot of his hand twisting the dial, however, Sailor finds a music station. Furthermore, it is playing the (now familiar) strains of 'Slaughterhouse' by Powermad. They instantly recognize the music of their favourite band and (after Sailor has somersaulted out of the car) begin to dance wildly to it, screaming aggressively, punching and kicking at the air.

It is through music that Sailor expresses his most profound feelings for Lula: he sings first Leiber and Stoller's 'Love Me', then Presley and Matson's 'Love Me Tender' in the style of 'E' (Elvis). His performance of 'Love Me' takes place at the Hurricane club, following a fight sequence that also warrants analysis.[17] When Sailor sees someone else try to dance with Lula, he raises his arm to the band and they stop playing instantly. When Sailor asks the man in question to apologize to Lula, he refuses and insults Sailor by making a derogatory remark about his snakeskin jacket. The ensuing fracas is introduced, and then accompanied, by the sound of cymbal crashes (played back in reverse) and snare, with Powermad's kit as a possible diegetic source (yet also a distinctly impossible one, given the cymbal sound's manipulation). The synchrony of these (musical) sounds to Sailor's movements is precise, creating a brief moment of 'mickey-mousing', otherwise rare in this soundtrack. Immediately after the fight, Sailor asks the band to join him in a song – 'Love Me'. As a result of this sequence, Sailor begins to be associated with the musicians: he becomes a kind of temporary member of the band, part of a collaborative musical team.

Direct synchronicity between music and image occurs on only two other occasions in *Wild at Heart*: in both instances, it is again associated with Sailor and violence. The first occurs at the start of the film with Sailor's defensive attack on Bobby Ray Lemon synchronized to the introduction to 'Slaughterhouse'; Sailor's violent acts achieve almost balletic status here. The other example occurs at the end of the film when Sailor is beaten by a gang in the street to the rhythm of a piece of blues-rock music: both the punches he receives and his subsequent collapse are synchronized with the music.[18] The composition of music to 'mickey-mouse' action on screen is usually a post-production task: when a final cut of the image exists, the music is composed to synchronize with it. However, in terms of the production of *Wild at Heart*, it is likely that in these two sequences the action was choreographed to the music.[19] Lynch often has music played through his headphones during production – along with any dialogue being recorded – and he sometimes also has the music played back on the set during rehearsals.[20] In this way, Lynch has a soundtrack of his own making in use during production. Thus, the production practice of these fight sequences owes more to the conventions of the Hollywood musical (that is, the choreographing of action or dance to music at the production stage) than to the post-production precision of 'mickey-mousing'.

After the fight in the Hurricane Club, Sailor turns to the band and praises them: 'You fellas have a lot o' the same power E [Elvis] had. Y'all know this one?' The singer/lead guitarist throws Sailor the microphone. Sailor starts to sing immediately, and, by the time he has finished the anacrustic introduction ('Treat me like a ...'), the band are with him ('... fool'). Clearly they do know 'Love Me', and moreover – as in the tradition of every good film musical – they play it instantly in the same key that Sailor sings it, without a word of discussion. They also sing the backing parts, and in this way further establish that, in this film, music is music, whether it be speed metal from the late 1980s, or 1950s crooning songs. Rather than seeing this scene as a mere parodic reference to the Hollywood musical, however, I would argue that it also both confirms Sailor's association with the band – his role as one of the musicians – and identifies him as a controlling figure around whom the music is played out.[21] This interpretation is further borne out by the fact that the only moments of direct (closely synchronized) correspondence between music and image appear in connection with Sailor. Furthermore, during the scene with the car radio, mentioned above, it is Sailor who takes control of the soundtrack: he can find music when Lula cannot.

At the very end of the film, Sailor sings 'Love Me Tender' to Lula: the song he said that he would only sing to his wife. The song's title completes both the title of the earlier 'Love Me' and also his relationship with Lula, by acting as a proposal of marriage. During his performance of 'Love Me' in the Hurricane Club, Sailor takes control of the diegetic soundtrack, in the form of the on-stage band. With 'Love Me Tender', he takes control of the nondiegetic soundtrack: he generates music out of thin air. No other characters in the film possess this ability. While, in some respects, Sailor appears to be a fugitive from a 1950s or 1960s Hollywood musical in which he plays the Elvis Presley character, he can also be considered to stand in for Lynch himself. That is, that Sailor's control of *Wild at Heart*'s soundtrack, in combination with his collaborative association with the film's diegetic musicians, can be seen as standing for Lynch's own collaborative mode of soundtrack production. As cited above, Lynch considers himself to be a member of a film sound team, rather than a director.

From his very earliest films, Lynch has been both deeply interested and directly involved in the scope of sound on film. With the 34-minute film *The Grandmother* (1970), for example, Lynch worked with specialist sound man, Alan Splet, for 63 days full-time, creating and recording the soundtrack (Rodley 1997, pp. 45–6). Splet officially started work on the soundtrack to *Dune* (1984) 19 days before the start of principal photography, although discussions with Lynch had started several months before that (Gentry 1984, p. 63). Subsequently, Lynch worked with engineers to produce the 'temp track' for an early screening of *Lost Highway* (1997). As discussed in the opening chapters, temp tracks are used to accompany a film through early stages of editing, usually before the composer has written the score and before the sound designers have created and mixed the sound effects. Pre-recorded music and library sound effects are used to give the producers and investors a broad idea of what the final cut will look and sound like. For the *Lost Highway* temp track, however, Lynch worked with engineers to create an approximation of what he actually wanted to use for the final cut: the temp track became an arena for experimentation.[22] He has said that he sees the mix as the 'real focus' of the editing process, and prefers to have the opportunity to continue to experiment at that stage, although he admits that this is expensive and thus something of a luxury.[23]

Lynch also believes that actors' voices have the potential to be 'like music'.[24] On set he listens both to the dialogue as it is recorded and to music on playback through his headphones (Rodley 1997, p. 133). During rehearsal and on occasion during recording, the actors hear the music too. If pre-existent songs have already been chosen for particular sequences he uses those and gives tapes of the music to the actors to listen to. Even if he later chooses to use different music, Lynch states that recording to music 'gives you a great indication' (ibid.).

On each of his first four features – *Eraserhead* (1976), *The Elephant Man*

(1980), *Dune* (1984), *Blue Velvet* (1986) – Lynch worked collaboratively with Alan Splet. On *Wild at Heart* he worked with Randy Thom.[25] Although Lynch has always been involved in the design and production of *sound* for his films, he states that before *Blue Velvet* (1986) – the film on which he first worked with composer-performer Angelo Badalamenti – he had been frustrated when it came to his films' scores (the implication being, that is, with the studio pictures, *The Elephant Man* and *Dune*).[26] Indeed, he believes that many more directors must also be frustrated by the system 'because you rarely get to sit down with the composer until late in the game – post-production':

> You meet him, you tell him what you want, he sees the film, comes back with the score, and there's no more time: you're mixing. And if it doesn't work, you don't have time to fiddle and to make it work. A lot of music just gets overlaid over sequences and it's the composer's sole interpretation of what you've done. And it may or may not marry. Sometimes it's painful to see what happens. It's better to pull it out. A scene might work better with no music. (Rodley 1997, p. 127)

With Badalamenti, however, Lynch found a composer who was willing, indeed happy, to discuss and play things through to him before, during, and after shooting: 'And he didn't mind me saying things. He liked me saying things. And so I'm, like, in seventh heaven ... You can do anything. You just have to say what you want. It's the best' (ibid., pp. 132–3). Many film composers would probably jump at the chance of working more closely with a director and film crew during production. It is primarily for economic (and pragmatic) reasons that this practice is much less common than that of introducing a composer to a film at the post-production stage. In general, it would appear that producers would rather spend money on a film's look than on its sound (though, as discussed below, this situation is changing).[27]

Nonetheless, as far as Lynch is concerned, Hollywood's industrial model of a highly specialized division of labour persists today, particularly in terms of a film's music (despite the fact that music personnel usually work freelance and are not on the producing studio's payroll). In general, a film's music and most of its sound effects remain post-production tasks in order to speed up the production process; composers and sound designers often have little or no opportunity for dialogue with the director at the production stage. As John Belton points out: 'Whereas initially the sound track was "recorded," now it is "built." ... The growth of post-production departments within the studio system institutionalizes the separation of sound and image that frees the former from its ties to the events that produced the latter' (1985a, p. 70). This institutionalized separation of sound and music production frequently leads to clashes between sound and music cues at the mixing stage.[28] By contrast, Lynch writes sound into his films' scripts and his direction of them.[29] As Michel Chion points out, his cinema 'is transformed by the central role allotted to the ear, to the passage through the ear. Even if he made silent films, his films would still be auditory' (1995, p. 169). In the next sections I suggest that, while the surface of a Lynch soundtrack glistens with the same high production values that usually signify Hollywood production, the Lynch soundtrack presents itself as something more musical due to the director's collaborative mode of production. I begin with a brief introduction to the developments in sound technology which accompanied the rise of the Hollywood blockbuster and return of classical scoring practice. This is followed by an exploration of sound as spectacle in theoretical terms.

The evolution of sonic spectacle: post-classical film sound?

Since the coming of sound, Hollywood's high production values have been evident in its soundtracks. Indeed, for a time in the late 1920s and early 1930s, the presence of synchronized sound *in itself* signified high production values.[30] The development of magnetic, stereo cinema sound in the 1950s also signified these values, although it proved unviable in economic terms.[31] High-definition stereo cinema sound did not become commonplace until the late 1970s; it followed the development of relatively inexpensive stereo optical sound which could be printed on to film – Dolby Stereo – in the mid-1970s. It has been suggested that since the late 1970s Hollywood soundtracks have offered pleasure to the viewer and that this is due, at least in part, to the high-definition sound-recording and theatrical playback equipment now available. Developments such as THX, Dolby Digital, Sony Dynamic Digital Sound and Digital Theatre Systems have not only resulted in a much wider range of possible frequency response and a huge reduction in unwanted noise; they have changed the nature of the soundtrack forever.[32]

Due to the limited number of tracks and the relatively poor quality of sound reproduction with optical soundtracks before Dolby Stereo, filmmakers tended to favour the use of stylized sound effects that would not obscure dialogue: the sound effects used were generic rather than specific (Chion 1994). One of the most noticeable effects of Dolby is that dialogue is still audible even when in competition with huge, apparently spectrum-wide, sound effects. At the other end of the scale, much quieter levels of sound are distinguishable which thus allows for a greater potential in dynamic contrast between high and low sound levels. Greater contrast in the representation of sound quality is also possible due to improvements in the definition of sounds in recording and reproduction. For example, a scene in Ridley Scott's *Alien* (1979) uses a representation of poor quality sound in combination with a representation of poor quality images. The investigation of an alien spacecraft – the source of a periodic sonic signal – by a team from the Nostromo spaceship provides the narrative motivation. The character Ash monitors the progress of the investigators from the Nostromo via headset microphones, speakers and small video cameras located inside and on top of the investigators' space suits. The pictures which Ash receives from the team are of a lower definition format than the rest of the film – probably video. The sound is also of poor quality with a low signal-to-noise ratio. At the point at which the team enter the alien craft Ash loses both visual and auditory contact with them. The frequent crosscutting between the two locations during the sequence emphasizes the contrast in sound quality. Such sequences work to confirm the classical soundtrack's ideology of transparency and the invisibility of the cinematic sound recording apparatus by implying – through demonstration *in the film's diegesis* – that sound-recording equipment presents only a poor quality, low-definition reproduction of sound.

Star Wars (1977), closely followed by Coppola's *Apocalypse Now* (1979), set new standards in sound recording, sound design and theatrical playback. Even though almost all of the film's 121 minutes are scored by John Williams's music, there is a good deal of dialogue and sound effects also play a central role. Ben Burtt, the film's sound designer, fully utilized the potential of the different channels for the speakers behind, to the left, and to the right of the audience, creating the impression that spacecraft whiz all over the space of the auditorium; from left to right, right to left, back to front, and so on. Since *Star Wars* a high production value soundtrack – particularly in terms of the big-budget summer event movies – is defined by all or most of the following elements: high-definition recording of dialogue, sound and music; appropriateness of acoustic perspective for diegetic sound and dialogue;[33] innovative sound design; use of Dolby stereo and surround sound (that is, the spatialization of sound within the auditorium); and use of extremes of frequency response, emphasizing clarity across the entire spectrum.[34]

Michel Chion has commented on the direct correspondence between changes in sound technology and the nature of recent soundtracks. He believes that recent Hollywood cinema has been experimenting with, and is in pursuit of, sensation: 'of weight, speed, resistance, matter and texture' (1994, p. 154).

> Recent American productions like John McTiernan's Die Hard (1988), Steven Spielberg's Indiana Jones and the Last Crusade (1989), or James Cameron's The Abyss (1989) have also added to this renewal of the senses in film through the playful extravagance of their plots. In these movies matter – glass, fire, metal, water, tar – resists, surges, lives, explodes in infinite variations, with an eloquence in which we can recognise the invigorating influence of sound on the overall vocabulary of modern-day film language. It is certainly looking as if an epic quality is returning to cinema, making its appearance in many films in the form of at least one fabulous sequence ... The sound of noises, for a long time relegated to the background like a troublesome relative in the attic, has therefore benefited from the recent improvements in definition brought by Dolby. Noises are reintroducing an acute feeling of the materiality of things and beings, and they herald a sensory cinema. (p. 155)

As Chion himself suggests, improvements of sound definition in recording and playback offer one reason why set-pieces which focus on the materiality of things – such as people jumping or falling through glass – have become such a frequent occurrence in recent cinema. Improvements in definition are the result of enhancements in high frequency response which enable greater detail and precision to be heard. Chion also points out that recent cinema sound varies from 'real world' sound in terms of what happens to it when it is amplified.[35] When a sound increases in intensity in the real world it generally distorts, resulting in changes to its 'nature, colour, resonance' (p. 101). In the amplified sound world of the cinema, sounds have as much clarity at extremely high amplitude levels as they do at very low ones. Acoustic verisimilitude is sacrificed in the name of exploiting the technology that is now available and which includes the spatialization of sound, for example.[36] Sound has finally caught up with the widescreen spectacle of the image and is itself able to be 'spectacular' in itself, at the stages of both production and exhibition. Indeed, following Roland Barthes ([1972] 1977; [1973] 1990), I would argue that moments of sonic spectacle offer the viewer of contemporary Hollywood cinema the opportunity to step out of the narrative to marvel at both the precision of the sound design and the technical capacity of the sound system.

In 'The Grain of the Voice' ([1972] 1977) and *The Pleasure of the Text* ([1973] 1990), Barthes emphasizes the materiality of the signifier as a source of sensual pleasure, in contrast to the conceptual content it signifies. In the former, he compares the singing style of the tenor Dietrich Fischer-Dieskau and the earlier French singer Panzera. Barthes prefers Panzera's performance to that of Fischer-Dieskau, which he considers to be over-precise in the articulation and expression of words and their meaning. Panzera focused instead on the diction of the vowels, in which 'lay the "truth" of language – not its functionality (clarity, expressivity, communication) – and the range of vowels received all the *signifiance* (which is meaning *in its potential voluptuousness*)' ([1972] 1977, p. 184; emphasis original).

Barthes turns to Julia Kristeva's distinction between genotext and phenotext to illustrate his point. In terms of sung performance he argues that the phenotext (here, pheno-song) refers to those qualities which serve 'communication, representation, expression', while the genotext (geno-song) refers to 'the space where significations germinate "from within language and in its very materiality"... It is ... the *diction* of language'(pp. 182–3; emphasis original). The geno-song is concerned with the expression of the linguistic material in and of itself, whereas the pheno-song is focused on the expression of the conceptual and symbolic character of these materials. Thus Barthes finds Fischer-Dieskau faultless in terms of pheno-song – that is, his expression of the song's representational meanings and emotions – but bland in terms of the geno-song.[37]

By contrast, in the singing of a Russian Cantor, a bass, Barthes detects something 'beyond (or before) the meaning of the words ... something which is directly the cantor's body' (p. 181). What he detects in the grain of the voice is individual to that body, is singular, unique. Rather than telling us of the specific singer's personality or subjectivity, it speaks of the physical nature of her/his body: 'The "grain" is the body in the voice as it sings, the hand as it writes, the limb as it performs' (p. 188). 'Grain' is not simply a reference to a sound's timbre, but to timbre as a signifier (*signifiance*) of the body of the sound's source. In vocal music, Barthes places this potential 'grain' of the voice at the boundary between language and music, but argues that it can also occur in instrumental music. Rather than evaluating performance on a performer's interpretation of a text's representational meanings and emotions, of their ability to conform to 'constraints of style' (p. 189), Barthes urges us to judge a performance on its ability to realize the body which sources it. Furthermore, it is our own body – rather than our conscious (or unconscious) self or subjectivity – which recognizes such embodiments in texts and experiences *jouissance*. Indeed, as Barthes explains in *The Pleasure of the Text*, *jouissance* cannot be expressed by words.[38]

In *The Pleasure of the Text* Barthes distinguishes between at least two kinds of readers' pleasures: *plaisir* (pleasure) and *jouissance* (bliss/orgasm).[39] The latter is more concerned with disruption, with texts' gaping 'cleavages', while the former functions both as a category of linguistic excess and also sometimes as a catch-all for both types of pleasure.[40] Barthes states that he gains pleasure from skipping ahead in a text, looking up from it, and returning to it to dip in: *la dérive*. He also takes pleasure from an excess of linguistic precision, of 'descriptive madness' (p. 26).[41] By contrast, *jouissance* is the experience of '*dissolve* which seizes the subject in the midst of bliss' (p. 6). It is experienced in reading when the 'body pursues its own ideas: for my body does not have the same ideas as I do' (p. 17). This body is separate from self or subjectivity, and the cultural identity which language creates. As such, this body is neither conscious nor unconscious.

Barthes suggests that cinema sound offers the experience of *jouissance* in the sensory intimacy of closely miked speech:

> In fact, it suffices that the cinema capture the sound of speech *close up* (this is, in fact, the generalised definition of the 'grain' of writing) and make us hear in their materiality, their sensuality, the breath, the gutturals, the fleshiness of the lips, a whole presence of the human muzzle (that the voice, granular and vibrant as an animal's muzzle), to succeed in shifting the signified a great distance and in throwing, so to speak, the anonymous body of the actor into my ear: it granulates, it crackles, it caresses, it grates, it outs, it comes: that is bliss. ([1973] 1990, p. 67; emphasis original)

Following Barthes, I would argue that two kinds of aural pleasures may be experienced by the audience of contemporary Hollywood: *plaisir* in the verisimilitudinous presentation of the diegetic world in sound; and *jouissance* in Barthes's notion of sensual bodily response to sounding signifiers, sonic materials in themselves. Barthes locates *jouissance* with disruption of, or difference from, meaning or expression, and with the body's recognition of another body. The body here recognized is not human, however, and the meaning such moments disrupt is the recognition of sound sources as suggested by the image. The narrative requires only that a sound's source event is recognized and that it is synchronized with the image of the event. Moments of sonic or aural spectacle as generated by high-definition (often spatialized) sound, on the other hand, divert the audience from the onward trajectory of the narrative as their bodies respond to a 'set-piece', the object of the sonic spectacle. The detail and precision offered by a high-definition recording (or generation) and playback of an explosion, for example, allows listeners to explore the interior of the sound – the many smaller events that make up the whole – and, in this way, withdraw from the sound's semantic meaning (the explosion) into the grain of the cinematic voice. David Lynch offers listeners many such opportunities in his films.

The soundtrack

> The borderline between sound effects and music is the most *beautiful* area.
> David Lynch, cited in Rodley 1997, p. 242

While most Hollywood blockbusters pride themselves on their sound design and effects, the quality of the music and dialogue recording, and perhaps also the name of the well-known film composer, in many cases there is little interaction or collaboration between the composer and the sound team.[42] By contrast, Lynch's films are planned so that sound effects may be considered musical, both in their own terms and in their relationship to music and dialogue. Indeed, dialogue is also considered to be a sound effect on occasion (Rodley 1997, p. 72). Dialogue, sound effects and music are integrated in such a way as to create a musical whole, with relationships created between the signifiers of the different sonic objects.[43] The most obvious examples that demonstrate the intricacy of sound, music and dialogue integration can be found in the music and sonic segues that overlap visual cuts.

In the case of music segues, the difference between two pieces of music which follow one another in quick succession is elided by a bridge which takes the form of a match in orchestration, pitch, rhythm, gesture or harmonic function. For example, the first music segue of the film takes the form of a modulation which bridges the fade-out of the introduction to 'Im Abendrot' by Richard Strauss, used for the opening credit sequence (discussed earlier), and the fade-in of a big band playing Glenn Miller's 'In the Mood'. The Strauss excerpt ends on the tonic (E♭). The introduction to the Miller starts with an arpeggio on the tonic of *that* piece: A♭ major. In retrospect, the transition from the Strauss to the Miller may be heard as a perfect cadence, with the Strauss ending on the dominant of the key of the Miller (E♭) and subsequently falling to the tonic (A♭).

The segue from the same extract from 'Im Abendrot', used later in the film, into a piece of bar-room pseudo-gypsy band music uses a match in orchestration and pitch.[44] This Strauss excerpt accompanies a shot of Lula and Sailor nondiegetically as they stand next to their car at the roadside in open country. During the excerpt, the camera pans steadily upward. As the lovers are lost from the frame, the horizon appears at the top, the sky red with the setting sun. As the camera stops, the shot is dissolved to that of a band playing on the stage in a New Orleans restaurant. The Strauss excerpt is faded out just after the dissolve, at a point at which the upper strings have just risen to a higher pitch (from bar 11 into 12; see Example 7.1). The band's violinist, shot centre-frame, plays several notes at this same pitch as the introduction to a new piece. As the supporting harmony of the Strauss excerpt is faded down beneath this solo violin line, the band begin to play. They play in a different key to that of the Strauss, but one which is consonant with the pitch played by the violinist, which acts as a bridge between the two pieces.[45]

Similarly to the music segues, the sonic segues involve movement from a sound in one shot to another in the next shot. More precisely, they usually involve the movement from a sound sourced by one object in one shot to a sound sourced by another in the next. The two sounds are usually physically similar, and it is this sonic isomorphism which forms the bridge between the two, masking the point of juncture. For example, a magnified close-up shot of a flame is cut to a close-up of the central yellow line of a road, shot as though from the bumper of a car moving at speed (with the dissolve of the yellow flame into the yellow line on the road also forming a visual segue over this cut). The sound of the burning flame in close-up – a broad band of noise at mid-range frequencies – forms a bridge to that of a car running on tarmac, recorded close to the source. A little later this same sound forms a bridge between a shot of Sailor and Lula's car and another of the lobby of the New Orleans hotel where Marietta and Johnnie are staying, with a visual cue implying that the sound issues from a vacuum cleaner in the lobby.[46]

There are also many examples of a high degree of integration between the film's sound and music, in which sound effects are used either in combination with, or as segues into or out of, music excerpts. For example, towards the end of the film there is a shot in which Lula slams the telephone down on her mother for the last time.[47] This is followed by a loud sustained scream of 'No!' from Marietta, which is underscored by a combination of high dissonant pitches from synthetic strings, very low in the mix, and the dialling tone of the telephone in her hand. Immediately after Marietta herself slams down the phone, there is a cut to a shot of Lula driving, in which she narrowly avoids an accident. The loud interruption of the other car's horn matches the pitch of the phone's dialling tone. The screeching of car tyres offers a structural approximation of Marietta's scream. This creates a sonic isomorphism organized around the cut (see Illustration 7.1).

Michel Chion points out that Randy Thom's sound design for *Wild at Heart* was considered controversial at the time of its release, not least for the strength of the

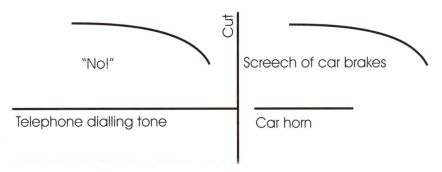

Illustration 7.1   The sonic isomorphism around the cut beginning at *c*. 1.45.36 (*Wild at Heart*)

sounds on this Dolby soundtrack (1995, p. 133). Yet, while moments of the film are loud, they are not especially so when considered in comparison with the persistent sound levels of action sequences in Bond movies, for example, or in each summer's Hollywood event movies. What *actually* upset critics was the degree of dynamic contrast used over a short timespan on this soundtrack. Chion highlights that we tend to forget that 'Dolby Stereo expands the cinema's sound field towards not only the very large but also the very small, by allowing the use of effects close to silence' (p. 134). In most of the sequences described above, cuts are elided through the work of the soundtrack, but during other sequences, cuts are emphasized by the soundtrack as a result of the contrast in successive sound levels. For example, in one scene we see an intimate shot of Sailor and Lula lying in bed. Lula says quietly, 'There's more'an a few bad ideas running around loose out there ...', at which point there is a cut to a four-second mid close-up of Marietta smearing lipstick aggressively across her face. This cut is also synchronous with the first presentation of an excerpt from Krysztof Penderecki's *Kosmogonia* (1970) at an extremely loud level (see Example 7.2).[49] This music uses all of an extended brass section and much of the percussion section at a loud dynamic. By contrast, the previous and subsequent shots are both very quiet: Sailor and Lula are seen in close-up, tucked up in bed whispering: a candle helps to set the intimate tone. Clearly the intention in this shot sequence is to link Marietta with the 'bad ideas running around loose out there'.[50]

Just as Lynch's images flaunt their physicality, their 'sensory impact', in the way in which images in Hollywood cinema tend not to (according to Nochimson, who points to the presentation of the Wicked Witch's crystal ball as an example of this), so Lynch's sonic constellations flaunt the sensory impact of their sounds, creating a rich, connective structure on a purely structural level.[51] The physical similarity of certain sounds used in *Wild at Heart* – as demonstrated, at local level, by sonic segues – is used to create a network of thematic and sonorous relationships that run throughout the film and form constellations. Improvements

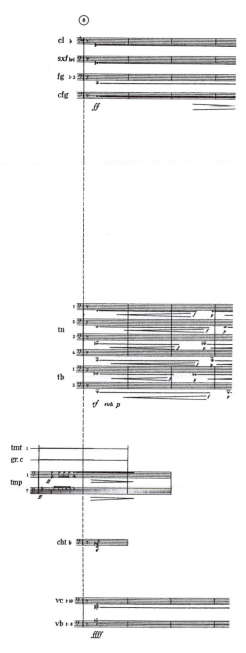

Example 7.2   Penderecki, *Kosmogonia* **(score figure 8). Reproduced with kind permission of the publisher, Schott Musik International, Mainz, Germany**

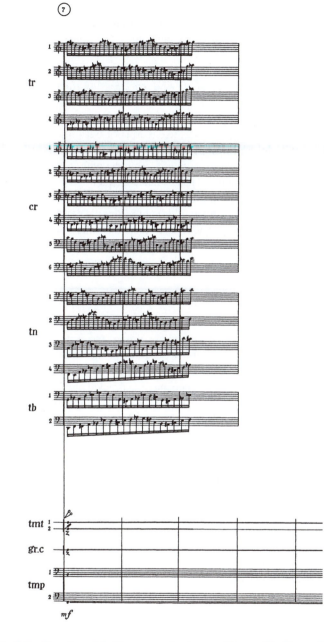

Example 7.3   Penderecki, *Kosmogonia* (score figure 7). Reproduced with kind permission of the publisher, Schott Musik International, Mainz, Germany

in sound definition not only enable sound designers to create highly specific sounds for each event – that is, an almost infinite number of different sonic possibilities – but also allow intricate connections to be made between individual sounds, in acoustic terms. In *Wild at Heart*, the most prominent of these constellations is centred around a short burst of broadband noise: it includes the auditory close-ups of flames, gusts of wind, cars passing Lula and Sailor as they drive (a sound that becomes associated with Santos), the cacophonous burst of orchestral 'noise' that occurs in the excerpts taken from Penderecki's *Kosmogonia* (see Example 7.3), and the excerpts of burning that we hear in the flashbacks to Clyde's murder.[2] This constellation is significant in its foregrounding of noisy sounds – that is, sounds with a high proportion of inharmonic spectral components. These sounds frequently interrupt scenes set in otherwise peaceful outdoor locations in broad daylight, or interiors lit with bright lights (for example, the desert in the middle of a sunny day, Marietta's garden, or her bathroom). Such disruptive noises also make thematic reference to the scene of the crime at the heart of the film – the burning of Clyde by Santos, at Marietta's instigation – which triggers the film's action: Marietta's attempts to murder Sailor.

In this chapter I have suggested that developments in sound technology which have improved the definition of sound recording and reproduction have thus improved the ability of the soundtrack to confirm the 'reality' of the diegetic world represented on screen. The enhancements have also created a situation in which the attention of a film's audience may be directed away from the narrative and the 'reality' of the diegesis, towards the soundtrack through moments of sonic spectacle. In the soundtrack to *Wild at Heart* such moments are also used to create a network of acoustic and thematic relationships which serve to further unify both the soundtrack and the filmic text as a whole. I would argue that Lynch's production techniques locate the director (and his work) deep *within* classical Hollywood practice, although they offer a radical reconfiguration of the institutionalized (and highly specialized) modes of production that have prevailed in Hollywood since the advent of the studio system. Rather than reinforcing the institutionally conventional alienation of sound, music and image production, Lynch builds collaborative links between them, and materializes these links within the frame. The potential for collaboration that was always a utopian possibility of the Hollywood studio system (though often unrealized) is an actuality of Lynch's work.

Notes

1. David Lynch, cited in Chion 1995, p. 169.
2. On the strength of his debut feature, *Eraserhead* (1976), Mel Brooks asked him to

direct *The Elephant Man* (1980), financed by Brooksfilms and Paramount. Lynch then went on to direct a film version of Frank Herbert's novel *Dune* (1984) which was financed as a package deal with Universal through Dino De Laurentiis. *Blue Velvet* (1986), Lynch's own project, was financed by De Laurentiis (then a mini-major).

3.   Lynch wrote the screenplay, adapting Barry Gifford's novel *Wild at Heart: the story of Sailor and Lula* (1990).

4.   As Nochimson also suggests: 'In music, Lula and Sailor find a fleeting cultural bridge to a better place that alters the condition of where they are, just as the Hurricane [music venue] does, even if it does not provide permanent shelter (1997, pp. 64–5).

5.   'Up in Flames' is the name of a song with lyrics by Lynch and music by Angelo Badalamenti. It is sung by Koko Taylor in *Wild at Heart* (*c*. 37 minutes into the film). The lyrics suggest that love is not always as powerful or constant as that which is shared by Sailor and Lula. In this song, 'our love' has gone 'up in flames'. There is also a reference here to Marietta's past act of sending her husband 'up in flames'.

6.   Lynch was at the very least involved in the production of the sound for *Wild at Heart*'s credit sequence created by Pacific Title. In a personal communication of 26 November 1998, Randy Thom stated that the Strauss had been Lynch's idea, while Thom himself 'supplied the sounds of fire'.

7.   0.48.59. As with the analysis of Godard's *Prénom: Carmen* in Chapter 4, timings are given in the format: hours.minutes.seconds.

8.   1.36.57. It is implied that this presentation of the Strauss excerpt is diegetic, however: at the start of the shot, as the music begins to get louder, we see Lula turn up the volume control of a radio at the side of her bed; the radio is also a mount for an ornamental horse.

9.   1.54.00.

10. Formal analysis of this track falls short of explaining the kinds of meaning it generates in this film. The track opens with a short, slow theme in metrically regular common time, played in a (melodic) minor key, in unison, by multiple electric guitars with heavy chorus effects. The second bar is completed by emphatic snare hits on the second, third and fourth beats. The theme is then repeated with the metrically regular snare hits replaced by a (metrically unstable) quintuplet across the same three beats of the bar. The whole section is then repeated a minor third higher. This forms the A section, which is then subsequently also repeated. The B section is based on the same thematic material, but develops its latent energy by articulating it in semiquavers and cutting the percussion breaks. A crescendo combined with a harsh vocal scream emphasizes the move into the second section. I have not mentioned the song's vocal line because Lynch uses only the instrumental sections of the song in the film. Interestingly, heard in its entirety (and available on the film's soundtrack album), the song is introduced by a narrative of sorts, with the approaching sound of heavily reverberant footsteps, and the unlocking and locking of prison cell doors. Similar sounds occur in *Wild at Heart* when Sailor is first 'locked up' at the Pee Dee Correctional Facility.

11. Chion 1995, p. 135. Of course, these pieces of music also carry with them a whole host of fairly stable meanings which we have come to associate with musical works (as generic signifiers) through convention.

12. 0.06.39.

13. 0.16.59.

14. 0.25.50.

15. 0.39.41.

16. 0.48.31.

17. 0.18.21.
18. 1.51.51.
19. In fact, in the case of Sailor's fight with Bobby Ray Lemon, Randy Thom has said that the sequence was choreographed to different music originally, with the 'Slaughterhouse' track grafted on top afterwards (personal communication, on 26 November 1998).
20. See Rodley 1997, p. 133.
21. It should, however, be noted that throughout the film there are a number of infamous allusions to one of the most famous of all Hollywood film musicals: *The Wizard of Oz* (1939). For example, Glinda (the good witch) appears to Sailor at the end of the film; Lula clicks the heels of her red stilettos together after an ordeal at the hands of Bobby Peru; both Sailor and Lula make reference to the Yellow Brick Road, Kansas and the Wizard of Oz; Lula has hallucinations in which her mother appears as a wicked witch, cackling as she rides a broomstick; and when Lula throws her drink at a photographic image of her mother at the end of the film, Marietta's picture fizzles away in a cloud of smoke (as did the Wicked Witch of the West when water was thrown at her).
22. For example, Lynch brought items from his home into the studio, pushed microphones up inside vacuum tubes and recorded music from loudspeakers placed at the other end of the tubes. When it came to re-recording this music in Prague for the final cut Lynch again worked with the recording engineers, this time using tubes borrowed from a nearby construction site, and large, empty wine bottles to create a similar kind of distortion. See Rodley 1997, pp. 240–41.
23. David Lynch, from video-taped interview with Larry Sider. First shown at the School of Sound Symposium held at the *Insitut Français*, London, April 1998.
24. David Lynch, ibid.
25. Splet was working on another picture at the time.
26. Lynch has worked with composer Angelo Badalamenti on virtually all of his films (and also the *Twin Peaks* [1989] television series) since *Blue Velvet*, and on the production of two albums of songs for Julee Cruise (who was featured as a singer at the Roadhouse in *Twin Peaks*): *Floating into the Night* (1989) and *The Voice of Love* (1993).
27. In addition, it has been suggested that the high fees charged by the relatively small number of well-known Hollywood composers contributes further to this situation. Even if such composers wanted to spend longer on score commissions, getting involved at the production stage, their fees would prevent it (from a discussion session with sound designer Randy Thom and other industry personnel, Second School of Sound Symposium, *Institut Français*, London, April 1999).
28. Such complaints were common among composers and sound personnel who had worked in Hollywood and spoke at the School of Sound Symposium, *Institute Français*, London, April 1998. Exceptions exist, however, and include film editor, sound designer and sound editor Walter Murch. Murch has worked almost exclusively for directors living in the San Francisco Bay area. These include Philip Kaufman (*The Unbearable Lightness of Being* [1987]), George Lucas (*American Graffiti* [1973]), and Francis Coppola (*Apocalypse Now* [1979]). Alan Splet suggested that there is a Bay Area approach to sound, which encourages an imaginative use of sound rather than a reliance on library sounds. He also stated that such directors spend longer than usual in post-production to get the soundtrack that they want (Gentry 1984). Gianluca Sergi suggests 'two major styles or schools' of post-classical film sound: 'the precise and detailed Bay Area sound, influenced by the electronic and esoteric stylizations of the 1960s, and the more gutsy New York Metropolitan sound, influenced, among other things, by rap and other forms of black

music' (1998, p. 161).

29. Lynch wrote the scripts for *Eraserhead* (1976), *Blue Velvet* (1986) and *Mulholland Drive* (2001), the screenplays for *Dune* (1984) and *Wild at Heart*, and co-wrote the scripts for *The Elephant Man* (1980), *Twin Peaks: Fire Walk With Me* (1992) and *Lost Highway* (1997).

30. As discussed in Chapter 1, before synchronized sound, the presence of a large orchestra to accompany film exhibition and other elements of the programme would similarly work to demonstrate high production values.

31. Magnetic stereo sound had a higher signal-to-noise ratio and enabled the recording and playback of a greater range of frequencies – higher definition sound – which, thus, made the stereo effect more audible since the recognition of sound localization is largely dependent on high-frequency sound. However, playback equipment was expensive both to install and to maintain, and the life-span of early magnetic media was considerably shorter than that of (monaural) optical sound. Fox initially made the conversion to magnetic stereo sound an obligatory part of conversion to their widescreen CinemaScope format. However, there were complaints from exhibitors about the exorbitant price (with the sound conversion comprising around 60 per cent of the total cost). There was also competition from Paramount's VistaVision format with Perspecta Sound, which gave exhibitors the option to exhibit films monaurally or buy extra equipment to exhibit in pseudo-stereo (that is, to simulate the stereo effect by panning a monaural track between two or more speakers). Eventually, Fox rescinded and made single-track optical sound prints of their films available. By 1956 (three years after the introduction of CinemaScope) less than a quarter of the 17 000 or so cinemas able to show films in CinemaScope had converted to magnetic sound. Gradually, fewer films were produced with magnetic sound and more with lower definition, monaural optical sound. See Hincha 1985; Belton 1985b; 1992a and 1992b.

32. Magnetic stereo sound of the 1950s offered many of the same developments as the later Dolby (optical) stereo, but for a number of reasons such as those discussed in the previous note, magnetic stereo became a 'frozen revolution' (Belton 1992b). For a consideration of the capabilities of Dolby stereo and subsequent development in sound technology and their impact on aesthetics see also Sergi 1998 and Allen 1998, pp. 116–19.

33. Though it should be noted that in order to fulfil the classical convention that dialogue *always* be audible, it is often placed higher in the mix than would be true of a wholly verisimilitudinous representation of a scene's sound levels. For more on this issue, see Williams 1980.

34. The name of a well-known film composer, or a smattering of popular music tracks might be added to this list.

35. See also Belton 1985a on this issue.

36. See Chion on the short promotional films which precede feature film exhibition in cinemas and which tell the audience which brand of sound system they are about to experience, for example (1994, p. 100).

37. It should be noted that vocal (and also instrumental) training often attempts to iron out such 'imperfections' (the 'grain') which may be considered to interfere with expression of music's representational meaning through the interposition of the body's presence.

38. '[P]leasure [*plaisir*] can be expressed in words, bliss [*jouissance*] cannot' (Barthes [1973] 1990, p. 21).

39. It should be noted that this distinction is by no means a clear one, however. *Jouissance* appears at times to be distinct from *plaisir*, and on other occasions to be a subset of the latter category.

40. As Johnathon Culler explains, 'Pleasure of the text, text of pleasure: these expressions are ambiguous because French has no word that simultaneously covers pleasure (contentment) and bliss (rapture). Therefore, "pleasure" here (and without our being able to anticipate) sometimes extends to bliss, sometimes is opposed to it' (1990, p. 19).

41. He cites, in particular, the sentence: 'Cloths, sheets, napkins, were hanging vertically, attached by wooden clothespins to taut lines', from a Robbe-Grillet novel (Barthes [1973] 1990, p. 26).

42. It is also clear that collaboration does occur on occasion, however: examples include the collaboration between sound designer Skip Lievsay, composer Carter Burwell, and Joel (director and co-writer) and Ethan Coen (co-writer) on *Barton Fink* (1991) (see Burwell 1999, pp. 24–7); and also between sound designer Randy Thom, composer Alan Silvestri and director Robert Zemeckis on *Contact* (1997) (see Shatkin 2000, p. 3).

43. This is not to say that no other Hollywood films exist that integrate their sonic elements in this way. Indeed, Robynn Stilwell (1997) argues that just such moments of integration can be found in John McTiernan's (1988) *Die Hard*; in particular, in Michael Kamen's reworking of Beethoven's 'Ode to Joy' from the Ninth Symphony as the underscore to a monologue by the film's villain, Hans. Nevertheless, a sizeable proportion of Hollywood cinema does not, in general, pay such consistent and careful attention to the integration of sonic elements for the duration of its films. Noël Burch ([1973] 1985) argues that other world cinemas, particularly the Japanese (with films by Kurosawa and Mizoguchi) and the French (through the work of sound man and director Michel Fano), approach such integration, although he also points out that the integration of all three sonic elements (dialogue, music and sound) is very rare and 'would obviously require the total collaboration of filmmaker and sound engineer [and composer!] throughout every stage of the conception and execution of a film' (p. 206).

44. 0.49.40.

45. Other musical segues include that from the pseudo-gypsy band music into the instrumental of Chris Isaak's 'Wicked Game' (0.51.55), and from the Strauss excerpt into 'Love Me Tender' at the end of the film (1.55.30).

46. 0.55.11.

47. The sound of the telephone being slammed is combined with that of heavily reverberant shotgun fire (and possibly also a piano lid being banged down) (1.45.36). Lula then throws a drink at a photograph of her mother. The sound of this impact is also combined with that of shotgun fire, the implication being that Lula has finally destroyed her mother – in effect, by shooting her twice.

48. Another example of similar integration occurs across the cut from the close-up shot of Lula's feet pounding the bed in a hotel into another close-up shot of her feet dancing to the music of Powermad in the Hurricane Club (0.16.56).

49. 0.41.32.

50. Other examples of contrast, include a 10-minute sequence during which extreme contrasts in sound level are exploited (this occurs roughly 30 minutes into the film). Chion suggests that each of the scenes within the sequence has a different 'tonality': 'The variations in rhythm, colour, and sound atmosphere among these grouped elements creates a striking impression of fatefulness, the ineluctable, because they play alternately on separation and return. We leave one sound atmosphere, then recover it, lose it again and so on, as if only a fleeting relation were possible' (1995, p. 134). The sequence is built up of parallel editing between shots set in different locations; it is notable because many other shots in the film have a somewhat languorous quality which matches the slow southern drawl of the protagonists'

accents.

51.   Nochimson 1997, p. 51. Despite the fact that high-definition sound quality is used throughout *Wild at Heart*, interestingly sonic spectacle is often created about its apparent opposite: noise.

52.   Chion also notes the prominence of these 'buffeting gusts' and suggests that they 'express the way in which Sailor and Lula's present happiness and freedom are doomed, not because of the wickedness of malevolent people, since the villains fail, but because they accentuate the fragility of their bodies and spirits, a fragility fatally determined by their life stories ... These gusts may also be taken, inversely, as the chink in the door, opening on to a source of eternal, fantastic power. What is at stake in the gusts is a sense of ambiguity, and depending on the way these gusts are presented, they may express different things: a fresh charge or energy, a breath which weighs upon your fate and presses you down, or a hole which opens in despair beneath your feet' (1995, p. 140).

Epilogue

This study is based on the idea that the analysis of film scores and soundtracks can operate as signifiers of institutional difference; that is, not only may the score and soundtrack of a Hollywood film be significantly different from those of a low-budget film financed outside of Hollywood, but they may also offer a further means by which institutional difference may be defined and recognized (along with production values, use of stars, adherence to particular narrative or filmmaking conventions, and so on). Such a view would seem fairly uncontroversial, I would suggest. However, the key argument discussed in this book extends this view: for films produced outside of Hollywood cinema or at its margins, alternative scoring and soundtrack practices offer a means by which a critical relationship to Hollywood cinema may be asserted by a film's creators. In the second half of the book, case-study analyses of four films and their scores and soundtracks were offered in support of this argument. Each of the films discussed was produced during the 1980s or early 1990s. I argued that in each case the interpretation of their soundtracks- and scores-as-critique reflected a reaction to the high-profile resurgence of classical scoring practices which accompanied the rise of the blockbuster from the mid-1970s, and the rise in Hollywood's market share of US and European box-office receipts through the 1980s and on into the 1990s.

The films discussed in the preceding four chapters are significantly different from one another, yet I would argue that their scores and soundtracks share a number of features. First, the organization of sonic elements is not as strictly hierarchical as one would expect of classical soundtrack practice in which dialogue is prioritized over sound effects, which are in turn prioritized over music in the main. In three of these films, other elements of the soundtrack are privileged over on-screen dialogue: in *Prénom: Carmen*, dialogue becomes one of several non-hierarchized sonic elements at certain moments; in *The Garden*, there is very little dialogue; and in *Wings of Desire*, the notion of on-screen dialogue is problematized by the presentation of characters' thoughts as heard by the angels, which thus occur without the confirmation of lip-synchronization. Although dialogue *does* play a major role as a conveyor of narrative information in *Wild at Heart*, it is also developed as a musical element and treated as a sound effect. Sounds, too, are made musical in Lynch's film: they are used to generate acoustic and thematic structures which recur during the film and thereby serve to unify the soundtrack further. The soundtrack to *The Garden* also uses sounds as music, though here to create the opposite effect: while the use of sound in *Wild at Heart* works to integrate the image- and soundtrack ever more closely, in *The Garden* the use of sound works to assert the potential liberation of the soundtrack from the image track.

In terms of scoring, through the intensification and exaggeration of classical scoring practices in Godard's *Prénom: Carmen*, the use of Beethoven String Quartets draws one's attention *to* these practices; practices such as providing continuity, for example, which are more usually organized around unobtrusiveness in classical scoring. The same is true of the ubiquitous presence of the diegetic quartet rehearsing – which has little apparent narrative motivation until this is revealed retrospectively in the film's finale – and the use of the same Beethoven quartets as nondiegetic score. Together, these practices problematize the classical score's conventional mobility across the diegetic–nondiegetic boundary. This boundary is thematized in Wenders's *Wings of Desire*, with different musical styles used to characterize the film's two ontological realms: diegetic rock (and circus) music is associated with the physical, sensual mortal realm; nondiegetic orchestral- and choral-scored art music associated with the angelic realm. Through their connection with these elements of the narrative (and their representation on screen), these musical styles become imbued with certain values. For example, the (diegetic/live) performance of rock music is valorized for the cathartic properties it offers to Marion (and, by extension, the film's director), and also because it is through this music that Damiel is able to locate Marion after the circus has closed.

Each of the films also includes apparently live diegetic musical performance. In *Prénom: Carmen* this role is played by the quartet, as discussed above. In the case of *The Garden*, several sequences are sung direct-to-camera and feature a slightly out-of-sync music track. On the one hand this form of address encourages audience identification through referencing conventions of live entertainment, while on the other it can work against identification and generate alienation and distance in its foregrounding of the apparatus and the film as constructed. Here, as with the musical numbers featured in other Jarman films, such sequences seem to hover somewhere between the two: foregrounding both the artifice of these constructed numbers, yet also encouraging a certain amount of audience identification. By contrast, neither Sailor's diegetic musical performances in *Wild at Heart* nor those of the bands featured in *Wings of Desire* involve direct-to-camera address: in *Wild at Heart* we watch Sailor as he sings songs to Lula, and in *Wings of Desire* we watch the band as they perform to the audience and unseen angels at the Esplanade. Although a number of classical (and post-classical) Hollywood films feature seemingly live musical performances, in general such performances operate under a different set of rules to those organized around the conventions of classical scoring practice: for example, live performances are often foregrounded and are clearly heard (and *seen*);[1] the narrative and the visuals often submit to musical logic during such numbers; the spectacle of these performances may halt narrative progression rather than driving it forward. Music and musical performance become the focus at such moments (rather than the film's narrative). In this way, the use of music during such sequences can be considered to work against some of the central tenets of classical scoring practice.

There are, however, plenty of examples of such moments in Hollywood films from the studio era on.[2] However, as with the examples in the Wenders and Lynch films discussed here, and with the exception of musicals, such performances are rarely shot direct-to-camera in Hollywood cinema, unlike the more 'radical' filming of musical performance in the Godard and Jarman films.

To discuss Hollywood cinema as an institution assumes that it may be clearly defined and understood as such. In the recent past, however, clear definitions of 'Hollywood' and 'non-Hollywood' cinemas have been complicated by a series of economic and other developments which have included the rise of the 'package deal', the majors' acquisition or development of smaller 'art' film production companies and the distribution deals between the majors and independent film production companies (as discussed in Chapter 2). The hybridization of genres, narrative conventions and filmmaking practices between Hollywood and other cinemas (art cinema, avant-garde cinema, 'Bollywood' cinema, and so on) has further confused the issue. While it is important to acknowledge the increase in such complicating factors, I would suggest that institutional differences between cinemas *are* still recognized and understood by film audiences in the main. However, to prove this assumption – and indeed to answer the more specific question of whether audiences recognize film scores and soundtracks in terms of institutional difference – would require that film musicology begin to adopt approaches from reception studies and sociological (and social-psychological) studies.

The apparent reticence to develop film musicology in this area may be due to the conception of 'good' film music proposed by a number of theorists of classical scoring practice: that is, that it should be 'unheard' at a conscious level by a film's audience, although its effect should be experienced. How useful would the standard qualitative methods of questionnaires, focus groups and interviews prove to be to film musicologists studying the unconscious effects of this music then? My own experience of cinema-going and of watching the response of others in cinemas suggests that film music may not be as unheard as we have tended to believe. Indeed, moments in which music moves to the fore in films may be far more frequent than has generally been suggested in theoretical terms. Sales of soundtrack albums – whether orchestral or pop – would appear to support this view. There are, of course, a great many other variables and questions to consider in relation to this issue: the different means by which people 'use' soundtrack albums outside of their experience of viewing a film; whether pop is 'heard' more than classical scoring; relatedly, whether evidence may be found to support Kassabian's thesis from *Hearing Film* with regard to the difference between affiliating and assimilating scores in experiments involving full-length movies in a standard cinema-going setting, for example.

There is also certainly plenty of scope for further research in identifying score and soundtrack practices across a range of cinemas in which the question of institutional difference has, as yet, been little discussed; up until now most such research has focused on Hollywood cinema, although a study of the use of popular music in British cinema has recently been published, for example (Donnelly 2001). In analysing the scores and soundtracks of various cinemas, both longitudinal (diachronic) and vertical (synchronic) approaches could usefully be undertaken, with analyses interpreted in relation to (and indeed, perhaps even contributing to the study of) changes in society and culture, and the impact of developments in technology and economics. Analyses of individual film scores and soundtracks have already begun to advance such work substantially.[3]

Recent studies such as those of Kassabian (2001) and Jeff Smith (1998) have usefully pushed forward the interrogation of ideological issues in terms of both the heard and the unheard in cinema scores and soundtracks. In developing this work further, and that of our understanding of the relationship between cinema soundtracks, film perceivers and album consumers, and also in broadening the range of film scores and soundtracks studied, film musicology could have a very fertile future.

Notes

1. There are occasions too when nondiegetic classical scoring is foregrounded (and which Claudia Gorbman associates with the generation of 'epic' feeling). However, in general, the sources of such cues remain nondiegetic and are thus not revealed onscreen.

2. For example, in Hawks's *To Have and Have Not* (1944), Lauren Bacall (along with Hoagy Carmichael) sings 'How Little We Know' (written by Carmichael and Johnny Mercer) and 'Am I Blue' (Harry Akst and Grant Clarke). It is possible that Bacall's vocals were dubbed by Andy Williams on the songs in this film. See http://www.warnerchappell.com/wcm/song_search/song_detail/songview.jsp?esongId=120503100 (url accessed 30 November 2002).

3. Such case-studies can be located in a range of journals, monographs and collections of essays. Some of the best examples include the series of book-length *Film Score Guides* initially published by Greenwood Press and to be continued by Scarecrow Press (series editor, Kate Daubney). These include Daubney 2000, Cooper 2001.

Bibliography

Adorno, T. ([1949]1973), *Philosophy of Modern Music*, trans. A. G. Mitchell and W. G. Blomster, London: Sheed & Ward.

―――― ([1970]1997), *Aesthetic Theory*, trans. R. Hullot-Kentor, London: The Athlone Press.

―――― (1976), *Introduction to the Sociology of Music*, trans. E. B. Ashton, New York: Seabury Press.

―――― (1982), 'On the Problem of Music Analysis, 1969', trans. M. Paddison, *Music Analysis*, **1** (2), 169–87.

―――― (1991), *The Culture Industry: selected essays on mass culture*, ed. with an introduction by J. M. Bernstein, London: Routledge.

Adorno, T. and Eisler H. ([1947]1994), *Composing for the Films*, London: The Athlone Press.

Adorno, T. and Horkheimer M. ([1944]1979), *Dialectic of Enlightenment*, trans. J. Cumming, New York: New Left Books.

Allen, M. (1998), 'From *Bwana Devil* to *Batman Forever*: technology in contemporary Hollywood cinema', in S. Neale and M. Smith (eds), (1998), pp. 109–29.

Allen, R. W. (1987), 'The Aesthetic Experience of Modernity: Benjamin, Adorno, and contemporary film theory', *New German Critique*, **40**, 225–40.

Althusser, L. (1971), *Lenin and Philosophy and Other Essays*, trans. B. Brewster, London: New Left Books.

Altman, R. (1980a), 'Introduction', *Yale French Studies*, **60**, 3–15.

―――― (1980b), 'Moving Lips: Cinema as Ventriloquism', *Yale French Studies*, **60**, 33–50.

―――― (1987), *American Film Musical*, Bloomington: Indiana University Press.

―――― (1992), 'Dickens, Griffith, and Film Theory Today', in J. Gaines (ed.), *Classical Hollywood Narrative: The Paradigm Wars*, Durham, NC: Duke University Press, pp. 9–48.

―――― (1997), 'The Silence of the Silents', *Musical Quarterly*, **80** (4), 648–718.

Armes, R. (1988), 'Entendre, C'est Comprendre: in defence of sound reproduction', *Screen*, **29** (2), 8–22.

Arnheim, R. (1933), *Film*, trans. L. M. Sieveking and I. F. D. Morrow, London: Faber & Faber.

―――― ([1938]1957), *Film as Art*, Berkeley: University of California Press.

Bachman, G. (1984), '"The Carrots are Cooked": a conversation with Jean-Luc Godard', *Film Quarterly*, **37** (3), 13–19.

Balio, T. (1998a), '"A major presence in all of the world's important markets": the globalization of Hollywood in the 1990s', in Neale and Smith (eds) (1998), pp. 58–73.

―――― (1998b), 'The art film market in the new Hollywood', in Nowell-Smith and Ricci (eds), (1998), pp. 63–73.

Bandy, M. L. (1992), 'Preface' in *Jean-Luc Godard: Son + Image: 1974–1991*, Bellour and Bandy (eds) (1992), pp. 7–8.

Barthes, R. ([1972]1977), 'The Grain of the Voice', in S. Heath (ed.), *Image, Music, Text*, London: Fontana, pp. 179–89.

—— ([1973]1990), *The Pleasure of the Text*, trans. R. Miller, Oxford: Blackwell.

Baudry, J.-L. ([1974–5]1986), 'The Ideological Effects of the Basic Cinematographic Apparatus', trans. A. Williams, in Rosen (ed.) (1986), pp. 286–98.

—— ([1976]1986), 'The Apparatus: Metapsychological Approaches to the Impression of Reality in the Cinema', trans. J. Andrews and B. Augst, in Rosen (ed.) (1986), pp. 299–318.

Bazin, A. ([1957]1985), 'On the *politique des auteurs*', trans. P. Graham, in Hillier (ed.) (1985), pp. 248–59.

—— (1967), *What is Cinema?*, trans. H. Gray, Berkeley: University of California Press.

Becce, G. (1919), *Kinobibliothek*, Berlin.

Bellour, R. and Bandy, M. L. (eds) (1992), *Jean-Luc Godard: Son + Image: 1974–1991*, New York: Museum of Modern Art.

Belton, J. (1985a), 'Technology and Aesthetics of Film Sound', in Weis and Belton (eds) (1985), pp. 63–72.

—— (1985b) 'CinemaScope: The Economics of Technology', *The Velvet Light Trap*, **21**, 35–43.

—— (1992a), *Widescreen Cinema*, London: Harvard University Press.

—— (1992b), '1950s Magnetic Sound: The Frozen Revolution', in R. Altman (ed.), *Sound Theory, Sound Practice*, London and New York: Routledge, pp. 154–67.

—— (2000), 'American cinema and film history', in Hill and Church Gibson (eds) (2000a), pp. 1–11.

Benjamin, W. ([1955]1992), *Illuminations*, ed. and with an intro. by H. Arendt, trans. H. Zohn, London: Fontana Press.

Bergala, A. (ed.) (1985), *Jean-Luc Godard par Jean-Luc Godard*, Paris: Cahiers du Cinéma/Éditions de l'Étoile.

Berger, J. (1972), *Ways of Seeing*, London: BBC and Penguin.

Betz, A. (1982), *Hanns Eisler Political Musician*, trans. B. Hopkins, Cambridge: Cambridge University Press.

Bloch, E. (1985), *Essays on the Philosophy of Music*, trans. P. Palmer, Cambridge: Cambridge University Press.

—— (1986), *The Principle of Hope*, trans. N. Plaice, S. Plaice and P. Knight, Oxford: Basil Blackwell.

Bordwell, D. (1979), 'The Art Cinema as a Mode of Film Practice', *Film Criticism*, **4** (1), 56–64.

Bordwell, D. and Thompson, K. (1990), *Film Art: An Introduction*, New York: McGraw-Hill.

Bordwell, D., Staiger, J. and Thompson, K. (1985), *The Classical Hollywood Cinema: Film Style and Mode of Production to 1960*, London: Routledge.

Branigan, E. (1992), *Narrative Comprehension and Film*, London: Routledge.

Branston, G. (2000), *Cinema and Cultural Modernity*, Buckingham: Open University Press.

Brown, R. S. (1994), *Overtones and Undertones: Reading Film Music*, Berkeley: University of California Press.

Buhler, J. and Neumeyer, D. (1994), 'Film Studies/Film Music', *Journal of the American Musicological Society*, **47** (2), 364–85.

Burch, N. ([1973]1985), 'On the Structural Use of Sound', in E. Weis and J. Belton (eds)

(1985), pp. 200–209.

Burlingame, J. (2000), *Sound and Vision: 60 years of motion picture soundtracks*, New York: Billboard Books.

Burwell, C. (1999), 'Music for the Films of Joel and Ethan Coen: Carter Burwell in conversation', in P. Brophy (ed.), *Cinesonic: the world of sound in films*, Sydney: Australian Film, Television and Radio School, pp. 15–39.

Carroll, N. (1982), 'The Future of Allusion', *October*, **20** (Spring), 51–81.

Caughie, J., (ed.) (1981), *Theories of Authorship: A Reader*, London: Routledge in association with the BFI.

Cavalcanti, A. ([1939]1985), 'Sound in Films', in Weis and Belton (eds) (1985), pp. 98–111.

Chabrol, C., Doniol-Valcroze, J., Godard, J.-L., Kast, P., Moullett, L., Rivette, J. and Truffaut, F. ([1963–64]1986), 'Questions About American Cinema: a discussion [extract]', in Hillier (ed.) (1986), pp. 172–80.

Chion, M. (1994), *Audio-Vision: Sound on Screen*, trans. C. Gorbman, New York: Columbia University Press.

———— (1995), *David Lynch*, trans. R. Julian, London: British Film Institute.

Clair, R. ([1929]1985), 'The Art of Sound', in Weis and Belton (eds) (1985), pp. 92–5.

Clarke, D. (1993), 'Parting Glances: Aesthetic solace or act of complicity? David Clarke reassesses the music of Arvo Pärt', *The Musical Times* (December), 680–84.

Claus, H. and A. Jäckel (2000), '*Der Kongress Tanzt*: UFA's Blockbuster *Filmoperette* for the World Market', in B. Marshall and R. Stilwell (eds), *Musicals: Hollywood and Beyond*, Exeter: Intellect Books, pp. 89–97.

Cockshott, G. (1946), *Incidental Music in the Sound Film*, London: BFI.

Comolli, J.-L. and Narboni, J. ([1969]1999), 'Cinema/Ideology/Criticism', in L. Braudy and M. Cohen (eds), *Film Theory and Criticism: Introductory Readings*, Oxford: Oxford University Press, pp. 752–59.

Cook, N. (1998), *Analysing Musical Multimedia*, Oxford: Oxford University Press.

Cook, R. F. (1997), 'Angels, Fiction, and History in Berlin: *Wings of Desire*', in R. F. Cook and G. Gemünden (eds), pp. 163–90.

Cook, R. F. and Gemünden, G. (eds) (1997), *The Cinema of Wim Wenders: Image, Narrative, and the Postmodern Condition*, Detroit: Wayne State University Press.

Cooper, D. (2001), *Bernard Herrmann's Vertigo: A Film Score Guide*, Westport, CT: Greenwood Press.

Corrigan, T. (1994), *New German Film: The Displaced Image*, Bloomington, IN: Indiana University Press.

Crafton, D. (1999), *The Talkies: American Cinema's Transition to Sound 1926–1931*, Berkeley: University of California Press.

Croft, J. (1997), 'Musical Traces: the limits of uncoded sound', in P. Howland (ed.), *Voices in Continuum*, Wellington, New Zealand: Victoria Postgraduate Association, Victoria University of Wellington, pp. 85–93.

Culler, J. (1990), *Roland Barthes*, London: Fontana.

Dack, J. (1994), 'Pierre Schaeffer and the Significance of Radiophonic Art', *Contemporary Music Review*, **10** (2), 3–12.

Daubney, K. (2000), *Max Steiner's Now Voyager: A Film Score Guide*, Westport, CT: Greenwood Press.

Davison, A. (1994), 'The Historical Moment of Musical Narrative', unpublished Masters dissertation, Music Department, University of Exeter.

Dayan, D. (1976), 'The Tutor Code of Classical Cinema', in B. Nichols (ed.) (1976), pp. 438–51.

De Grazia, V. (1989), 'Sovereignty and the Star System: The American Challenge to the European Cinemas, 1920–1960', *Journal of Modern History*, **61** (1), 53–87.

———— (1998), 'European cinema and the idea of Europe, 1925–95', in Nowell-Smith and Ricci (eds) (1998), pp. 19–33.

Derrida, J. ([1972]1982), 'Difference' in *Margins of Philosophy*, trans. with additional notes by A. Bass, Chicago, IL: University of Chicago Press, pp. 3–27.

———— (1973), *Speech and Phenomena, and Other Essays in Husserl's Theory of Signs*, trans. with an introduction by D. B. Allison, Evanston, IL: Northwestern University Press.

Doane, M. A. (1980), 'The Voice in Cinema: The Articulation of Body and Space', *Yale French Studies*, **60**, 33–50.

———— (1985), 'Ideology and the Practice of Sound Editing and Mixing', in Weis and Belton (eds) (1985), pp. 54–62.

Donnelly, K. J. (1998), 'The classical film score forever? *Batman*, *Batman Returns* and post-classical film music', in Neale and Smith (eds) (1998), pp. 142–55.

———— (2001), *Pop Music in British Cinema: a chronicle*, London: BFI.

Duchen, J. (1997), *Erich Korngold*, London: Phaidon.

Dyer, R. (1977), 'Entertainment and Utopia', *Movie*, **24**, 2–13.

Eisenstein, S. (1942), *The Film Sense*, trans. J. Leyda, San Diego, CA: Harcourt Brace & Company.

———— (1949), *Film Form: Essays in Film Theory*, trans. J. Leyda, San Diego, CA: Harcourt Brace & Company.

Eisenstein, S., Pudovkin, V. I. and Alexandrov, G. ([1928]1985), 'Statement [on Sound]', trans. J. Leyda, in Weis and Belton (eds) (1985), pp. 83–5.

Ellwood, D. W. and Kroes, R. (eds) (1994), *Hollywood in Europe: Experiences of a Cultural Hegemony*, Amsterdam: VU Press.

Elsaesser, T. (1975), 'The pathos of failure: American films in the 70s – notes on the unmotivated hero', *Monogram*, **6**, 13–19.

———— (1997), 'Spectators of Life: Time, Place, and Self in the Films of Wim Wenders', in Cook and Gemünden (eds) (1997), pp. 240–56.

Fenlon, I. (ed.) (1989), *The Renaissance. Man and Music*, Basingstoke: Macmillan.

Feuer, J. (1982), *The Hollywood Musical*, London: Macmillan/BFI.

Flinn, C. (1992), *Strains of Utopia: Gender, Nostalgia, and Hollywood Film Music*, Princeton: Princeton University Press.

———— (1999), 'The Legacy of Modernism: Peer Raben, Film Music and Political After Shock', in P. Brophy (ed.), *Cinesonic: The World of Sound in Films*, Sydney: Australian Film, Television and Radio School, pp. 171–88.

Frith, S. (1998), *Performing Rites: Evaluating Popular Music*, Oxford: Oxford University Press.

Garncarz, J. (1999), 'Made in Germany: Multiple-Language Versions and Early German Sound Cinema', in A. Higson and R. Maltby (eds), *'Film Europe' and 'Film America': Cinema, commerce and cultural exchange 1920–1939*, Exeter: University of Exeter Press, pp. 249–73.

Gentry, R. (1984), 'Alan Splet and the Sound Effects for *Dune*', *American*

Cinematographer, **65** (11), 62–72.

Gibson, J. J. (1966), *The Senses Considered as Perceptual Systems*, London: Unwin Bros.

——— (1979), *The Ecological Approach to Visual Perception*, Hillsdale, NJ: Lawrence Erlbaum.

Godard, J.-L. (1984), 'Screenplay to *Prénom: Carmen*', *L'Avant-Scene du Cinéma*, **323–4**, 20–68.

Gomery, D. (1986), *The Hollywood Studio System*, London: BFI/Macmillan.

——— (1998), 'Hollywood corporate business practice and periodizing contemporary film history', in Neale and Smith (eds) (1998), pp. 47–57.

Gorbman, C. (1980), 'Narrative Film Music', *Yale French Studies*, **60**, 183–203.

——— (1987), *Unheard Melodies: Narrative Film Music*, Bloomington, IN: Indiana University Press and BFI.

——— (1991), 'Hanns Eisler in Hollywood', *Screen*, **32** (3), 272–85.

Handzo, S. (1985), 'Appendix: A Narrative Glossary of Film Sound Technology', in Weis and Belton (eds) (1985), pp. 383–426.

Hansen, M. (1981), 'Introduction to "Adorno – Transparencies on Film"', *New German Critique*, **24–25**, 186–98.

Hansen, M. B. (2000), 'The mass production of the senses: classical cinema as vernacular modernism', in C. Geldhill and L. Williams, *Re-inventing Film Studies*, London: Arnold, pp. 332–50.

Hayward, Susan (2000), *Cinema Studies: The Key Concepts*, London: Routledge.

Heath, S. (1977–78), 'Notes on Suture', *Screen*, **18** (2), 48–76.

——— (1981), *Questions of Cinema*, London: Macmillan.

Herman, E. S. and McChesney, R. W. (1997), *The Global Media: The New Missionaries of Corporate Capitalism*, London: Cassell.

Hill, J. and Church Gibson, P. (eds) (2000a), *American Cinema and Hollywood: critical approaches*, Oxford: Oxford University Press.

Hill, J. and Church Gibson, P. (eds) (2000b), *World Cinema: critical approaches*, Oxford: Oxford University Press.

Hillier, J. (ed.) (1985), *Cahiers du Cinéma – The 1950s: Neo-Realism, Hollywood, New Wave*, London: Routledge & Kegan Paul.

——— (1986), *Cahiers du Cinéma – 1960–68: New Wave, New Cinema, Re-evaluating Hollywood*, London: Routledge and BFI.

——— (2001), 'Introduction', in J. Hillier (ed.), *American Independent Cinema: A Sight and Sound Reader*, London: BFI, pp. ix–xviii.

Hincha, R. (1985), 'Selling CinemaScope: 1953–1956', *The Velvet Light Trap*, **21**, 44–53.

Hoberman, J. (1991), *Vulgar Modernism: Writing on Movies and Other Media*, Philadelphia: Temple University Press.

Hoskins, C., McFadyen, S. and Finn, A. (1997), *Global Television and Film: An Introduction to the Economics of the Business*, Oxford: Clarendon Press.

Hughes, S. (2000), 'Mission: Music', *The Guardian*, 25 May, Screen Section, 8–9.

Jameson, F. (1971), *Marxism and Form*, Princeton, NJ: Princeton University Press.

Jarman, D. and Sooley, H. (1996), *Derek Jarman's Garden*, New York: Overlook Press.

Jarvie, I. (1998), 'Free trade as cultural threat: American Film and TV exports in the post-war period', in Nowell-Smith and Ricci (eds) (1998), pp. 34–46.

Jay, M. (1994), *Downcast Eyes: The denigration of vision in twentieth-century French thought*, Berkeley: University of California Press.

Jeancolas, J.-P. (1998), 'From the Blum-Byrnes Agreement to the GATT Affair', in Nowell-Smith and Ricci (eds) (1998), pp. 47–60.

Jenkins, H. (1995), 'Historical poetics' in J. Hollows and M. Jancovich (eds), *Approaches to Popular Film*, Manchester: Manchester University Press, pp. 99–122.

Kalinak, K. (1992), *Settling the Score: Music and the Classical Hollywood Film*, Madison, WI: University of Wisconsin Press.

Kaplan, E. A. (2000), 'Classical Hollywood film and melodrama', in Hill and Church Gibson (eds) (2000a), pp. 46–56.

Kassabian, A. (2001), *Hearing Film: Tracking Identifications in Contemporary Hollywood Film Music*, London: Routledge.

Kerman, J. (1967), *Beethoven String Quartets*, London: Oxford University Press.

Kermode, M. (1995), 'End Notes', *Sight and Sound*, September, 71.

Klinger, B. (1989), 'Digressions at the Cinema: Reception and Mass Culture', *Cinema Journal*, **28** (4), 3–19.

Kolker, R. P. (1988), *A Cinema of Loneliness: Penn, Kubrick, Scorsese, Spielberg, Altman*, New York: Oxford University Press.

Kolker, R. P. and Beicken, P. (1993), *The Films of Wim Wenders: Cinema as Vision and Desire*, Cambridge: Cambridge University Press.

Kovacs, K. S. (1990), 'Parody as "Countersong" in Saura and Godard', *Quarterly Review of Film and Video*, **12**, 105–24.

Kramer, J. (1988), *The Time of Music*, London: Schirmer Books.

Krämer, P. (1998), 'Would you take your child to see this film?: The cultural and social work of the family-adventure movie', in Neale and Smith (eds) (1998), pp. 294–311.

——— (2000), 'Post-Classical Hollywood', in Hill and Church Gibson (eds) (2000a), pp. 63–83.

Leicester, H. M. Jr (1994), 'Discourse and the Film Text: four readings of *Carmen*', *Cambridge Opera Journal*, **6** (3), 245–82.

Lippard, Chris (ed.) (1996), *By Angels Driven: The Films of Derek Jarman*, Trowbridge: Flicks Books.

London, Kurt (1936), *Film Music: a summary of the characteristic features of its history, aesthetics, technique; and possible developments*, trans. E. S. Bensinger, with a foreword by Constant Lambert, London: Faber & Faber.

MacCabe, C. (1974), 'Realism and Cinema: Notes on Some Brechtian Theses', *Screen*, **15** (2), Autumn, 7–32.

——— ([1976]1986), 'Theory and Film: Principles of Realism and Pleasure', in Rosen (ed.) (1986), pp. 179–97.

Maltby, R. (1995), *Hollywood Cinema: An Introduction*, Oxford: Blackwell Publishers.

——— (1998), '"Nobody knows everything": post-classical historiographies and consolidated entertainment', in Neale and Smith (eds) (1998), pp. 21–44.

Marks, M. M. (1997), *Music and the Silent Film*, Oxford: Oxford University Press.

Mattelart, A. (2000), 'European Film Policy and the Response to Hollywood', in Hill and Church Gibson (eds) (2000b), pp. 94–101.

McCann, G. (1994), 'New Introduction', in T. Adorno and H. Eisler, *Composing for the Films*, new edn, London: The Athlone Press, pp. vii–xlvii.

McClary, S. (1992), *Georges Bizet: Carmen*, Cambridge: Cambridge University Press.

Metz, C. ([1975] 1980), 'Aural Objects', trans. G. Gurrieri, *Yale French Studies*, **60**, 24–32.

———— ([1975]1982), *The Imaginary Signifier: Psychoanalysis and the Cinema*, trans. C. Britton, A. Williams, B. Brewster and A. Guzzetti, Bloomington, IN: Indiana University Press.

Meyer, L. (1967), *Music, the Arts, and Ideas: patterns and predictions in twentieth-century culture*, London: University of Chicago Press.

Miller, T. (2000), 'Hollywood and the World', in Hill and Church Gibson (eds) (2000a), pp. 145–55.

Monaco, J. (1976), *The New Wave: Truffaut, Godard, Chabrol, Rohmer, Rivette*, New York: Oxford University Press.

———— (1979), *American Film Now*, New York: New American Library.

Morrison, J. (1998), *Passport to Hollywood: Hollywood Films, European Directors*, Albany, NY: State University of New York.

Mulvey, L. ([1975]1986), 'Visual Pleasure and Narrative Cinema', Rosen (ed.) (1986), pp. 198–209.

———— (1992), 'The Hole and the Zero: The Janus Face of the Feminine in Godard', in R. Bellour and M. L. Bandy (eds), *Jean-Luc Godard: Son + Image: 1974–1991*, New York: Museum of Modern Art, pp. 75–88.

Murphie, A. (1996), 'Sound at the End of the World As We Know It: Nick Cave, Wim Wenders' *Wings of Desire* and a Deleuze-Guattarian Ecology of Popular Music', *Perfect Beat*, **2** (4), 18–42.

Musy, F. (1984), 'Les Mouettes Du Pont D'Austerlitz: Entretien avec François Musy', *Cahiers du Cinéma*, **355**, 12–17.

Naha, E. (1984), *The Making of Dune*, London: W. H. Allen.

Narboni, J. and Milne, T. (eds) ([1972]1986), *Godard on Godard*, with foreword by Annette Michelson, New York: Da Capo Press, Inc.

Neale, S. (1985), *Cinema and Technology: Image, Sound, Colour*, London: Macmillan.

———— (1998), 'Widescreen composition in the age of television', in Neale and Smith (eds) (1998), pp. 130–41.

Neale, S. and Smith, M. (eds) (1998), *Contemporary Hollywood Cinema*, London: Routledge.

Nelson, R. (1946), 'Film music: color or line?', *Hollywood Quarterly*, **2** (1), 59–62.

Nichols, B. (ed.) (1976), *Movies and Methods: an anthology Vol. 1*, London: University of California Press.

———— (1992), 'Form Wars: The Political Unconscious of Formalist Theory', in J. Gaines (ed.), *Classical Hollywood Narrative: The Paradigm Wars*, Durham, NC: Duke University Press, pp. 49–77.

Nochimson, M. (1997), *The Passion of David Lynch: Wild at Heart in Hollywood*, Austin, TX: University of Texas Press.

Nowell-Smith, G. (1998), 'Introduction', in Nowell-Smith and Ricci (eds) (1998), pp. 1–16.

Nowell-Smith, G. and Ricci, S. (eds) (1998), *Hollywood and Europe: Economics, Culture, National Identity 1945–95*, London: BFI.

O'Pray, M. (1996), *Derek Jarman: Dreams of England*, London: BFI.

Paddison, M. (1993), *Adorno's Aesthetics of Music*, Cambridge: Cambridge University Press.

———— (1996), *Adorno, Modernism and Mass Culture: essays on critical theory and music*, London: Kahn & Averill.

Pearl, M. (2000), 'Zero Patience: AIDS, Music and Reincarnation Films', in B. Marshall and R. Stilwell (eds), *Musicals: Hollywood and Beyond*, Exeter: Intellect Books, pp. 141–6.

Peterson, R. A. and Berger, D. D. ([1975]1990), 'Cycles in Symbol Production: The Case of Popular Music', in S. Frith and A. Goodwin (eds), *On Record: rock, pop, and the written word*, London, pp. 140–59.

Petrie, D. (ed.) (1992), *Screening Europe: Image and Identity in Contemporary European Cinema*, London, BFI.

Pudovkin, V. I. ([1929]1985), 'Asynchronism as a Principle of Sound Film', in Weis and Belton (eds) (1985), pp. 86–91.

Rapee, E. ([1924]1970), *Motion Picture Moods for Pianists and Organists: A Rapid Reference Collection of Selected Pieces Adapted to Fifty-Two Moods and Situations*, New York: Arno.

Rodley, C. (ed.) (1997), *Lynch on Lynch*, London: Faber and Faber.

Rosen, P. (1980), 'Adorno and Film Music: Theoretical Notes on *Composing for the Films*', *Yale French Studies*, **60**, 157–82.

——— (ed.) (1986), *Narrative, Apparatus, Ideology: A Film Theory Reader*, New York: Columbia University Press

Rosenmann, L. (1955), 'Notes on the score to *East of Eden*', *Film Music*, **14** (5), 3–12.

Ryan, M. and Kellner, D. (1988), *Camera Politica: The Politics and Ideology of the Contemporary Hollywood Film*, Bloomington: Indiana University Press.

Sabaneev, L. (1935), *Music for the Films*, trans. S. W. Pring, London: Pitman.

Sandahl, L. J. (1987), *Encyclopedia of Rock Music: a viewer's guide to three decades of musicals, documentaries and soundtracks 1955–1986*, Poole, Dorset: Blandford Press.

Sanjek, R. ([1988] 1996), *Pennies From Heaven: The American Popular Music Business in the Twentieth Century*, updated by D. Sanjek, New York: Da Capo Press.

Schaeffer, P. (1967), *Traité des Objets Musicaux*, Paris: Seuil.

Schamus, J. (1998), 'To the rear of the back end: the economics of independent cinema', in Neale and Smith (eds) (1998), pp. 91–105.

Schatz, T. (1993), 'The New Hollywood', in J. Collins, H. Radner and A. Preacher Collins, *Film Theory Goes to the Movies*, New York: Routledge, pp. 8–36

Schoenberg, A. ([1911]1978), *Theory of Harmony*, trans. R. Carter, London: Faber & Faber.

——— (1975), *Style and Idea: Selected Writings of Arnold Schoenberg*, ed. L. Stein, trans. L. Black, London: Faber & Faber.

Schopenhauer, A. (1966), *The World as Will and Representation*, trans. E. F. J. Payne, New York: Dover Publications.

Screen ([1970]1972), 'A collective text by the Editors: [John Ford's] *Young Mr Lincoln*', **13**, 5–44.

Sergi, G. (1998), 'A cry in the dark: the role of post-classical film sound', in Neale and Smith (eds) (1998), pp. 156–65.

Shatkin, E. (2000), 'Randy Thom, Sound Designer, *What Lies Beneath*', *Post Industry* (3 August 2000), url: www.postindustry.com/article/mainv/0,7220,112676,00.html (accessed 20 January 2001).

Sheer, M. (2001), 'The Godard/Beethoven Connection: On the Use of Beethoven's Quartets in Godard's Films', *Journal of Musicology*, **18** (1), 170–88.

Shohat, E. and Stam, R. (1994), *Unthinking Eurocentrism*, London: Routledge.

Silverman, K. (1983), *The Subject of Semiotics*, New York: Oxford University Press.

——— (1988), *The Acoustic Mirror: The Female Voice in Psychoanalysis and Cinema*, Bloomington: Indiana University Press.

Sinn, C. E. (1911), 'Music for the Picture', *Moving Picture World*, **8** (2), 76.

Smalley, D. (1992), 'The Listening Imagination: Listening in the Electroacoustic Era', in J. Paynter, T. Howell, R. Orton and P. Seymour (eds), *The Routledge Companion to Contemporary Musical Thought*, London: Routledge, pp. 514–54.

——— (1994), 'Defining Timbre – Redefining Timbre', *Contemporary Music Review*, **10** (2), 35–48.

Smith, J. (1996), 'Unheard Melodies? A Critique of Psychoanalytic Theories of Film Music', in D. Bordwell and N. Carroll (eds), *Post-Theory: Reconstructing Film Studies*, London: University of Wisconsin Press, pp. 230–47.

——— (1998), *The Sounds of Commerce: Marketing Popular Film Music*, New York: Columbia University Press.

Smith, M. (1998), 'Theses on the Philosophy of Hollywood History', in Neale and Smith (eds) (1998), pp. 3–20.

Smith, P. J. (1993), 'Blue and the outer limits', *Sight and Sound*, **3** (10), 18–19.

Stam, R. (2000a), *Film Theory: An Introduction*, Oxford: Blackwell Publishers.

Stam, R. (2000b), 'Alternative Aesthetics: Introduction', in R. Stam and T. Miller (eds), *Film and Theory: an anthology*, Oxford: Oxford University Press, pp. 257–64.

Stilwell, R. (1997), '"I just put a drone under him ...": Collage and Subversion in the Score of *Die Hard*', *Music and Letters*, **78**, 551–80.

Tagg, P. and Clarida, B. (forthcoming), *Ten Little Tunes*, New York: Mass Media Music Scholars' Press, Inc.

Tasker, Y. (1993), *Spectacular Bodies: Gender, Genre and the Action Cinema*, New York: Routledge.

——— (1996), 'Approaches to New Hollywood', in J. Curran, D. Morley and V. Walkerdine (eds), *Cultural Studies and Communications*, London: Arnold, pp. 213–28.

Ten Hoopen, C. (1994), 'Issues in Timbre and Perception', *Contemporary Music Review*, **10** (2), 61–73.

Truffaut, F. ([1954]1976), 'A Certain Tendency in French Cinema', in B. Nichols (ed.) *Movies and Methods: an anthology Vol. 1*, pp. 224–37.

Vincendeau, G. (1999), 'Hollywood Babel: The Coming of Sound and the Multiple Language Version', in A. Higson and R. Maltby (eds), *'Film Europe' and 'Film America': Cinema, commerce and cultural exchange 1920–1939*, Exeter: University of Exeter Press, pp. 207–24.

——— (2000), 'Issues in European Cinema', in Hill and Church Gibson (eds) (2000b), pp. 56–65.

Vincenzi, L. (1986), 'The Sound of *Blue Velvet* – interview with Alan Splet', *Millimeter*, **14**, 121–4.

Wasko, J. (1994), *Hollywood in the Information Age, Beyond the Silver Screen*, Cambridge: Polity Press.

Weber, M. (1958), *The Rational and Social Foundations of Music*, trans. D. Martindale, J. Riedel and G. Neuwirth, Carbondale, IL: Southern Illinois University.

Weis, E. and Belton, J. (eds) (1985), *Film Sound: Theory and Practice*, New York: Columbia University Press.

Wenders, W. (1989), *Emotion Pictures: Reflections on Cinema*, trans. S. Whiteside in association with M. Hofmann, London: Faber & Faber.

—— (1991), *The Logic of Images: Essays and Conversations*, trans. M. Hofmann, London: Faber & Faber.

—— (1997), *The Act of Seeing: Essays and Conversations*, trans. M. Hofmann, London: Faber & Faber.

Williams, A. (1980), 'Is Sound Recording Like a Language?', *Yale French Studies*, 60, 57–66.

—— (1982), 'Godard's Use of Sound', *Camera Obscura*, **8–9–0**, 193–208.

Wills, D. (1986), 'Carmen: Sound/Effect', *Cinema Journal*, **24** (4), 33–43.

Windsor, L. (1995), 'A Perceptual Approach to the Description and Analysis of Acousmatic Music', unpublished PhD thesis, Music Department, City University, London, UK.

—— (2000), 'Through and Around the Acousmatic: The Interpretation of Electroacoustic Sounds', in S. Emmerson (ed.), *Music, Electronic Media, and Culture*, Aldershot: Ashgate Publishing, pp. 9–35.

Wishart, T. (1985), *On Sonic Art*, York: Imagineering Press.

Wyatt, J. (1994), *High Concept: Movies and Marketing in Hollywood*, Austin, TX: University of Texas Press.

—— (1998), 'The formation of the "major independent": Miramax, New Line and the New Hollywood', in Neale and Smith (eds) (1998), pp. 74–90.

Young, R. (1996), 'The Soundtrack Syndrome', *The Wire*, **153** (November), 26–30.

Discography

The Best of Nick Cave and the Bad Seeds, Nick Cave and the Bad Seeds, LCDMUTEL4

The Garden, original soundtrack album, Ionic 5 CD (Mute Records)

Live Blue Roma (The Archaeology of Sound), Simon Fisher-Turner, CDSTUMM149 (Mute Records)

Wings of Desire: a film by Wim Wenders, soundtrack album, Ionic 2 CD (Mute Records)

Your Funeral, My Trial, Nick Cave and the Bad Seeds, CD STUMM 34 (Mute Records)

Index